The American Sentence

The American Sentence

From Pulpit to Pulp Fiction

Ira Nadel

BLOOMSBURY ACADEMIC
LONDON • NEW YORK • OXFORD • NEW DELHI • SYDNEY

BLOOMSBURY ACADEMIC

Bloomsbury Publishing Plc, 50 Bedford Square, London, WC1B 3DP, UK
Bloomsbury Publishing Inc, 1385 Broadway, New York, NY 10018, USA
Bloomsbury Publishing Ireland, 29 Earlsfort Terrace, Dublin 2, D02 AY28, Ireland

BLOOMSBURY, BLOOMSBURY ACADEMIC and the Diana logo are trademarks
of Bloomsbury Publishing Plc

First published in Great Britain 2026

Copyright © Ira Nadel, 2026

Ira Nadel has asserted his right under the Copyright, Designs and
Patents Act, 1988, to be identified as Author of this work.

For legal purposes the Acknowledgments on p. viii constitute an
extension of this copyright page.

Cover illustration and design by Rebecca Heselton

All rights reserved. No part of this publication may be: i) reproduced or
transmitted in any form, electronic or mechanical, including photocopying,
recording or by means of any information storage or retrieval system without
prior permission in writing from the publishers; or ii) used or reproduced in
any way for the training, development or operation of artificial intelligence (AI)
technologies, including generative AI technologies. The rights holders expressly
reserve this publication from the text and data mining exception as per Article
4(3) of the Digital Single Market Directive (EU) 2019/790.

Bloomsbury Publishing Plc does not have any control over, or responsibility for,
any third-party websites referred to or in this book. All internet addresses given
in this book were correct at the time of going to press. The author and publisher
regret any inconvenience caused if addresses have changed or sites have ceased
to exist, but can accept no responsibility for any such changes.

A catalogue record for this book is available from the British Library.

A catalog record for this book is available from the Library of Congress.

ISBN:	HB:	978-1-3504-7309-6
	PB:	978-1-3504-7308-9
	ePDF:	978-1-3504-7310-2
	eBook:	978-1-3504-7311-9

Typeset by Integra Software Services Pvt. Ltd.
Printed and bound in India

For product safety related questions contact productsafety@bloomsbury.com.

To find out more about our authors and books visit www.bloomsbury.com
and sign up for our newsletters.

For Gideon, Levi, and Coby,

American sentence-makers

Contents

Acknowledgments viii

Prelude: The Blue Air 1

Introduction: The Architecture of the American Sentence 17

1 American Voices: The Pulpit, the Sermon, the Jeremiad 41

2 The Telegram: American Speed 65

3 Criminal Sentences: The Press 99

4 American Pieces: The Screen 141

Conclusion: Dancing Periods 187

Bibliography 203
Index 220

Acknowledgments

In 1856, Flaubert noted that "sentences themselves are adventures." Working on this project has made that clear but it could not have been undertaken without the support of readers and friends who have listened, questioned, corrected, and encouraged beginning with Ben Doyle, Jesse Tisch, Michael Earley, Steven Zipperstein, and Aimee Pozorski. Ryan, Isabelle, Dara, Jon, and the three caballeros have also contributed. Anne has, again, been a wonderful support bringing sharpness, clarity, and understanding to the project and its composition. Two editors have also played important roles: Olga Panova, editor of *Literature of the Americas*, published by the Gorky Institute of World Literature, Moscow and Priscilla Walton, editor of the *Canadian Review of American Studies* at Carleton University, Ottawa. All have contributed to my grasp of the American Sentence and discovery, in the words of Gertrude Stein, how a sentence "thinks loudly."

Prelude: The Blue Air

There was the time when all we could talk about was sentences, sentences—nothing else stirred us.
                JONATHAN LETHEM, "THE KING OF SENTENCES" (2007)

While sentences and their origin have been the subject of literary histories, cultural narratives, and personal writings, they have rarely been examined as a singular subject. There is no history of the sentence, nor theoretical analysis, although multiple titles address their composition. Stanley Fish's *How to Write a Sentence* (2011), Jan Mieszkowski's *Crises of the Sentence* (2019), Joe Moran's *First You Write a Sentence* (2019), and Brian Dillon's *Suppose a Sentence* (2020) are representative. But wrestling with the nature of the sentence has been a writerly preoccupation for generations as Donald Barthelme illustrated. His 1970 short story/essay, "Sentence," is a meandering sentence of 2,569 words without a period, although parentheses, question marks, semicolons, two exclamation marks, and assorted commas appear. It begins with a self-conscious interrogation of its own form:

> Or a long sentence moving at a certain pace down the page aiming for the bottom—if not the bottom of this page then some other page—where it can rest, or stop for a moment to think out the questions raised by its own (temporary) existence, which ends when the page is turned, or the sentence falls out of the mind that holds it (temporarily in some kind of embrace).[1]

But what of the American sentence? What is its history, its poetics? What, in fact, *is* an American sentence and how has it changed?

The following chapters address stages in the unfolding story of the American sentence oriented around a particular form of communication: the sermon, the telegraph, the newspaper, and the screen (movie, computer, and smartphone). The social construction of the American sentence, drawing on communication technology, might be one way of conceptualizing the project. Sound might be another, what Robert Frost called "vocal reality."[2] The study will consider how words must be situated in relation to each other to produce both affect and meaning. A sonic and physical resemblance must emerge, frequently a contest between cadence and meaning. Words in a sentence vibrate and destabilize themselves as Gertrude Stein emphasized.[3] Juxtaposing similarity and difference in a sentence becomes inimical for Stein as in "[s]ugar any sugar, anger every anger, lover sermon lover, centre no distractor, all order is in a measure." "Act," she advises, "so that there is no use in a center," all from *Tender Buttons*. A new American form supplements new American content "not unordered in not resembling."[4]

A singular example from Norman Maclean best known for his novella, "A River Runs through It" (1976). Here, dramatized nature gains unexpected impact in a single sentence through the imagery of a thunderstorm:

> By three-thirty or four, the lightning would be flexing itself on the distant ridges like a fancy prizefighter, skipping sideways, ducking, showing off but not hitting anything.[5]

Movement and frustration unite, nature and mankind dance in a way that accumulates force until it deflects its energy "not hitting anything." The opening sentence of the novella introduces the blended clarity of relationships that exist throughout the story: "In our family, there was no clear line between religion and fly fishing" (River 1). Here, a shadowy Puritan ethos converges with the American wilderness.

Individual writers will record stages in the development of the American sentence: Benjamin Franklin, Henry James, and Gertrude Stein to start followed by David Foster Wallace, Don DeLillo, Cormac McCarthy, Lydia Davis, and Colson Whitehead. They all participate in the quest for the American Sentence. But the quest can fail. The LA writer John Fante made this clear in *Ask the Dust* (1939):

> The lean days of determination. That was the word for it, determination. Arturo Bandini in front of his typewriter two full days in succession, determined to succeed; but it didn't work, the longest siege of hard and fast determination in his life, and not one line done, only two words written over and over across the page, up and down, the same words: palm tree, palm tree, palm tree, a battle to the death between the palm tree and me, and the palm tree won: see it out there swaying in the blue air, creaking sweetly in the blue air. The palm tree won after two fighting days, and I crawled out the window and sat at the foot of the tree. Time passed, a moment or two, and I slept, little brown ants carousing in the hair on my legs.[6]

Writing offers no guarantees and sentences are always dangerous, beginning with disorder and misdirection. The process is similar to what James Salter describes in his novel, *Light Years* (1975). In a commentary on the lives of his two central characters, he indirectly describes the act of writing sentences:

> Their life is mysterious, it is like a forest; from far off it seems a unity, it can be comprehended, described, but closer it begins to separate, to break into light and shadow, the density blinds one. Within there is no form, only prodigious detail that reaches everywhere: exotic sounds, spills of sunlight, foliage, fallen trees, small beasts that flee at the sound of a twig-snap, insects, silence, flowers.[7]

Norman Mailer was less poetic. Critiquing his early success, *The Naked and the Dead* (1948), he praises its immediacy and timing—everyone was ready "for a big war novel"—but, he admits, the book was

> sloppily written in many parts (the words came too quickly and too easily) and there was hardly a noun in any sentence that was not holding hands with the nearest and commonly available adjective—*scalding* coffee and *tremulous* fear are the sorts of thing you will find throughout. Over-certified adjectives are the mark of most best-seller writing.[8]

Nevertheless, the book had "vigour ... the felicity of good books by amateurs." Mailer's remarks confirm the awareness of authors concerning the success or failure of their own sentences.

i

Sentences themselves are adventures
FLAUBERT (C. 1856; CORR II 665)

I wish I could say everything there was to say in one word.
I hate all the things that can happen between the beginning of a sentence and the end.
LEONARD COHEN, THE FAVORITE GAME (1963)

A short history of the sentence to begin, starting with this question: "Does a sentence require a minimum number of words?" There is certainly no absolute answer and linguistic historians vary as to responses. It can be as long as those found in Proust—one sentence in *Sodom and Gomorrah* is 958 words—but as short as 6 as in Hemingway. Henry James in *The Golden Bowl* (1904) uses sentences to amplify character and thought; Lydia Davis concentrates on one or two expressions, anticipated by the intense brevity of Cormac McCarthy. Length does not offer a guide, nor does syntax or the traditional subject/verb/ predicate order. Sentences mix words with disorder, sometimes structured in code. A sentence can be understood from tone or emphasis alone: "Stand!" "Turn!" "Walk!" echo moments in *Waiting for Godot*.[9]

Critics often flounder, however, when concentrating on sentences as their subject. Barthes's 1957 essay on seven sentences in Flaubert, precisely titled "Flaubert and the Sentence," or Ian Watt's essay on the opening sentences of *The Ambassadors* are two examples. Barthes emphasizes the "labor of style" which commits the writer to "the structure of language as a passion," although he concentrates on the corrections of style, one vertical, the other horizontal. The former are substantive changes, metaphorical; the latter are associative, metonymic[10] (Barthes, 71, 72). His focus is far from the nature of the sentence which begins to exhibit metaphysical properties: "the sentence is at once a unit of style, ... and a unit of life" (Barthes).

Barthes then presents the Flaubertian sentence is a work's "double *reflection*," a history of the work on a micro level but also a de facto representation of the writer, presenting itself as a finite object: "Flaubert's sentence is a *thing*" which has a history (Barthes 76). Complexly, while the sentence possesses a finitude, it is also expansive and does not end unless the writer assiduously works at it. Flaubert believes a sentence is never finished; it merely stops (Barthes 77). This might be summarized as the philosophy of sentences. One labors to construct what is ultimately an endless sentence, more in the mode of Borges rather than Flaubert. In a sense, Barthes has removed the sentence from the page.

Watt does the opposite, drilling down into the opening paragraph of James's 1903 novel. He concentrates on "the delayed specification of referents" partly the result of non-transitive verbs and abstract nouns used as subjects of main or subordinate clauses arguing that James's late style is typically abstract with his verbs expressing states of being, not finite actions.[11] This is acutely summarized at the end of the second paragraph. After assessing how he will explain to Waymarsh their intentionally delayed meeting in Chester and his genuine pleasure at having some time to himself, the narrator describes the burden of Strether's "double consciousness," disturbed at delaying Waymarsh but elated with his freedom. The narrator then perceptively writes, "[T]here was detachment in his zeal and curiosity in his indifference," outlining the "double consciousness."[12] But again, on Watt's part, no consensus as to the structure, form, or length of a Jamesian sentence or what a sentence could or couldn't be. Yet commitment to the sentence is unwavering in both James and Flaubert who proudly wrote, "I'd rather die like a dog than rush my sentence through, before it's ripe ... I'm going on again, then, with my dull and simple life ... in which the sentences are adventures" (in Barthes 76 nt.1).

But memorable sentences persist, from Scott Fitzgerald's poetic, final sentence of *Gatsby*, offering hope mixed with struggle—"So we beat on, boats against the current, borne back ceaselessly in to the past"—to the worrying opening of Pynchon's *Gravity's Rainbow*: "A screaming comes across the sky. It has happened before, but there is nothing to compare it to now."[13] Experiments are constant, the "unverbed sentence" one example. Elizabeth Hardwick casually creates a vivid scene without verbs: "In the hotel lobby, tired bandsmen, dark glasses, ashen sleeplessness, oppressive overcoats, their wives, blond and tired" or "the creamy lips, the oily eyelids, the violent perfume—and in her voice the tropical l's and r's."[14] One more from the first page of her incomplete novel, *Sleepless Nights* (1979): "Every morning the blue clock and the crocheted bedspread with its pink and blue and gray squares and diamonds."[15] Sentences without verbs are effective but they challenge conventional grammar and definitions of what a sentence might be.

A passage by Wayne Koestenbaum on Elizabeth Hardwick may capture the variability of the sentence noting that Hardwick's sentences are

> strange and wayward. They veer, they avoid the point. Sometimes they are specific, but often they grow soft-focused and evasive at the crucial moment. They fuzz out by adopting a tone at once magisterial and muffled. When I was writing my biography of Andy Warhol, I told myself, "Imitate Elizabeth Hardwick." By that advice, I meant: *be authoritative, but also odd.*

He goes on to say "every gesture is gloved" noting that tone rather than clarity is the key to her sentences enfolded by syntax both graceful and stumbling.[16] This modern, or postmodern, understanding of what a sentence might be stretches Barthes's view of the sentence as a "unit of life." A sentence becomes an act of self-discovery: "[T]he deeper I become entangled in the process of getting a sentence right in its syllables and rhythms, the more I learn about myself," a character writes in Don DeLillo's *Mao II*.[17]

The oldest known sentence written in the first alphabet is on a comb of the Canaanites, although the idea of the sentence is relatively new. In the medieval period, there was never any conception of the sentence as a syntactic unit.[18] Units of thought and figures of speech ruled, while logic and rhetoric confronted each other. The stanza dominated, unlike anything resembling a sentence. Nevertheless, following the Latin *sententia* (sense), it became common in Middle English, although its meaning was not grammatical but other: it meant opinion, an authoritative statement or decision. By the early sixteenth century, however, the sentence began to mean a grammatical term implying sense or sense worth remembering (Robinson 15). But when a character in Ben Jonson's *Poetaster* says, "Thou speakest sentences," he means that another character is offering an authoritative comment, not a clearly defined syntactic unit (Robinson 16). Logic, not grammar, controlled efforts to define the nature of a sentence. Classical orators, following principles of logic in their presentations, and medieval scholars, seeking systems of expression, disregarded ideas of the sentence as a syntactic unit. Not even Cicero seemed aware of the nature of the grammatical sense of a sentence.

Punctuation may have had a role, extending its importance to phrase-marking, helping the voice to phrase and shape words. In Greek and Latin, strings of letters were unseparated, as were other units shorter than a paragraph (Robinson 21). Punctuation was introduced to aid the "performance" of a text. Punctuated books became known as *codices distincti,* writing with marked divisions. However, word divisions were then forgotten but reinstated by Irish monks who, when writing Gaelic, produced phrases, not simply words. For medievalists, a whole book might be a single long sentence.[19] But the punctuation itself was uncertain: different punctuations of the same passage were commonplace, these differences creating changes in interpretation. Some understood sentences in I Corinthians as questions; others rephrased them as statements (Robinson 23–4). The shift was from phrasal to syntactic prose which likely took place first in Italy, removing a kind of "syntactic drift," although Robinson suggests a theoretical change in the attitude toward sentences occurred in the mid-seventeenth century (Robinson 24, 29, 33). Grammatical assumptions about punctuation then formulated the modern concept of the sentence. Formalized grammar, not speech, shaped sentence forms.

But what of the American Sentence? Can one recognize it? Is it a unique syntactic unit with American references in a distinct American voice and tone—or is it simply an utterance by an American writer? Is resemblance between one American writer and another a link? Could the sentences of Emily Dickinson and Gertrude Stein connect? Both pursued the freedom to explore making new language networks, Susan Howe explaining that "connections between unconnected things are the unreal reality of Poetry."[20] Might that also apply to prose?

Furthermore, what is the role of the American language in shaping the sentence? What stayed, what strayed? "English in America/American English," a section in Ezra Tawil's *Literature, American Style* (2018) helps. Outlining the impact of Noah Webster in the creation of an American vocabulary and syntax, Tawil argues not for the corruption of English but for its renewal beginning in 1607 with the founding of the first permanent English-speaking settlement at Jamestown.[21] The transfer of English to North America was a milestone but soon to be reinvented. In his dictionary, Webster stressed regional differences, privileging the New England farmer, not the Virginia planter. He also emphasized the Puritans and their New England locale over migrants to Chesapeake Bay and Virginia (Tawil 73). In fact, he criticized what he believed to be the alliance of pronunciation between Londoners and Virginia or "fashionable Londoners and American slaveholders" (73). According to Webster, the London theaters and court were responsible for the artificial, if not affected, pronunciation of British English in contrast with the natural, democratic pronunciations of America (74).

Samuel Johnson, however, thought that the transfer of English meant absolute degeneracy, the American dialect ensuring deficiencies. In a review of 1755 on essays focusing on language, Johnson wrote that the work was elegantly written "tho' not without some mixture of the American dialect, a tract of corruption" (in Tawil 68). Such assertions prompted Noah Webster to mount "a counteroffensive," claiming that English in America is purer and more honest than that in Britain; America is actually the preserve of pure British English, untainted (Tawil 69). And the transfer point is 1729, the year of the founding of the Massachusetts Bay Colony.

The origin of the American Sentence is complex as is the move to the concise style but both may have their beginnings in the "rhetoric of sensation." This involves John Locke and Book III on language in *An Essay on Human Understanding,* in which he divorced words from natural or spiritual reality; Bishop Berkeley and his ideas of language as a social convention; and Jonathan Edwards who preached in Puritan New England that language functions only to provoke the emotions.[22] If words substituted for actuality and were separated from ideas, language could best operate not by communicating anything but by "the raising of some passion" (Berkeley in Miller, 180). The best way to do so was through the incisive sentence, an arrow to the heart. Edwards soon believed that an idea was not a concept but an emotion. Accepting sensational psychology meant a commitment to the elimination of the ambiguity of words. Figures of speech, tropes, and allusions only complicated and obscured language meant to present unvarnished ideas to the emotions. And for Edwards, an emotional response was an intellectual response. Miller explains: "a passionate grasping of meaning from a thing or a word" became for Edwards "as much an idea ... as a theoretical grasping" (Miller 181). And when a word is apprehended emotionally, as well as intellectually, an idea "can be more readily and more accurately conceived" (Miller 181). It is a short step from this perception to the decisive style of the Puritan/ American Sentence.

Franklin and Crèvecoeur followed Edwards. Franklin understood the importance of plain speaking to his fellow men and in works like *Poor Richard's Almanac* and *Autobiography* aimed to make his writing accessible. There was no attempt to write above the intelligence of his readers. His vocabulary and syntax were direct: Plain talk was his *métier*.

"Hold your Council before Dinner; the full Belly hates Thinking as well as Acting." 535
"Many have quarrl'd about Religion, that nevr practis'd it." 537
"A lean Award is better than a fat Judgment." 537 (Poor Richard's Almanac)
"By my rambling Digressons I perceive my self to be grown old. I us'd to write more methodically,—But one does not dress for private Company as for a publick Ball. This perhaps only Negligence"—(Autobio. 576).[23]

Crèvecoeur's *Letters from an American Farmer* had a similar intent, although written by the son of a marquis who became a naturalized American and gentleman farmer in the Catskill Mountains of New York until imprisoned by the British as a suspected spy and shipped back to France during the American Revolution. There, he revised his writings on American agriculture and life into a series of letters to a fictional English recipient. The tone is relaxed and casual. Writing of his admired bees, he studies their "government, their industry, their quarrels, their passions, always present me with something new."[24] But when attacked by a kingbird, he kills the bird and rescues 171 bees. Laying them on a blanket in the sun, to his surprise fifty-four "returned to life, licked themselves clean, and joyfully went back to the hive" where they likely told their companions of their adventure and escape "as I believe never happened before to American bees!" His emotional pleasure marks his connection with nature but in a natural manner (Crèvecoeur 27). The letters appeared in London in 1782; his third letter, "What is an American?" is his best-known.

In clear language, it emphasizes self-reliance, individualism, and hard work and set the tone for a series of later writers including James Fenimore Cooper and Mark Twain. Crèvecoeur's style was understood as distinctly American with its emphasis on place and a loose epistolary, natural style, creating what many believe to be a foundational work of American Literature where subject matter dictates method (Tawil 88–90). The style is organic and parallel to speaking but acknowledged by Crèvecoeur as "incorrect" because of the narrator's admitted shortcomings as a writer. But in origin, the act of "writing America" is transatlantic: not only were the letters written by a Frenchman after his return to France but the work first appeared in London (Tawil 106, 88–91).

The history of the sentence is not a linear narrative. It may only register emotional expression through arranged words but without a Lockian sense of order. It is experienced, not programmed. It may emerge from sound and then image initially pinned to a linguistic formula of subject–verb–predicate. But not always—and that's the delight. But having stated this cloudy history, there are differences, especially between the literary style of the United Kingdom and the United States, although words and meaning, movement and inaction, often unite in unexpected ways:

> She wasn't doing a thing that I could see, except standing there leaning on the balcony railing, holding the universe together.
>
> J. D. Salinger, "A Girl I Knew"

ii

He couldn't write without seeing the writing; though he could picture what the sentences pictured, he couldn't picture the sentences unless he saw them unfold and fasten one to the other.

ROTH, *ANATOMY LESSON*

It is, of course, a challenge to clarify differences in sentence structure and style between the forceful American sentence of the twentieth century and the more reticent twentieth-century sentence style of British and Irish writers. A variety of factors have shaped these variances as Gertrude Stein understood. Americans changed their language by choosing words they liked better than others, she wrote, "by putting words next to each other in a different way than the English way, by shoving the language around .... we use the same words as the English do but the words say an entirely different thing."[25] Writers, whether from the United Kingdom or United States, pick up inflections, syntactic forms, and vocabulary from British traditions or American streets—and differences remain, generalized in that the American sentence tends to be emotive, the British discursive.

The American Sentence is dramatic, terse, and direct in an effort to be affective and avoid evasion. The British less so, preferring lengthy, complex sentences with various subordinate clauses and qualifiers that sometimes do not know when to stop. The adverbial clause is a favorite. Lily Briscoe in Woolf's *To the Lighthouse* (1927), for example, thinks of her painting as it nears completion in this fashion:

> Beautiful and bright it should be on the surface, feathery and evanescent, one colour melting into another like the colours on a butterfly's wing; but beneath the fabric must be clamped together with bolts of iron.[26]

Conjunctions operate to extend the sentence which remarkably couples a butterfly's wing and bolts of iron metaphorically suggesting lyricism and force. An earlier sentence in the novel shows an emphasis on depiction as the narrator describes a "phantom kitchen table ... whose virtue seems to have been laid bare by years of muscular integrity, which stuck there, its four legs in air" joining the abstract with the concrete (To L 22). Details pile up in a set of dependent clauses to unravel the abstractions and reinforce independent statements.

Other examples of the prolonged sentence are evident in John Banville's *The Infinities* (2009) when the protagonist has been introduced to a Madame Mac who does not impress:

> Perhaps it was the contrast between the stillness of her broad grey flat face and the frantic movements of the bush behind it and the scraps of fluttering silk about her person, but what she reminded me of most strongly was an electric fan, with its warning tassel tied to the mesh, turning its bland, tilted head slowly from side to side, and the blades behind the mesh a motionless blur as they spun and spun and spun.[27]

Conjunctions, dependent clauses, repetition, and a character presented as an object, rule.

Similarly, in Zadie Smith's *Swing Time* (2016):

> We knew American YTV had been built, in part around her [the performer, Aimee] legend, like a shrine to a pixie god, and the fact that she should even deign now to enter our own, British, far lowlier place of worship was considered a great coup, it put everybody on our version of high alert.[28]

An even longer sentence on the "crazed buoyancy to YTV in those dying days of the nineties" appears on p. 85.

Broadly speaking, the British sentence is hesitant to state its meaning directly pointedly addressed by North Partiger in Woolf's *The Years*: "Why do we hide all the things that matter?"[29] The British sentence resists exposing its feelings, although there are exceptions, when stress and pressure force the character/author to release pent up emotions. Heathcliff in *Wuthering Heights* or Jude in *Jude the Obscure* comes to mind, but situations (psychological as well as physical) have to force characters to reveal themselves. It's as if Jane Austen set the tone and style of feelings clothed in decorum, good manners, and proper behavior that lead, the reader hopes, to some form of restrained resolution. But it requires complicated syntactic structures to hide the emotions often behind other thoughts or objects.

To generalize, things make up the British sentence, feelings of the American.[30] It's Thackeray's focus on buttons in *Vanity Fair* vs. Jack Kerouac's determination to enter America's threatening emotional and physical landscape in *On the Road*.[31] Objects form the subject of the British sentence, while feelings express that of the American conveying immediacy as seen in two passages from Don DeLillo. In *Underworld* (1997), Bobby Thomson hits the pennant-winning home run where the Giants miraculously defeat the Brooklyn Dodgers, an act inspiring disbelief. De Lillo writes:

> Pafko at the wall. Then he's looking up. People thinking where's the ball. The scant delay, the stay in time that lasts a hairsbreadth.[32]

At this moment of suspense, there is syntactic and psychological drama equal to the drama on the field.

Underworld actually begins with a sentence that defines and embodies its Americanness: "He speaks in your voice, American, and there's a shine in his eyes that's halfway hopeful" (Underw. 11). Voice and optimism reign, the phrasing and directness echoing Bellow and the first sentence of *Augie March* (1953): "I am an American, Chicago born—Chicago, that somber city—and go at things as I have taught myself, free-style, and will make the record in my own way."[33] "As I have taught myself"—the American way—"free style." "Here they come, marching into American sunlight" is the appropriate opening of DeLillo's *Mao II* (Mao 3). Perhaps, we should move out of the way.

By contrast is the first page of *Earthly Powers* (1980) by Anthony Burgess:

> I retired twelve years ago from the profession of novelist. Nevertheless, you will be constrained to consider, if you know my work at all and take the trouble now to reread that first sentence, that I have lost none of my old cunning in the contrivance of what is known as *an arresting opening*.[34]

Self-conscious and not entirely convincing.

Generalities are dangerous. Only examples can clarify. There *are* differences between the rhetorically anchored British sentence and the free-floating, singularity of the American. One is left wondering, as North does in Woolf's *The Years*, "why not down barriers and simplify" (Years 389)? But the challenge is the same: "Making a living is nothing; the great difficulty is making a point, making a difference—with words."[35]

Notes

1. Donald Barthelme, "Sentence," *New Yorker* March 7, 1970. https://www.newyorker.com/magazine/1970/03/07sentences.
2. Robert Frost, "Interview," with William Stanley Braithwaite. *Boston Evening Transcript* May 8, 1915. https://udallasclassics.org/wp-content/uploads/maurer_files/Frost.pdf.
3. See Gertrude Stein, *How to Write* (1931; West Glover, VT: Something Else Press, 1973); Garielle Lutz, "The Sentence Is a Lonely Place," *The Believer* 59 (January 2009) [5]. Lutz believes "that the sounds of letters composing words—not their meanings or the images they compromise—take precedence over everything," writes Vincent Czyz, "Book Commentary: Hooked on Phonics? A Brief Reply to Gary Lutz's 'The Sentence Is a Lonely Place," *The Arts Fuse* (Boston) March 9, 2012.
4. Gertrude Stein, *Tender Buttons, Objects, Food, Rooms* (New York: Claire Marie, 1914) 75, 63, 9. "A wideness makes an active center" she also believed (77).
5. Norman Maclean, *A River Runs through It and Other Stories* (Chicago: University of Chicago Press, 1976) 145. Hereafter River.
6. John Fante, *Ask the Dust* (1939; New York: Harper Perennial, 2006) 17.
7. James Salter, *Light Years* (New York: Random House, 1975) 23.
8. Norman Mailer, "Introduction to the 50th Anniversary Edition," *The Naked and the Dead & Selected Letters, 1945–1946*. Ed. J. Michael Lennon (New York: Library of America, 2023) 796.
9. These terms suggest Pozzo's commands to Lucky: "Forward! … Turn! … Done it!" Beckett, *Waiting for Godot* (New York: Grove, 1982) 30a.
10. Roland Barthes, "Flaubert and the Sentence," *New Critical Essays*, tr. Richard Howard (New York: Hill and Wang, 1980) 71, 72. Barthes notes that Proust adds endlessly, while Flaubert subtracts and erases; For Barthes, Flaubert's writing *is* erasure (70).
11. Ian Watt, "The First Paragraph of *The Ambassadors*: An Explication," *Essays in Criticism* Vol.X No.3 (July 1960): 255.

12 Henry James, "The Ambassadors," *Novels 1903–1911* (New York: Library of America, 2010) 24.

13 F. Scott Fitzgerald, *The Great Gatsby* (New York: Scribner's, 1925) 218. Thomas Pynchon, *Gravity's Rainbow* (1973; New York: Bantam, 1974) 3.

14 Elizabeth Hardwick in Brian Dillon, *Suppose a Sentence* (New York: New York Review of Books, 2020) 191; Hardwick, "Billie Holiday," *New York Review of Books* March 4, 1976. https://www-nybooks-com.eu1.proxy.openathens.net/articles/1976/03/04/billie-holiday/. Two other memorable sentences on Holiday: "The sheer enormity of her vices. The outrageousness of them." "Still, even with her, authenticity was occasionally disrupted." Ibid.

15 Elizabeth Hardwick, *Sleepless Nights* (1979; New York: Vintage Books, 1980) 3.

16 Wayne Koestenbaum, "'Every gesture is gloved': Wayne Koestenbaum on Elizabeth Hardwick," Pen America, Blog PEN America, Blog. November 17, 2007. http://penamerica.blogspot.com/2007/12/every-gesture-is-gloved-wayne.html. Hereafter Kostenb.

17 Don DeLillo, *Mao II* (New York: Viking 1991) 48.

18 Ian Robinson, *The Establishment of Modern English Prose in the Reformation and the Enlightenment* (Cambridge: Cambridge University Press, 1998) 13.

19 On the problem of the re-punctuation of medieval and even Renaissance prose, see Robinson, 32–3. For a detailed account in classical sources on the formation of the sentence, see Robinson, "The History of the Sentence," *The Establishment of Modern English Prose* 166–84.

   Jan Mieszkowki outlines the problematics of a history of the sentence in *Crises of the Sentence* (Chicago: University of Chicago Press, 2019) 12–14. He especially challenges the persistent investment, philosophically and grammatically, in subject–predicate thinking. He also opposes the "stark opposition" between the syntactic and semantic (29) and argues that the rules of grammar are actually the site of "an ideological struggle" (34).

20 Susan Howe, *My Emily Dickinson* (Berkeley: North Atlantic Books, 1985) 97. Hereafter My.

21 Ezra Tawil, *Literature, American Style, The Originality of Imitation in the Early Republic* (Philadelphia: University of Pennsylvania Press, 2018) 67. For the "English in America/ American English" section, see 66–79. Hereafter Tawil.

22 Perry Miller outlines these concepts in, "The Rhetoric of Sensation," *Errand into the Wilderness* (Cambridge, MA: Belknap Press, 1956) 167–183. Hereafter Miller. The essay first appeared in 1950.

23 Benjamin Franklin, "Poor Richard's Almanac," *Autobiography, Poor Richard, and Later Writings*, ed. J. A. Leo Lemay (New York: Library of

America, 1997) 535, 537. "The Autobiography," ibid., 576. Also of interest is Franklin's December 26, 1789 letter to Noah Webster on the occasion of *Dissertations on the English Language*. See *Autobiography* (1997) 433–8.

24 Hector St. John Crèvecoeur, *Letters from an American Farmer*, Intr. W. Barton Blake (New York: E.P. Dutton & Co., 1951) 29–30.
25 Gertrude Stein, *Wars I Have Seen* (New York: Random House, 1945) 171.
26 Virginia Woolf, *To the Lighthouse*, ed. David Bradshaw (Oxford: Oxford University Press, 2006) 141.
27 John Banville, *The Infinities* (London: Picador, 2009) 222.
28 Zadie Smith, *Swing Time* (London: Hamish Hamilton, 2016) 83–4.
29 Virginia Woolf, *The Years*, Ed. Hermione Lee (Oxford: Oxford University Press, 2009) 391.
30 For an introductory discussion of differences, see Weijie Liu, "Linguist Features of British and American Literary Works from a Cross-cultural Perspective," *International Journal of Art Innovation and Development* Vol.1 No.3 (2020): 45–56.
31 From Kerouac, *On the Road*: "He didn't have a care in the world and had the hugest regard for everybody. I said to myself, Wham, listen to that laugh. That's the West, here I am in the West." *Road Novels 1957–1960*, ed. Douglas Brinkley (New York: Library of America, 2007) 19. And later, "I walked around, picking butts from the street. I passed a fish-'n-chips joint on Market Street and suddenly the woman in there gave me a terrified look … she apparently thought I was coming in there with a gun" (*Road Novels,* 155).
32 Don DeLillo, *Underworld* (New York: Scribner, 1997) 42. Hereafter Underw.
33 Saul Bellow, *Adventures of Augie March* (New York: Viking, 1953) 3.
34 Anthony Burgess, *Earthly Powers* (London: Hutchinson, 1980) 7.
35 Elizabeth Hardwick, "Grub Street, New York," *The Collected Essays of Elizabeth Hardwick*, Sel. Darryl Pinckney (New York: New York Review Books, 2017) 125.

Introduction: The Architecture of the American Sentence

She was up like a bull and like a bull she charged. Her head struck me in the stomach (setting off a flash in that forest of nerves) and then she drove one powerful knee at my groin (she fought like a prep-school bully) and missing that, she reached with both hands, tried to find my root and mangle me.
                    NORMAN MAILER, *AN AMERICAN DREAM* (1965)

i

Here unleashed is the full force of the American Sentence—tough, brutal, strong—written by a man but featuring a woman. It punches and punishes both the reader and the character, mixing literalism with metaphor ("forest of nerves"). It aims high and low simultaneously. From Mailer's *An American Dream* (1965), the excerpt embodies the strength and precision of the modern American Sentence.

Another example, by Hemingway, turns on the emotions:

Everything was gone inside of me. I did not think. I could not think. I knew she was going to die and I prayed that she would not. Don't let her die .... Please, please, please, dear God, don't let her die. Dear God, don't let her die. Please, please, please don't let her die.[1]

Short sentences, repetition, and anguish converge in this passage from *A Farewell to Arms* (1929), emphasizing the ability of the American Sentence to convey emotion as well as action. The attributes are the same in both examples: urgency, will, insistence, and power expressed in syntax that ignites reaction. The colloquial rules, supported by adaptation of spoken, concrete language. The story of the American Sentence is precisely this process of variation and change transferring the kinetic (physically and emotionally) to the page which, in turn, animates the energy and vitality of disparate, often conflicting, voices.

According to *The Cambridge Dictionary*, a sentence is "a group of words, usually containing a verb, which expresses a thought in the form of a statement, question, instruction, or exclamation and starts with a capital letter when written." *The American Heritage Dictionary* has a different view: a sentence is "a grammatical unit that is syntactically independent and has a subject that is expressed or, as in imperative sentences, understood and a predicate that contains at least one finite verb."[2] These formal origins, implying a predictive order, began in America with the Puritans but were radically altered by the time of the Beats.

In practice, American writers have long challenged the rationalist definition of a sentence described by the *Cambridge Dictionary*. The statement in the *American Heritage Dictionary,* with its keyword "independent," is closer to the radical forms and unorthodox shapes of the unit, ranging from one-word sentences to sentences incomplete, upside down, and illegible that have collectively determined the design of American Sentences.[3]

But can one trace the habits and idiosyncrasies of the American Sentence? What is there about Thoreau, Twain, Dreiser, or Dos Passos, as well as Gertrude Stein, Cormac McCarthy, Joyce Carol Oates, or George Saunders that is quintessentially American? Is there a distinct American style/ language or syntax? Is it possible to claim that many writers do not write texts but compose sentences which, when accumulated, form an American script? What are the qualities of the American Sentence and how might it function as a compositional unit? Allen Ginsberg thought he knew.

Inspired by the Japanese haiku, Ginsberg created an American Sentence which is a single sentence of seventeen syllables. He took the tradition of the 5, 7, 5 syllables of the haiku to add 5+7+5 to create his prose form, in essence a prose poem. Two examples: "Put on my tie in a taxi, short of breath, rushing to meditate" (Ginsberg Nov. 1991); "That grey-haired man in business suit and black turtleneck thinks he's still young" (December 19, 1992).[4] Further examples: "Taxi ghosts at dusk pass Monoprix in Paris 20 years ago." "Bearded robots drink from Uranium coffee cups on Saturn's ring." These seventeen-syllable sentences first appeared in *Cosmopolitan Greetings* (1994), mixing a defined form with remarkable imagination.[5] But definitions are fluid as the concept of the American Sentence demonstrates, alternating in form and meaning.

Yet the sentence possesses its own poetic as Louise Glück noted in her 2017 essay "Ersatz Thought" from her collection, *American Originality*: "The sentence deploys emphasis to create readings complementary to, or at variance with, the logical. It works magically, electrically … the sentence is the Bible and the Talmudic commentary." The sentence constantly creates dramas and suggests "variety through its concreteness, its presentness."[6] It proposes and comments on itself simultaneously becoming both a text and its own analysis, stating and questioning at the same time.

Related to the topic is length. Should the American Sentence have a limit? The quick answer is "no" as evidenced by differences between Hemingway and Faulkner who at one time supposedly wrote the longest sentence in literature, a 1288-word example found in *Absalom, Absalom*! (1936).[7] The works of David Foster Wallace and Lucy Ellmann have carried on the practice. Wallace's *Infinite Jest* (1996) contains powerful sentences of immoderate length extending for pages. Ellmann's *Ducks, Newburyport* (2019) is a work of more than one thousand pages without block paragraphs and no indentation after page 1. Formally, it contains only eight sentences.[8] Offsetting such style is Cormac McCarthy or, in its extreme, what has been called "micro fiction." Hemingway was an early practitioner with this six-word story: "For sale: baby shoes. Never worn."[9]

But how did such polarity over length come about? Did postwar American fiction become trapped by a schism between maximalist and minimalist compositions, the need to recover excess vs. a wish to shed the old and start over with the new? This became a contest between a so-called mandarin and a plain style, the former emphasizing periodicity and sinuosity, qualities originating in sets of dependent clauses, the latter concentrating on unornamented expressions, simple and direct.[10]

But this may be too programmatic a proposal. The American Sentence has operated more like a pendulum alternating between the elaborate rhetoric of a Thomas Wolfe or Saul Bellow and the pared-down style of a Raymond Carver or Cormac McCarthy. Alfred Kazin sensed the problematics of the sentence when he wrote in 1942 that modern American prose writing contained an inherent paradox: writers were absorbed "in every last detail of their American world together with their deep and subtle alienation from it."[11] To be a part of, and yet apart from, the culture creating an irregular, alternating system of sentence forms is to understand the shift from the complex structures of Melville or James to the more direct writing of J.D. Salinger or Lydia Davis. The oscillating nature of the American Sentence shifts between the "spool of ... rhetoric," with classical epithets and allusions, to the freedom of the direct utterance or word. Kazin links this change to the moral life of America claiming that developments with the American Sentence may actually express a "moral history." The conflict between traditionalism and innovation, conservatism and experimentation summarizes the struggle (Kazin x).

Attributes of the American Sentence in the twentieth century were clear: the drive toward compression and coherence, broadly related to the search for the direct, redemptive meaning of America. For the Puritans, taking the reformation overseas needed justification in the new Promised Land. The American Sentence began, then, with a distinctive, elaborate, rhetorical quest rooted in biblical and oratorical sources with its writing becoming a determining historical force with new content: America itself. Displacing the authority of scripture by the authority of a secular place and an unscripted history identified as American became the launching pad for the American Sentence. A natural voice and plain style soon replaced the imported pulpit style with the symbolic substituting for the biblical. Place, itself, became a sacred book with America the new figure of redemption.[12] The rhetoric of American identity became embedded in the sentence which moved from Protestant hermeneutics to American symbolism. This is the beginnings of an American syntax and sentence discovering rhetorical energy and verbal confidence initiated by Edwards and Puritan preachers and then extended by a multitude of others including Franklin, Crèvecoeur,

Hawthorne, and Twain but then altered by their heirs. Replacing the Puritan sense of mission was the quest, often to confront evil, as Ahab showed in his futile pursuit of the White Whale.[13] "Neversink" is the appropriate name of the American frigate that defeats an English man-of-war in Melville's *White-Jacket*.[14]

The travel narrative was part of the corrective, anti-Puritan process. Brisk, descriptive narratives of discovery, beginning with Crevècoeur's *Letters from an American Farmer* (1782), the journals of Lewis and Clarke (1803–6), Washington Irving's *Sketch Book* (1820)—"My native country was full of youthful promise; Europe was rich in the accumulated treasures of age"—revealed this new voice and style at work. Thoreau's *Week on the Concord and Merrimack Rivers* (1849), Twain's *Innocents Abroad* (1869), and even Kerouac's *On the Road* (1957) contributed to the emphatic directness of the American Sentence. Thoreau expressed this when he wrote in January 1842 that "I want to see a sentence run clear through to the end, as deep and fertile as a well-drawn furrow."[15] Use of the land as a metaphor was fundamental.

Travel became a secular mission reflected in its language of expectation and movement: "I could hear a new call and see a new horizon, and believe it at my young age ... I wanted to take off," says Sal Paradise in Kerouac's *On the Road,* echoing Twain's Huck Finn.[16] Travel meant sharing new experiences in new forms, resisting the deadening styles and isolating formulae of the predictable and conservative American Sentence. The sentence became, like the road for the Beats, "a space that radically juxtaposed fixed domestic [forms] with something new."[17] In twentieth-century fiction, this meant replacing Dreiser or Sinclair Lewis with Dos Passos, Ralph Ellison, or Norman Mailer.

Travel brought a new sentence style duplicating the impact and surprise of travel itself which became both a metaphor and an act. As Gertrude Stein showed in a passage from *Useful Knowledge,* the exchange between travel and style, movement and syntax, united: "Iowa means much. Indiana means more. More more more. Indiana means more. As more. Kansas means most and most and most and most. Kansas means most merely."[18] Stein destabilizes boundaries borders, facts, constants, and syntax.

But the space within the sentence was soon in dispute, Robert Frost declaring that it should be a "vocal reality." The essence of a sentence for Frost is its sound because "to me a sentence is not interesting merely in conveying a meaning of words. It must do something more; it must convey a meaning by sound."[19] Philip Roth opted for sound plus rhythm, for what he calls in *The Counterlife* the "jumpy beat of American English." For Roth, the sentence was all, as a disillusioned character in his novel *Deception* ironically reveals: "[A]ll the time I thought you loved me for my body when in fact it was only for my sentences."[20] And the new style? Summarized by a Dutch critic when he said, "everything that can be left out is left out, but the theme is huge …. it's mostly what's not said or not written that makes it so strong."[21]

ii

American culture is most "American" in what lies hidden in its mixture of modes, thus it's hard to tell who the hell had his hand in the mixing.
    RALPH ELLISON, OCTOBER 30, 1987 *SELECTED LETTERS*

What makes an American Sentence American? Might it be the "fleeting conjunctions of vernacular and cultivated style," Ralph Ellison notes where "the comic, cathartic action occurs" to the "earing eye and eyeing ear of a vulgar, vernacular-bred Oklahoman" (where Ellison was born)? Or is it the individual self-expression promoted by Emerson and Whitman?[22] By the nineteenth century, the sentence had escaped the Church and State taking control of itself. Released from the confines of the subject–verb–object format and the elaborate clauses fencing in ideas and expressions, regional features appeared in a dialect of emotion and energy expressed by independent and dependent clauses. Voice became the reaction against authority, order, and any governing social, religious, or historical forces. Freedom meant the rejection of prescriptive forms. It is both the desire to say things clearly and directly, and the refusal to become something other than one's self. It is in the dialogue of *Huck Finn,* the simple style of *Winesburg, Ohio* or the truncated exchanges in *Absalom, Absalom*. Damn the restraints and celebrate the incomplete expressed by the vernacular and colloquial rhythms of speech. The sentence controls itself whether through dialect, slang, neologisms, shouts, or murmurs. Non-literary words soon find a valuable place in literary texts.

The new methods include asymmetry, disjointedness, and aphoristic expressions, extending an anti-Ciceronian practice. No longer cool, neutral sentences in fixed arrangements but vibrant, energetic, experimental, personal, often incomplete statements. Not amplification but deflation; subjectivity, not objectivity; one does not describe something, one *is* that something through authority over the prose. In Saussurian terms, *parole* has replaced *langue*. The sentence is no longer literary and veers toward silence: "Shh. No more talking" the father tells the son in Cormac McCarthy's *The Road*.[23]

Prose form becomes inconsistent and the value of words questioned: "Rub out the words!" .... "Reduce ... Sentence Spell," writes the impatient William Burroughs.[24] Words simply get in the way, leading to silent or almost silent pages as Mark Danielewski presents in *House of Leaves* (2000). A number of its over-sized pages have no more than three words or perhaps just one.[25] Placement of the single word becomes crucial, possessing rhetorical and dramatic effect. Page 230 has only "door" at the bottom, while in the topmost right corner of p. 287 is the word "top?" printed upside down. "Transition and the old grammar forms no longer useful," Burroughs wrote, skipping a verb. "All writing is in fact cut ups," he announced.[26]

With its reduction in diction and shifts in syntax, American writing became more forceful, confident in its independence. Transferred to the page, words became concrete, syntax more simplified. Being curt became the mean, often a masculine mean as the vernacular began to dominate, something which absorbed Ellison who believed that the vernacular held an essential position "in structuring American culture." In *Going to the Territory*, he argues that the vernacular is no less than "a gesture toward perfection."[27] Hemingway depended on "concrete objects for the body and movement of his prose," but the vernacular is what gives the objects agency.[28] Dashiell Hammett's spare, crisp style with its renderings of urban America idioms and rhythms confirmed the effectiveness of such prose paralleled by Raymond Chandler. A passage from Chandler's short story "Trouble Is My Business" makes this clear. A gangster surprises the detective Philip Marlowe in his office:

"So you killed my pal," he said.
He stood up slowly, came across the room slowly and leaned the .22 against my throat …. He reached quietly under my coat

and took the Luger. I might as well leave it home from now on. Everybody in town seemed to be able to take it away from me.

Silence, careful action matched by careful thought, expanded by repetition and irony, guarantees tension and surprise with a minimal amount of words:

> Park the body, friend. No false moves. No moves at all. You and me are at the jumping-off place. The clock's tickin' and we're waiting to go.[29]

American fiction writers acknowledged the power of speech acts, adopting the performative nature of speaking and writing.[30] This conceptual platform provides the foundation for the construction and iteration of the architecture of the American Sentence.

Deviation and diversion, surprise and the unexpected become the new norms much like that of the journeyman in Thomas Nashe's *The Unfortunate Traveller* (1594): "Towards Venice we progrest, and tooke Roterdam in our waie, that was cleane out of our waie."[31] No progression of events, just a sudden turn where the narrator meets Erasmus and More. This is Burroughs and *The Ticket That Exploded* (1962) with its cut-up method summarized in a September 5, 1960 letter to Allen Ginsberg and expanded in Burroughs's *The Third Mind* (1978; Rub 44–5). Lionel Essrog embodies the method in Jonathan Lethem's *Motherless Brooklyn* (1999) with his frequently disjointed and seemingly nonsensical outbursts because of his Tourette's. Conventional phrases become surprising new sounds: "[W]hen a television pitchman said *to last the rest of a lifetime* my brain went *to rest the lust of a loaftomb,* that when I heard 'Alfred Hitchcock', I silently replied 'Altered Houseclock' or 'Ilford Hotchkiss'."[32] This is also a world where guns establish a grammar of understanding: "Tony held the gun floppily between us, using it to gesture, to signal punctuation. I only hoped he understood how literally it could punctuate" (MB 184). Unsurprisingly, in this world verbs disappear and the American Sentence dissolves, although meaning emerges from its incoherence (MB 91).

Distinct properties define the Americanness of the American Sentence beginning with its specificity noted by Philip Roth: "This passion for specificity, for the hypnotic materiality of the world one is in, is all but at the heart of the task to which every American novelist has been enjoined: ... to discover the most arresting, evocative verbal depiction for every last American thing."[33] The drive to be specific defines the nature of the American Sentence which seeks to be sharp, exact, detailed, brief, and short. Mixing incompleteness with exactness is the new style: disjointed syntax rules. Even without logical, syntactic connections, precision is the goal. To be precise is to be American.

As part of this gesture was the emerging view that every sentence had the force and feel of a climax. Gordon Lish, *Esquire* fiction editor and then editor at Knopf, promoted this view and sponsored literary minimalism, although he disliked the term. Mentoring a series of American authors through lectures and workshops, he developed a strong following. Don DeLillo dedicated *Mao II* (1991) to him, repeated by Amy Hempel in the dedication to her short story collection *Reasons to Live* (1985). Raymond Carver also benefited greatly from Lish's editorial directives. Creative writing programs at universities, ranging from the Iowa Writers' Workshop to Stanford, similarly promoted the redacted style.[34] Every sentence became a performance providing an archaeology of the present and past simultaneously: what the author wrote (past) and what the reader understands (present). It does double time. Sentences became contingent narratives where enjambment became the new rule, syntactic conformity a curse. The poet Ron Silliman called this "the new Sentence," matched by Lish's observation from his two-volume *English Grammar*: "[T]he growing tempo of modern life changes language."[35] The preference is for shortcuts rather than syntactic complexity. Updike vs. Cormac McCarthy, Joyce Carol Oates vs. Donald Barthelme might be the shorthand match ups between the old and new styles.

D.H. Lawrence identified several additional characteristics of the American Sentence in *Studies in Classic American Literature* when he wrote that "the essential American soul is hard, isolate, stoic and a killer. It has never yet melted."[36] Such a description suggests the determination to be free from the imposing forms American writers inherited—highly structured, intensely rhetorical, and possessing a heavy, moralistic, religious tone. It was writing that was prophetic, oracular with sentences that broadcast rather than exposed. They reported rather than revealed what the author sought to say with the foregrounding of style rather than content as a new freedom of form expressed a political need for American independence. Richard Poirier outlined this in *A World Elsewhere* when he wrote that "the classic American writers try through style … to free the hero (and the reader) from systems, … from social forces which are ultimately the undoing of American heroes and quite often of their creators."[37] The American writer, in dispossessing the past, creates an "existence only in style" which becomes his only authority (Poirier 17). Rejecting the past in a quest for originality led to new prose forms, parallel to the effort of American fictional heroes to free themselves from the conventions of historically rooted environments. Style itself, Poirier argues, became the hero of the text.

Ellison's *Invisible Man* pinpoints this notion of self-discovery. In the Epilogue to the novel, the narrator explains that his problem was he "tried to go in everyone's way but my own."[38] No one, he adds, "really wished to hear what I called myself" (IM 564). He rebelled but became an "*invisible* man," hibernating (IM 564). Nevertheless, with "all boundaries down, freedom was not only the recognition of necessity, it was the recognition of possibility" (IM 491).

But that, too, was unsatisfactory and he returns to the principles "on which the country was built" (IM 564). This was the independence of spirit and voice that led to the rejection of imposed stylistic and social forms. A new voice emerges through Ellison's complex style with multiple subordinate clauses, colons/semicolons, and multiple prepositional phrases modeled on Faulkner:

> I wanted to stop the car and talk with Mr. Norton, to beg his pardon for what he had seen; to plead and show him tears, unashamed tears like those of a child before his parent; to denounce all we'd seen and heard; to assure him that far from being like any of the people we had seen, I *hated* them, that I believed in the principles of the Founder with all my heart and soul, and that I believed in his own goodness and kindness in extending the hand of his benevolence to helping us poor, ignorant people out of the mire and darkness.
>
> (IM 97)

Two semicolons, eight subordinate clauses, and ten prepositional phrases. The complexity of the sentence reinforces the stress experienced by the Invisible Man.

The speaker begins the novel with optimism but experience brings pessimism. Yet in his cellar, he waits in a world of "infinite possibilities" (IM 567). For the writer, this was the chance to employ new structures and shapes of expression: "all life is divided and that only in division is the true health," he thinks, rejecting the passion and pressure "to make men conform to a pattern" (IM 567). "Diversity is the word," syntactically and formally (IM 567). "I'm shaking off the old skin and I'll leave it here in the hole," the narrator announces on the final page of the novel (IM 572).

Unpredictability is one glorious result. The excitement of discovery through prose in its most contemporary American style provides a new energy for writers and readers. It parallels the architectural movement from the formalized style of a Louis Sullivan or Daniel Burnham to the excitement of a Frank Lloyd Wright or Frank Gehry. The unexpected defines the new.

iii

The basic work is built around the sentence. This is what I mean when I call myself a writer. I construct sentences.
DON DELILLO, *PARIS REVIEW*, 1993

In general terms, the goal of a new American style was to release previously "unexpressed dimensions of the self into space where it would encounter none of the antagonistic social systems which stifle it,' reshaping the American element of the American Sentence (Poirier 40). Personality became pronounced and action sought union with language. For characters, success became inward and invisible but expressed through language, but ironically, the ultimate American Sentence, as it moves from the elaborate and lengthy to the precise and brief, maybe silence, generating what Thomas Hardy once called "silent speaking words." It is the father in Cormac McCarthy's *The Road* telling his son, "No more talking," repeated by the son late in the novel. To his dying father, he says "It's okay, Papa. You don't have to talk. It's okay" (Road 115, 279). Preceding such silence is Carson McCullers in *The Heart is a Lonely Hunter* about two deaf mutes in Georgia who are still able to communicate.[39] It is Susan Sontag in "The Aesthetics of Silence," and the silence that controls the action or inaction in Toni Morrison's *Beloved*. "The art of our time is noisy with appeals for silence," wrote Sontag.[40] America is a sentence yet to be written, yet to be heard. But silence can amplify its composition.

Silence may, in fact, be the fate of the American Sentence, the result of the breakdown of language into syllables described by Mark Danielewski in *House of Leaves* (2000) when the narrator explains:

> Words filling my head. Fragmenting like artillery shells. Shrapnel, like syllables, flying everywhere. Terrible syllables. Shap cracked. Travelling at murderous speed.
>
> (H of L 71)

The narrator had just written that "the rest is in pieces. A scream, a howl, a roar. All's warping, or splintering … Everything falls apart" (H of L 71).

Lionel Essrog, anti-hero of Jonathan Lethem's *Motherless Brooklyn*, constantly embodies the seemingly breakdown of words as he remakes words into sentences reducing the American Sentence to sounds. His neologisms possess sound but not meaning, a form of vocalized silence. When a policeman asks the hero if he would describe himself as a friend of the deceased, he replies with "Trend the decreased" and then "Mend the retreats!" Essrog constantly recreates words and statements. Reconstituted, "a guy walks into" becomes "*whrywhroffsinko*" (MB 31). Sentences have become single words of oral, not semantic, value and are best understood when read, not heard; they are no longer literary, rhetorical displays with allusions, references, imagery, or languages of the past. Syntax and imagery disintegrate into utterances that are visual collages with the text generating an acoustic, subtext not so much written as notated without conventional words.

But how does one build an American Sentence? What is its foundation, framing, plumbing, insulation, fixtures, and finishes? Who designs it? What demolition and excavation are necessary? What is the framing package and windows? And is punctuation the mortar, syntax the lumber, spelling the foundation? And will it be one story or two, a home or a retail outlet, a school or a cathedral? Architecture as a metaphor for the construction of a sentence and its construction is useful. The metaphor relates to Richard Poirier's argument that American writers were constantly seeking homes for their heroes, the quest for a home a repeated theme. But tangential questions persist: how long to build and how large should it be? And what about roofing, siding, painting, trim, lighting, and plumbing fixtures, plus landscaping and driveway? These features relate to syntax, dialect, length, and the substitution of one word for a phrase associated with the breakdown or decomposition of language, technically called "desegmentalization" (Traugott 17). Collectively, the mortar might be summarized as the narrative grammar of the text, grammar defined as "the Art of expressing the Relation of Things in Construction, with due Accent in Speaking, and Orthography in Writing"[41]

Broadly speaking, these changes in construction occurred because of the move from oral to written forms, from the pulpit to print, from the platform to the literary marketplace where, by the mid-nineteenth century, American literature became a product of labor not inspiration. This naturally influenced style.[42] But the reverse also happened. Not only the means of production but the spoken language, whether of Los Angeles (Chandler), Harlem (Whitehead), or Chicago (Bellow), soon shaped the structure of the American Sentence. Yet where imperatives, exclamations, and even anger took over, there was a paradoxical sense of restraint, similar to that described by Professor St. Peter in Willa Cather's *The Professor's House.* Reading Tom Outland's diary, he writes that "through this austerity [of words] one felt the kindling imagination, the ardour and excitement of the boy, like the vibration in a voice when the speaker strives to conceal his emotion by using only conventional phrases"[43] A new, "charged simplicity" takes over, an economy that strips away excess without sacrificing the powerful feeling of the experience itself.[44]

Cather, and later Hemingway and Dos Passos, provided innovative approaches to American prose style, one where implication rather than explicit statement ruled. As Cather stressed in a 1920 essay, "On the Art of Fiction," the writer finds what conventions of form and detail one can eliminate and "yet preserves the spirit of the whole" (in Love 297). In *Death in the Afternoon,* Hemingway would write that "if a writer of prose knows what he is writing about he may omit things that he knows and the reader ... will have a feeling of those things as strongly as though the writer had stated them."[45] Omission is a form of knowledge reflecting in the sentence's revised and shortened structure where emphasis replaces order. "It is the inexplicable presence of the thing not named

... that gives higher quality to the novel" or to the sentence Cather wrote in 1922 (in Love 297).

In the final section of *The Professor's House*, the short sentences and clauses lack sequentiality or the logic of subordination, anticipating the technique of Burroughs, Carver, or Danielewski. Writes Cather, "He was a primitive ..... wherever sun sunned and rain rained and snow snowed .... Desire under all desires, Truth under all truths" (Cather 260). The language seems primal and almost a denial of style. The essence of the sentence is its utterance not its form. The style of the American Sentence withholds more and more approaching, in *The Professor's House*, a state of silence coupled with the "rhetoric of obliteration" (Love 306).

Others have noted this move in the construction of the American Sentence, notably Edmund Wilson in "The Chastening of American Prose Style" from *Patriotic Gore* and Richard Bridgman in *The Colloquial Style in America*. Wilson argues that the change to word reduction occurs in the middle of the nineteenth century as prose became more efficient and functional, the pace firmer and faster. The old inflated style was gone. A "florid American rhetoric," with classical allusions and quotations from Shakespeare or Milton, disappeared.[46] The polysyllabic had no place in American ears but short words and plain speaking did with Lincoln the model. Directness and precision would provide new force often coupled with disequilibrium: the reader will be caught off-guard.

Journalism was a spur to this change; both Cather and Hemingway, of course, were journalists early in their careers and responded positively to the emphasis on brevity and concreteness. And with concision came omission, creating a new dynamism of understanding as readers worked to understand what was missing and yet what was there in a text. As Wilson summarizes, "[T]he cultivation of brevity was no doubt the result of the speeding-up of everything in American life" (PGore 649). He also explains that the experience of the war combined with the mechanical age increased Northern efficiency and had an impact on American style. The speaking style of Grant and Lincoln reinforced this approach defined as lucid, precise, and terse (PGore 649). Furthermore, their military and administrative positions required a quick and decisive prose style (PGore 650). They had no time to waste. There was an "accent of decisiveness" marked by a trenchant and concise manner showing self-confidence (PGore 650). Henry Adams and Henry James reflected the opposite: ambiguity, prolixity, and irony reflecting a certain lack of self-confidence or diffidence. But soon, grammatical subordination and complexity disappeared; in the new brevity, words became dispensable.[47]

iv

We played it just like we would tell it.
    JAMES M. CAIN, *THE POSTMAN ALWAYS RINGS TWICE* (1934)

Voices from the street increasingly formed the page as the colloquial took control. The street spoke and authors listened, satisfying what Whitman in *Democratic Vistas* called the need for a more Native American voice. Combined with this was the emergence of a broader readership, impacting on the forms of writing with high-speed access to reading through the papers. One rejected literary gentility to express the energy of the democratic dream. For Whitman, "the priest departs; the divine literatus comes."[48] Professionalism replaced decorum, affecting style.

Writing also became more mimetic than moral as realism advanced with modern professional writers emerging into a new "mass market of words" (Wright 13; E. Wilson, P G 636). The author became a paid writer best seen in reporters, magazine writers, writers-for-hire, and writers who actually received advances and had substantial periodical sales. This new literary professionalism seeped into the prose which became urgent, intense, and energetic. There were deadlines and new expectations: one had to produce. Writing for print changed the actual nature of American prose and American Sentences. The architecture of the sentence became more functional, immediate, and purposeful with variety altering the textual topography. Each sentence offered a different linguistic and rhetorical perspective.[49] Efficiency defined the relationship between words and form embodied, in part, by the telegraph, the topic of Chapter 2, expanded to the newspaper in Chapter 3, and the screen (movie, laptop, and smartphone) in Chapter 4.

Mixing accuracy with incompleteness soon became the new style as disjointed syntax replaced syntactic order in a search for prose freedom. William Burroughs outlined this in *The Ticket That Exploded:*

This is a novel presented in a series of oblique references... shave?.. did he?.. an amputation.. three young burglars one wearing a black overcoat stopped on the stairs by two English detectives.. *One of the thieves is nicknamed Genial* ....

or

Blue notes of Pan trickled down silver train whistles—calling the imprisoned Jinn from copulation space suits that clung to his muscle lust and burning sex skin ....[50]

Echoing Céline in the use of ellipses and absence of logical syntactic connections, the goal is still precision: to be precise is actually to be American in language and dialog.[51] At the same time, it is a search for power, Miezkowski insightfully asking, "[H]ow powerful can a single sentence be?" (Mieszkowski 35).

And just as there are ways of writing American sentences, there are ways of American speaking. The narrator of Ralph Ellison's *Invisible Man* (1952) explains that "here in the North I would slough off my southern ways of speech. Indeed, I would have one way of speaking in the North and another in the South" (IM 161). American speech clearly shapes the format, tone, and even length of the American Sentence, as noted by the linguist John McWhorter. In a 2021 column, he complains of the steady "coarsening" of American talk, noting that four-letter words often appear as punctuation (although he defends this saying that "profanity is no longer as profane as it used to be," although certain taboo words remain). He cites other shifts in American speech beginning with so-called uptalk, the habit of turning statements into questions and the overuse of "like," acknowledging the novelty of such constructions but suggesting that these colloquialisms are leading to a new level of understanding and politeness. Language, he believes, is becoming more considerate.[52]

Resisting formulaic dialogue, the American Sentence's post-1945 dialogue, curt and minimal, frequently decompresses over the course of a text, reducing itself to cyphers and eventually silence. Danielewski actually has a page in Braille, while the title of an Amy Hempel story is "*Beg, Sl Tog, Inc, Cont, Rep*." Meaningless? No. They are knitting instructions. The fate of the American Sentence may be its reduction to codes, not words, the "loss of language" Lionel Essrog experiences on the edge of the Maine shore in *Motherless Brooklyn*. But not completely. He needed "to reply in some new tongue," ever an *"Alphabet Tuningfreak!"* (MB 264, 295). The way to regain power is by the erasure and remaking of inherited language forms or as Gertrude Stein succinctly declared: "make it plain."[53] Dismantling the past, dismantling syntax, and dismantling words become the first steps in creating new sentences. "America is a poem in our eyes," Emerson said but it is also a sentence yet to be completed.[54]

Notes

1. Norman Mailer, *An American Dream* (London: Andre Deutsch, 1965) 37–8. Ernest Hemingway, *A Farewell to Arms* (1929: London: Jonathan Cape, 1933) 347.

2. *Cambridge Dictionary*. https://dictionary.cambridge.org/dictionary/english/sentence. *The American Heritage Dictionary of the English Language*. https://www.ahdictionary.com/word/search.html?q=sentence.

3. Virginia Woolf contrasted the logic-built sentence with this description of sentence-making in a letter to Via-Sackville West:

   > A sight, an emotion, creates this wave in the mind, long before it makes words to fit it … and then, as it breaks and tumbles in the mind, it makes words to fit it.
   >
   > (Virginia Woolf March 16, 1926, *Letters* Vol. III [New York: Harcourt Brace, 1978])

   She further wrote that every great work is "based on the sentence that was current at the time," *A Room of One's Own* (London: Hogarth Press, 1929) 115.

4. Sue Walker, "The American Sentence," Blog, Negative Capability Press, April 5, 2015. http://www.negativecapabilitypress.org/blog/theamericansentence. Paul E. Nelson maintains an American Sentence website with numerous examples stressing the imagistic quality of the form. See https://paulenelson.com/american-sentences-2/.

5. The poet Paul E. Nelson took this directive to heart, publishing *American Sentences: One Sentence, Every Day, Fourteen Years* (2015). It records his writing one seventeen-syllable sentence a day for eleven years. See the vol. at https://www.paulenelson.com/wp-content/uploads/2014/12/1.-American-Sentences-MS-10.27.14.pdf.

6. Louise Glück, "Ersatz Thought," *American Originality: Essays on Poetry* (New York: Farrar, Strauss and Giroux, 2017) 25–6, 27.

7   See "When William Faulkner Set the World Record for Writing the Longest Sentence in Literature," *Open Culture*, March 14, 2019. https://www.openculture.com/2019/03/when-william-faulkner-set-the-world-record-for-writing-the-longest-sentence-in-literature.html. A competitor is a sentence in Jonathan Coe's the *Rotter's Club* which ends with a 33-page-long example of 13,995 words.

8   Additional novels of one sentence include Bohumil Hrabal's *Dancing Lessons for the Advanced in Age* (1964) and Georges Perec's *The Art of Asking Your Boss for a Raise* (1968), this last uncapitalized, unpunctuated, and unparagraphed. An algorithm was the model, the text similar to that produced by a computer program. Proust, noted for long sentences, has a 447-word sentence on a sofa in *The Captive* and a 958-word sentence in *Cities of the Plain I*.

9   Legend suggests Hemingway wrote the story to win a bet. For a comic take on the story, see Zack Wortman, "Ernest Hemingway's Six-word Sequels," *New Yorker* September 11, 2016. https://www.newyorker.com/humor/daily-shouts/ernest-hemingways-six-word-sequels.

10 Mark McGurl argues for such a situation in *The Program Era, Postwar Fiction and the Rise of Creative Writing* (Cambridge, MA: Harvard University Press, 2011) 377. A recent obituary of Lewis Lapham, editor, documents his mandarin style and manners, his prose constantly demonstrating, balance, restraint, understatement, and elegance to perhaps be contrasted with the emphatic style of Hunter S. Thompson or the controlled, non-fictional writing of Joan Didion. See Christian Lorentzen, "Lewis Lapham Knew That a Great Editor Was an Artful Thief," *The Washington Post*, July 26, 2024. https://www.washingtonpost.com/books/2024/07/26/lewis-lapham-appraisal/.

On the broader question of style in fiction, see Geoffrey Leech and Mick Short, *Style in Fiction, A Linguistic Introduction to English Fictional Prose*, 2nd. Ed. (London: Routledge, 2007). The emphasis in the text is stylistics, described as "the study of the relation between linguistic form and literary function" (Leech and Short 3).

11 Alfred Kazin, *On Native Grounds, An Interpretation of Modern American Prose Literature* (1942; Garden City, NY: Doubleday Anchor Books, 1956) ix. Hereafter Kazin.

12 On this topic see Sacvan Bercovitch, *Puritan Origins of the American Self* (New Haven: Yale University Press, 1975) *passim*.

13 For a discussion of this position, see Charles Feidelson, Jr. *Symbolism and American Literature* (Chicago: University of Chicago Press, 1953) and such subsequent studies as Barbara Foley, "From New Criticism to Deconstruction: The Example of Charles Feidelson's Symbolism and American Literature," *American Quarterly* Vol.36 No.1 (1984): 44–64. Feidelson linked the symbolist method to American literary independence

with symbolism as a mode of perception rather than a technique. Consequently, the language in a symbolist work is the reality, not the expression of another reality apart from the speaker. The linguistic medium itself becomes the actual subject of symbolist literature. See Feidelson, 45, 49. Edward Said complained about this situation: "In achieving a position of mastery over man, language has reduced him to a grammatical function." People do not write texts, language writes them Said in Frank Lentricchia, *After the New Criticism* (Chicago: University of Chicago Press, 1980) 162.

14 A sentence from *White-Jacket*, appropriate to mid-nineteenth-century sentence structure, combining a series of linked clauses, is the following:

> At length, having lost her fore and main-topmasts, and her mizzen-mast having been shot away to the deck, and her foreyard lying in two pieces on her shattered forecastle, and in a hundred places having been *hulled* with round shot, the English frigate was reduced to the last extremity

Tension generated by the set of introductory clauses builds up until the main clause, the defeat of the English ship. But the diction is formal and inexact, although there are attempts at being specific (the foreyard "lying in two pieces"). Melville, "White-Jacket," *Herman Melville, Redburn, White-Jacket, Moby Dick*, ed. G. Thomas Tanselle (New York: Library of America, 1983) 678.

More characteristic is the lengthy sentence that ends chapter 1 of *Moby Dick*:

> By reason of these things, then, the whaling voyage was welcome; the great flood-gates of the wonder-world swung open, and in the wild conceits that swayed me to my purpose, two and two there floated into my inmost soul, endless processions of the whale, and, midmost of them all, one grand hooded phantom, like a snow hill in the air.
>
> (Ibid., 800)

Symbolism is rampant and the sentence grows by accumulation until the final, mysterious image. Two hundred pages later, Melville displays his virtuosity again, writing, "Is it that by its indefiniteness it shadows forth the heartless voids and immensities of the universe, and thus stabs us from behind with the thought of annihilation, when beholding the white depths of the milky way?" (ibid., 1001).

The chapter sequences and clusters, offset with balancing, factual chapters, may anticipate the structures of the American Sentence on a macro scale. See Walter Bezanson, "Moby Dick: Work of Art," *Moby Dick*, Norton Critical Edition, 2nd ed. ed. Hershel Parker and Harrison Hayford (New York: Norton 2001).

15 Henry David Thoreau, "Journal Passages," January 1842. American Transcendentalism Web. https://archive.vcu.edu/english/engweb/transcendentalism/authors/thoreau/index.html.

16 See Jack Kerouac, *On the Road*, ed. Douglas Brinkley (New York: Library of America, 2007), 10.

17 See Deborah Paes de Barros, "Driving That Highway to Consciousness: Late Twentieth-century American Travel Literature," *The Cambridge Companion to American Travel Writing*, Ed. Alfred Bendixen and Judith Hamera (Cambridge: Cambridge University Press, 2009) 231.

18 Gertrude Stein, *Useful Knowledge* (New York: Payson & Clarke, 1928) 38.

19 Robert Frost, "Interview," with William Stanley Braithwaite. *Boston Evening Transcript* May 8, 1915. https://udallasclassics.org/wp-content/uploads/maurer_files/Frost.pdf.

20 Philip Roth, *The Counterlife* (New York: Farrar Straus Giroux, 1986) 53; Roth, *Deception* (New York: Vintage Books, 1990) 194.

21 Victor Schiferli, "Marga Minco… dies at 103," *The New York Times* July 15, 2023. https://www.nytimes.com/2023/07/15/books/marga-minco-dead.html?action=click&module=Well&pgtype=Homepage§ion=Obituaries.

22 Ralph Ellison, *Selected Letters*, ed. John Callahan and Marc C. Conner (New York: Random House, 2019) 938. Hereafter Ellison.

23 Cormac McCarthy, *The Road* (New York: Vintage Books, 2006) 115, Hereafter, Road.

24 William Burroughs, *Rub Out the Words, The Letters of William S. Burroughs 1959–1974,* Ed. Bill Morgan (New York: Ecco, 2012) 28, 27, 34, 38. Hereafter Rub. For a parody of this and other "post-modern" methods, see Gilbert Sorrentino, *Mulligan's Stew* (1979). As part of the text, Sorrentino includes a selection of rejection letters he received for the novel.

Nicholas Rougeux in *Between the Words: Exploring the Punctuation in Literary Classics* (2016), a poster, went further. He stripped out all words, numbers, and spaces from well-known literary works and left only the punctuation marks, a text of pure signs.

25 Mark Z. Danielewski, *House of Leaves*, 2nd. Ed. (New York: Pantheon Books, 2000) 214, 217, 220–4. Hereafter HofL.

26 Rub 7. William Burroughs and Brion Gysin, *Third Mind* (New York: Viking, 1978) 32. For a contemporary analysis of the method see *Burroughs Unbound, William S. Burroughs and The Performance of Writing*, ed. S.E. Gontarski (London: Bloomsbury, 2023).

27 Ellison. Letter of June 5, 1991 in *Sel. Letters* 972 where he also cites a series of titles addressing the tension between the vernacular and cultured style. Ellison, *Going to the Territory* (New York: Vintage Books, 1987) 140. Ellison writes that the vernacular for him is "a dynamic *process*" where the "refined styles from the past are continually merged with the play-it-by-eye-and-by-ear improvisations which we invent in

our efforts to control our environment and entertain ourselves" (139). In this way, "the high styles of the past are democratized" (139). This was originally a talk given on September 20, 1979, at Brown University.

On the general topic of the importance of the vernacular, see Sieglinde Lemke, *The Vernacular Matters of American Literature* (New York: Palgrave Macmillan 2009).

28 Richard Bridgman, *The Colloquial Style in America* (New York: Oxford University Press, 1966) 212. Bridgman also notes that Hemingway economized so that his briefest statements bore his meaning; they, in fact, became his meaning (226). Prepositions were also key.

29 Raymond Chandler, "Trouble is my Business," *Stories and Early Novels* (1934; New York: Library of America, 1995) 552–3. A passage from *Farewell, My Lovely* conveys the drama of the plain style: "I kicked my stool back and stood up and jerked the gun out of the holster under my arm. But it was no good. My coat was buttoned and I was too slow. I'd have been too slow anyway, if it came to shooting anybody." Chandler, "Farewell, My Lovely," *Stories and Early Novels*, ed. Frank MacShane (New York: Library of America, 1995) 880.

30 See Elizabeth Closs Traugott, *A History of English Syntax* (New York: Holt, Rinehart and Winston, 1972) 26–7. Hereafter Traugott. J.R. Searle's *Speech Acts* is useful, preceded by the work of J.L. Austin.

31 Thomas Nashe, *The Unfortunate Traveller,* Intro. Edmund Gosse (London: Chiswick Press, 1892). Project Gutenberg. https://www.gutenberg.org/files/21338/21338-h/21338-h.htm.

32 Jonathan Lethem, *Motherless Brooklyn* (1999; New York: Vintage Books, 2000) 46. Hereafter MB.

33 Philip Roth, *Philip Roth at 80* (New York: Library of America, 2014) 53–4.

34 Mark McGurl discusses this thoroughly in *The Program Era, Postwar Fiction and the Rise of Creative Writing* (Cambridge, MA: Harvard University Press, 2011). An earlier discussion is Bob Perelman, "Parataxis and Narration: The New Sentence in Theory and Practice," *American Literature* Vol.65 No.2 (1993): 313–24.

35 See Ron Silliman, *The New Sentence* (New York: Roof Books, 1987); Lish in McGurl 288.

36 D.H. Lawrence, *Studies in Classic American Literature* (1923; New York: Viking, 1964) 62.

37 Richard Poirier, *A World Elsewhere, The Place of Style in American Literature* (New York: Oxford University Press 1966) 5. Hereafter, Poirier.

38 Ralph Ellison, *Invisible Man* (New York: Modern Library, 1994) 564. Hereafter IM.

39 For earlier examples, see "The Sphynx" chapter of *Moby Dick* with Ahab gazing at a decapitated head of a whale, Poe's "Silence: A Fable" or Emily Dickinson's poem beginning with "Silence is all we dread."

40 Susan Sontag, "The Aesthetics of Silence," *Styles of Radical Will* (New York: Farrar Strauss and Giroux, 1969) Sect. 6. 12–13.

41 Anne Fisher, *A Practical New Grammar* (London, 1759) in Cynthia Wall, *Grammars of Approach, Landscape, Narrative, and the Linguistic Picturesque* (Chicago: University of Chicago Press, 2019) 1. For Wall on the elements of a sentence, see 224. Hereafter Wall.

42 See Christopher P. Wilson, *The Labor of Words Literary Professionalism in the Progressive Era* (Athens: University of Georgia Press, 1985) *passim*.

43 Willa Cather, "The Professor's House," *Later Novels* (New York: Library of America, 1990) 258. Hereafter Cather.

44 Glenn A. Love, "*The Professor's House*: Cather, Hemingway and the Chastening of American Prose Style," *Western American Literature* Vol.24 No.4 (1990): 305. Hereafter Love.

45 Ernest Hemingway, *Death in the Afternoon* (New York: Scribner's 1932) 192.

46 Edmund Wilson, *Patriotic Gore, Studies in the Literature of the American Civil War* (1962; New York: Norton, 1994) 638, 639. Hereafter PGore.

47 Critics have noted that in *The Professor's House* the text shifts from third person in Book One to first person in Book Two to interior monologue in most of Book three, a progression toward muteness. See Glenn A. Love, "The Professor's House: Cather, Hemingway and Chastening of American Prose Style," *Western American Literature* Vol.24 No.4 (1990): 305.

48 Walt Whitman, "Democratic Vistas," *The Portable Walt Whitman*, ed. Mark Van Doren (New York: Viking, 1945) 393.

49 More specifically, changes in syntax marked the alterations, the principal shift in the variable forms of the American Sentence the choice between simplification or elaboration. Simplification is the "loss of a pattern or rule" such as the number, gender, and case of nouns (Traugott 14). Simplification reduces redundancy, semantically and structurally.
Choice in grammar is a condition of simplification marked in the radically different dialogue of, say, James or Wharton versus that of Joseph Heller or Colson Whitehead. By contrast, elaboration involves increased complexity often marked by the addition of a pattern. The restructuring of syntax almost always involves simplification. But as Traugott observes, simplification in one part of grammar may cause elaboration in another. Such changes, however, become the building blocks of the revitalized or at least altered American Sentence.

50 William S. Burroughs, *The Ticket That Exploded* (New York: Grove Press, 1967) 13, 31.

51 Using quantitative metrics, a 2017 study of dialogue in the novel *c*. 1790 to 1999 showed that authors add roughly one quote per thousand words every twenty-five years, "equivalent to just under one more quote per page every century." Their model of dialogism was based on grammatical categories not genre. See G. Muzny, M. Algree-Hewitt, D. Jurafsky, "Dialogism in the Novel: A Computational Model of the Dialogic Nature of Narration and Quotations," *Digital Scholarship in the Humanites* Vol.32, Issue suppl_2 (December 2017): ii 31–ii 52, https://doi.org/10.1093/llc/fqx031. For a detailed, algorithmic analysis of dialogue see https://academic.oup.com/dsh/article/32/suppl_2/ii31/3978683.

52 John McWhorter, "The Softening of American Conversation," *The New York Times* August 27, 2021. https://www.nytimes.com/2021/08/27/opinion/uptalk-English-language-coarsening.html. In certain ways, McWhorter echoes Walker Gibson's, *Tough, Sweet & Stuffy, An Essay on Modern American Prose Styles* (Bloomington, IN: Indiana University Press, 1966). Gibson has several passages on diction, sentence length and structure. In the "Tough Talk," section, he suggests that the length of sentences has been "reduced almost to the disappearing point" (83). Voice, tone, and persona are Gibson's concerns; he is especially clear on the sentence constructions of Hemingway (34–7).

Matthew Krumholtz's 2015 dissertation at Princeton, "Talking Points," explores different categories of dialog and their political valences: straight talk, small talk, cross talk, and smooth talk relating each to a set of particular authors. See https://dataspace.princeton.edu/handle/88435/dsp01cc08hh93k.

53 The full statement reads "anybody knows the difference between explain and make it plain." Gertrude Stein, "Henry James," *Four in America*, Intro. by Thornton Wilder (Freeport, New York: Books for Libraries Press, 1947) 125.

54 Emerson, "The Poet," *Essays Second Series* (1844) 21. Emerson Central. https://emersoncentral.com/ebook/The%20Poet.pdf.

Chapter 1
American Voices: The Pulpit, the Sermon, the Jeremiad

His way of Preaching was plain, aiming to shoot his Arrows not over his people's heads, but into their Hearts and Consciences.
          INCREASE MATHER ON HIS FATHER, RICHARD MATHER

Increase Mather's description of his father Richard Mather's pulpit style aimed for directness: "[I]n handling the deepest Mysteries he would accommodate himself to Vulgar Capacities, that even the meanest might learn something." This was not, however, always the case. The origin and change that preceded this shift in the rhetoric, delivery, and style, to later dominate American prose, found their beginnings in biblical prose with the sermon as the keynote form of American communication.[1]

This chapter concentrates on the building of the American sentence from its Puritan foundations expressed in the sermon to its eighteenth- and nineteenth-century forms. Drawing from ideas presented by a range of scholars, from Sacavan Bercovitch in the *Puritan Origins of the American Self* (1976) to Andrew Delbanco's *The Puritan Ordeal* (1989), Larzar Ziff's *Puritanism in America* (1973), Patricia Roberts-Miller's *Voices in the Wilderness: Public discourse and the Paradox of Puritan Rhetoric* (1999), and Kenneth and William Hopper's *The Puritan Gift* (2007), as well as Robert Alter's *Pen of Iron, American Prose and the*

King James Bible (2010), it will show how the sermon and the Jeremiad introduced, in addition to a new rhetoric of American identity and expression, a new channel of communication.

i

"The principal action of the day," Perry Miller writes in summarizing the practices of early American Puritan settlements, was

> the delivery of a public sermon before all the society, in which the minister, the spokesman for the community, would set forth the issues of occasion, review the affliction, and make articulate the determination of the group ... to banish whatever sins had brought the distress upon it.[2]

The sermon as an oral newspaper became a source of community news, although its language was biblical and its message theological. A prophetic tone fashioned the delivery, while biblical references and allusions provided its content and shaped its sentences. It mixed an inherited formality with a determination to correct. It commanded, directed, and entertained no stylistic deviations, although that would change.

As a communication tool, the sermon and the preacher became the dominant voice of New England's moral and political authority. Views on faith, society, social action, and politics found a truth component in the form of the sermon, the dominant means of communicating with a forceful rhetoric of action and power. It "stood alone in local New England contexts as the only regular (at least weekly) medium of public 'communication' combining religious, education and journalistic functions," writes Harry Stout at the opening of *The New England Soul* (Stout 3). The sermon became "a channel of information," regularly uniting a community while conveying spiritual and even secular news to its audience (Stout 3). Over time, it became "the dominant ritual of social order" (Stout 147). The church covenant and belief that the New Englanders were the chosen of God reconfirmed the authority of the minister's voice and texts. In this way, the continuity and strength of the church and preaching remained echoed in the repeated and sacred triumvirate of piety, power, and liberty. The religious dimension of republicanism was the point of revolution (Stout 310).

Community gatherings in seventeenth-century America often became a ritual to address "communal humiliation" when people in church acknowledged their sins and promised to reform, while praying for relief ("Declension"16). The sermon brought hope as well as news, both spiritual and communal. The Calvinist theology meant all action was under the providence of God. Natural law did not exist and moral judgments upon "a sinful people" were acts of God. The formula was simple and spelled out repeatedly in the sermon: if people are sinful, they suffer; if they are virtuous they prosper. The aim was to establish a covenant with God to ensure right behavior ("Declension" 17–19). The constant emphasis in a standardized sermon was devoted exclusively to an analysis of the sins of the people; denouncing the sins of corruption was their message. But the importance of the sermon as a form of communication, shouted out to a willing audience, was less religious than stylistic becoming an early American guide to linguistic practice often duplicated in conversation and other texts.

Denouncing the spread of corruption took further form identified in an angry American voice as the jeremiad, a lament on the decline or declension of New England Puritanism. Tirades against a lengthening list of sins formed its content. Its pattern became a public review of the shortcomings of the society at large to be verbalized on formal occasions. The method soon became "fixed and stereotyped as the funeral sermon or Latin oration" ("Declension" 23). This would be, in legal terms, "an arraignment of public evils" which were often printed and circulated throughout the colonies ("Declension" 23). These tabulations of sins replaced any discourse on doctrine or grace. Jonathan Mitchell's *Nehemiah on the Wall* (1667) and William Stoughton's *New England's True Interests* (1668) are two definitive jeremiads with new sins added yearly. The jeremiads of the 1670s, Miller writes, were "the literary triumphs of the decade," two successes Samuel Danforth's *A Brief Recognition of New England's Errand into the Wilderness* (1670), followed by Increase Mather's *The Day of Trouble Is Near* (1673) ("Declension" 24).

Sacvan Bercovitch furthered the concept and form of the jeremiad in his 1978 study, *The American Jeremiad*, noting its persistence through the eighteenth century and how it joined "social criticism to spiritual renewal, public to private identity," playing a major role in "fashioning the myth of America."[3] "American Puritan rhetoric," Bercovitch's label, becomes the formative base for the early American Sentence. But what were its features?

To begin, there was an inheritance of the English/Anglican pulpit style soon amplified and altered in America, substituting optimism for vengeance, affirmation for sin (Bercovitch 7). They did not sacrifice divine retribution but intensified it with a switch: "God's punishments were *corrective*, not destructive .... his vengeance was a sign of love" (Bercovitch 8). Scriptural phrases provide the mechanics, oral delivery the syntax, America ("the wilderness") the vision. The result was a fusion of the secular and sacred creating a prophetic history with a sense of mission. In relation to content, there was a scheme: a precedent from Scripture setting out communal norms, then a set of condemnations that detail the actual state of the community and "finally a prophetic vision that unveils the promises" (Bercovitch 16). This "three-part configuration" became the standard rhetorical and stylistic format for almost two centuries.

The formality of the sentences reflects a progressive, syntactic build-up, increasing in cadence and climax. There was no room for play or experiment as long there was a message to project, a message that joined promise with condemnation. The decline of Puritan theocracy, however, loosened the sentence structures and allowed for personalization, subjectivity, even lyricism. Sentences became varied, fluid, elastic, and casual. Conflict may have defined the modus operandi of the predominant sermon but consensus and then consolidation replaced it often generated by ambiguity. The language and form of the sermon became devalued as theocracy declined with new immigrants, the drive for independence and a quest for freedom partly expressed through laissez-faire capitalism. Rapid social change meant rapid stylistic change. A homogeneous style dissolved as the plain style replaced the biblical, and a new Yankee style, with its idioms and diction, overtook the Puritan in the late seventeenth century.[4]

The rhetorical force of the "political sermon," another phrase for the jeremiad, came from a single source: the Bible. In terms of diction, syntax, parallelism, and structure—the ground-work of the sermonic style was fixed. Anaphora (repeating a sequence to establish rhythm with similar but not exact words) dignified the language, while creating impact. The sentence absorbed formality from its rhetoric supported by its elevated diction. The King James Version of the Bible (1611) triumphed (with modification) in the wilderness. The foundation of the American sermonic sentence is scriptural, compelling preachers and writers to assume a tone and set of images often out-of-step with the direct experience of the early Americans seeking to evolve a culture from the wilderness. But the imposition of the formal structures was precisely to regulate and order the spiritual and literary landscape. It is no surprise to learn that Hebrew (not Greek) was required for all first-year students at Harvard when it was founded in 1636.

The language of the Old Testament, as Robert Alter has suggested, suffused the writing of nineteenth century and later American writers. Their sentences assumed a semi-prophetic, oratorical nature, often favoring a periodic construction, partly echoing the prominence of the American Greek Revival style.[5] Think Hawthorne, think Melville, think Faulkner. But gradually, resistance to the canonical occurred, plain and precise language substituting for biblical typology and symbolic language to sustain audiences. A divide occurred between the archaic language of the Bible and contemporary American usage, An adjustment in style was needed. Replacing biblicizing phrases was speech, the natural replacing the artful. "Speaking intellect" imposed itself on written style.[6] The "technologies of the word" influenced what and how a statement, a declaration, or even a question was uttered.[7]

Performance and voice became essential in preaching, the speaker often employing contrapuntal diction drawing on a biblical lexicon—but it was soon surpassed by an emphatic antithesis in succinct, parallel clauses replenishing elevated biblical structures. Monosyllabic words, originating in the Anglo-Saxon world, competed with diction derived from Greco-Latin language elements, largely polysyllabic. But the aim remained the same: to use reason to encourage faith as it affected this life and the next. Exhortation, threats, conciliation, and a core biblical text were the lynchpins, strongly expressed in formulaic sentences. Doctrine and practice ruled in an effort to explicate the Word following the triple division of Doctrine, Reason, and Use. Citations were biblical, not classical and each sermon attempted to identify, from the text, an axiom of theology and to discuss its practical applications. The text was then dismantled by analysis into its component parts and usually set out again as a proposition. After the logical analysis of the passage, the practical appeal was made by the pastor who attempted to make the Bible applicable to real life.

The aim, according to the seventeenth-century theologian Richard Baxter, was "first to convince the understanding and then to engage the heart. Light first, then heat."[8] A sentence from Isaiah 58:1 conveys the energy to be transmitted: "Cry aloud, spare not, lift up your voice like a trumpet; declare to My people their transgression, to the house of Jacob their sin." Parallel clauses following the semicolon add heft to the challenge of "Cry aloud, spare not." The sentence accelerates from long expressions to short.

For the Puritans, the Reformation did not go far enough. They demanded that the Church reduce ritual and foster the preaching of sermons to educate parishioners about Scripture. The canons of the Church of England prescribed only four sermons a year and Elizabeth I tried to restrict preaching to short homilies. But sermon attendance increased, often meeting secretly to hear preachers. By 1592, a work entitled the *Art of Prophecying,* by William Perkins outlined four practice rules: (1) read the text out-loud from the Canonical Scriptures (often from the annotated Geneva Bible); (2) offer a brief explication (texts) followed by (3) a statement on Doctrine; and (4) a final section on Use, showing the practical application of the Doctrine. Logic joined rhetoric in the presentation of the ideal sermon often delivered from memory or outline notes.[9]

Extemporaneous preaching was rare until the late eighteenth century, a stricture duplicated in the style of writing: formal, precise, repetitive, and mechanical. The so-called "plain style," noted by Perkins, stressed clarity but did not renounce figures of speech or erudition. Eliminating the ostentatious was the goal. Publication of the sermon quickly became desired so that parishioners could review and study what the preacher said. To that end, members of congregations often took down entire sermons in shorthand or made notes. The delivery of sermons usually occurred on Sunday morning and again on Sunday afternoon, as well as a lecture sermon usually given on Thursday. All sermons normally lasted an hour and were also given on special occasions such as annual elections, funerals, fast days, and public executions. These occasional sermons were more likely to be published to educate and remind the public of their social responsibilities. The so-called Sunday sermons (morning and afternoon) were not published, yet they were considered to be the more important: they were heard by more, concentrated on salvation, and had a greater impact on the theological life of Colonial America.[10] The sovereignty of God reigned over the concept of free will, while the church was a community of the elect formed in a covenant with God. But each church in the colonial period required a spiritual exam from every candidate for membership.

The ornate style of presentation served to prove the art of the preacher with the performance more important than the tents of faith. But the weakness of this method was that it apparently did not penetrate the hearts and minds of the audience; they switched to the more appealing "plain style" in contrast to the eloquent sermons of Anglican bishops. The Puritan preference for austerity and simplicity found expression in the rigid, rational form of the sermon with its managed language. The plain style transformed the Puritan sermon into a lecture designed to inculcate principles of the Gospel. In "Preach like a Puritan," Obbie Tylor Todd explains that the Puritan opened by expounding the context and setting of a passage. This included an explanation of grammar and the rhetoric of the text. Next, the preacher proclaimed the doctrine in a straightforward way contained in the text. In his preaching textbook, *The Art of Prophecying*, Perkins outlined this highly methodical form, and the benefit of topics and subtopics. Ultimately, rewording texts into doctrinal statements was one of the accomplishments of Puritan preaching "designed to make a highly developed argument for the reasonableness of Gospel truths." Further characterizing the Puritan plain style were short words, direct statements, and references to everyday objects.[11]

The Puritans were logo-centric, *sola scriptura.* Scripture was God speaking and preaching was largely expository. The sermon exists inside the Word of God; the sermon is in the text and partly explained through the agent of the Word, Christ. The Bible and Christ's word were the grammar of Puritan preaching which became, in the words of Martyn Lloyd-Jones, "logic on fire," constantly stressing form and structure. Discussions of doctrine always required examples or testimonies from Scripture. Here is a description by Leland Ryken, literary editor of the *English Standard Version* of the *Bible* (2001):

> The Puritan sermon was planned and organized. It may have been long and detailed, but it did not ramble. It was controlled by

a discernible strategy and it progressed toward a final goal. The methodology ensured that the content would be tied to Scripture, that the sermon would involve an intellectual grasp of the truth, and that theological doctrine would be applied to everyday living.

The Puritan sermon quotes the text and 'opens' it as briefly as possible, expounding circumstances and context, explaining its grammatical meanings, reducing its tropes and schemata to prose, and setting forth its logical implications; the sermon then proclaims in a flat, indicative sentence the "doctrine" contained in the text or logically deduced from it, and proceeds to the first reason or proof. Reason follows reason, with no other transition than a period and a number; after the last proof is stated there follow the uses or applications, also in numbered sequence, and the sermon ends when there is nothing more to be said.[12]

Grace, they knew, entered the heart through the mind. And there were no distractions or digressions. Truth came by definition.[13] But length, volume, and syntax—all had a crucial role. But the plain style was rhetorically never plain. It followed a firm structure of exegesis, doctrine, proof, and uses as Perkins had outlined. It was often prolix and scholastic and measured success only by its results. Plainness did not mean lack of complexity. Simplicity of speech and logic, not necessarily brevity or anti-complexity, was the new style. The Puritans did not favor a pastiche of quotations or embellished language (Ryken 40).

The printed sermon became a popular form of knowledge distribution, circulating for study, home reference, repeated discussion, and reading. People saw what was said. Print itself restructured communication, while the form of expression provided rigorous *textual* authority for what they heard. Writing offered a private, not communal, domain for knowledge separate from communal interaction, creating an "inward turn." It altered relationships between the known and the knower. The objectivity of thought generated by print created information as a commodity, data which could be manipulated. The printed sermon became an agency of culture *and* literary change centering text as a critical part of American religious life, evolving from the pulpit to the page. Supplementing it were religious tracts, newsletters, self-help books, and editions of the Bible.

By 1776, Congregational ministers in New England were delivering over two thousand sermons a week, publishing them at a rate that outnumbered secular pamphlets from all the colonies by a ratio of more than four to one (Stout 6). In revolutionary New England "ministers continued to monopolize public communications" using Scriptures to justify resistance (Stout 7). The idea of a "national covenant" provided the "liberties" New Englanders would die protecting, while the sermon became a public call to arms. Within the covenantal perspective, resistance to England "was only secondarily about constitutional rights and political liberties" (Stout 7). The primary objection was religious. Printed sermons became the "Pulpit of the American Revolution," the title of John Wingate Thornton's 1860 collection of early American sermons that related political liberty with religious truths.

Generating the attack on England was anger at Great Britain in setting itself alongside the word of God as a competing sovereign. Such tyrannical demands gave New Englanders no choice but to resist. The providential mission of pulpit discourse invigorated the public imagination and eased the acceptance of the Revolution and republican principles. Radical changes in social and political organizations meant that the Revolution was not a rejection but fulfilment of the original dream to create a holy nation subject to the claims of God. The "exegetical inventiveness of their ministers" preserved the myth that New England audiences were special people maintaining continuity with the past. New Englanders, Stout writes, perceived themselves as "the predestined founders of the American republic" (Stout 9). But the error was to read America as New England "writ large" (Stout 9). The Middle Colonies and Chesapeake showed that the atypical New Englander was in certain economic, political, and demographic respects out-of-step with the young country. Nonetheless, "the influence of Puritan rhetoric on the American identity" was formidable (Stout 9). Messianic destiny and national elections guided religious beliefs.

The preeminence of the sermon in the continuity of New England culture insured its role as the primary form of communication read and heard by many.[14] Sermons were events to experience as well as objects to be studied. Biblical Israel became the typological starting point for understanding New England's special, national covenant with God. And while occasional sermons were given on lecture days during the week, as well as Thanksgiving, militia, and election days, it was the Sunday salvation sermons, admonishing the nation, that mattered most. As early as 1626, it was understood that "faithful ministers are the defenders of states, churches and commonwealths," the term "defender" a euphemism for critics (in Bush 138). Expanding the spiritual role of the preacher was the public who, by the mid-eighteenth century, became promoters of increased opposition to British authority. Tyranny was to be resisted.

In the midst of these debates over the politics of the sermon, Colonial printing grew to address the scarcity of religious literature and biblical texts. The printed sermon became the gateway to such popular publications. As early as 1638, Cambridge, in the Massachusetts Bay Colony, had a printing press to offer reading material of a spiritual nature. Its first publication was the *Bay Psalm Book* (1640), although with type (with remarkably uniform font) and paper still imported from England. However, by 1690, a paper mill was established in Germantown, PA.[15] By 1725, the printer William Bradford, formally of Philadelphia, who began with religious tracts, moved to New York and established its first newspaper, the *New York Gazette*. The first regularly published newspaper printed in British North America, however, was the *Boston News-Letter*, first issued in 1704. There were no newspapers in the colonies before 1700; printed sermons carried the social and religious news. The Mathers, father and son, would often distribute their sermons as pamphlets during pastoral visits, as well as to ships' officers for the benefit of their sailors. Increase Mather set up the first press in Boston in 1675. Its first book was his *A Wicked Man's Portion* (1675). The text was a sermon linked to the hanging of two men for murder delivered the year before. The words "sermon" and "murder" often appeared together on title pages to titillate readers. The most popular books from New England presses from 1638 to 1713 were execution sermons and captivity narratives. Printers aggressively sought sermons to print; they knew they had a ready audience.

The Sunday sermon communicated not only God's word but, when necessary, a critique of society, government, and the nation. In this way, it became a tool of cultural, as well as religious, messaging. One of the most controversial and yet popular was *An Arrow Against Profane and Promiscuous Dancing. Drawn out of the Quiver of the Scriptures* (1686), largely written by Increase Mather. The occasion for *An Arrow* was the arrival of dancing master in Boston in 1685 who offered classes for men and women during times normally reserved for church meetings. With appropriate biblical, classical, and historical examples, and support from Church Fathers and reformed theologians, Mather compiles arguments and precedents for the prohibition of mixed or "Promiscuous Dancing," men and women together. Such behavior would absolutely lead to sin: adultery and other sexual acts were only a few short steps from the dance floor. "The unchast Touches and Gesticulations used by *Dancers,* have a palpable tendency to that which is evil."[16] The tone is admonitory, the syntax hortatory.

But as communication technology shifted, so, too, did written style, specifically the American Sentence as used in the Sermon. It became more relaxed, responding to a restless audience that did not want to be lectured to. It reflected, through the next century, new complexities, as Abraham Joshua Heschel would later describe: "God has moved out of the fortress of pedestrian certainties and is dwelling in perplexities." He has "entered our spiritual agony, upsetting dogmas."[17] With print, knowledge turned into a product to be consumed as information and fact. But soon, a new emphasis on speed emerged, related to the arrival of electric communication, specifically the telegraph and telephone which objectified the voice. However, Mark Twain, like others, had doubts about this transition: "The moment you pick up a pen, you begin to lose the spontaneity of the personal relation which contains the very essence of interest." But despite Twain's complaint, print culture advanced, again in contrast to Twain's hesitations: "With a pen in the hand the narrative stream is a canal; it moves slowly, smoothly, decorously, sleepily …. it is too literary, too prim, too nice; the gait and style and movement are not suited to narrative."[18] Matching his views, Twain did not write but dictate his *Autobiography*.

While the biblical tone and structures of Puritan language at first dominated American discourse, the material of the American sentence quickly became the difference between the rhetorical excesses of Cotton Mather in his *Magnalia Christi Americana* (1702) with its Greek and Latin quotations, learned references, wordplay, italic type, and profusion of capital letters and that of Benjamin Franklin who outlined his own casual writing practice:

> I … sometimes jumbled my Collections of Hints into Confusion, and after some Weeks endeavour'd to reduce them into the best Order, before I began to form the full Sentences & compleat the Paper.[19]

Forms of expression gradually became informal, relaxed, with plainness and lucidity the new aim. Mather, however, unites the self and the nation into an imaginative construction, projected in American heroes defined by conquering the land and, if necessary, its indigenous people as seen in James Fenimore Cooper. As Bercovitch outlines, to be an American meant assuming a prophetic identity. Think of Melville, Faulkner, Richard Wright, Saul Bellow, or Toni Morrison where the prophetic infuses their sentences with energy.

America became its own fulfilment, the figure of, rather than just the setting for, redemption. Its language, and specifically its prose, blended self, history, and nation. This inverted traditional Puritan hermeneutics. The shift was from the Bible to America; writers and readers were not merely Americans but America itself, a radically subjective perception projected through the syntax and form of what became the American, not Puritan, sentence. It was free from the prescriptions of any sacred text and responded to the immediate needs of the new populace and its engagement with the "wilderness," the title of Perry Miller's classic study of the rhetoric and language of the Puritans, *Errand into the Wilderness* (1956).

But where would the sentence go? And what did it mean to write like an American? Was it actually original prose or did it refashion its European, notably English, antecedents? Recent analyses of literary originality complicate clear answers but on the page, it is possible to see change as American history, technological developments and a widening democracy released the sentence from its biblical confinement.[20] Coordinated with these changes was Noah Webster's 1789 *Dissertation on the English Language*, an effort to differentiate American from British English. It is necessary for Americans to find their own standard or system, he argues: "Great Britain … should no longer be *our* standard; for the taste of her writers is already corrupted, and her language on the decline."[21] And in his *An American Dictionary of the English Language* (1828), Webster's first definition of "sentence" is legal: "a judgment pronounced by a court." Only his sixth definition relates to grammar: "a number of words containing complete sense or a sentiment, and followed by a full pause."[22]

In his essay "An American Language," Perry Miller understood the rigidity of the Puritan outlook and style fashioned by ideas of predestination and the search for salvation. But their influence on

American Literature, Miller came to believe, was "a curse" and repressed the literary conscience.[23] This occurred because the movement was not genuinely Puritan "and instead became merely didactic." Substituting for life as an ordeal was a new, almost cheery, moralism. Life remained earnest but revolt was inevitable. Hemingway, in fact, criticized the New England poets (Longfellow, Whittier) as substituting a withered speech for the language of the everyday, "the words that survive in language." Instead of bodies, they had minds, "nice, dry, clean minds" (in Miller Amer. 234). They wrote for "edification" not life and lacked a common voice. In Miller's language, they became "the orthodox poets of American households" in contrast to the dark worlds and sentences of a Hawthorne, Poe, or Melville (Miller Amer. 235).

Into this maelstrom between formal and informal, stepped Twain who pretended to write a boy's book by using, of all choices, dialect, generating candor, spontaneity, curiosity, and adventure. Huck speaks with a natural authority about violence, misbehavior, and deception. He also addresses what is noble and self-sacrificial without resorting to moralistic language or posturing in sentences that are immediate and direct. A naive bravado captures the reader for this special American life presenting an American "linguistic realism" that is unhidden and perhaps at times, unhinged (Miller Amer. 236). This romance in the plain style even captures the differences in inflection between states like Arkansas, Louisiana, and Missouri, plus those of a disenfranchised and uneducated Black man. But the goal of the plain style, the foundation for the American Sentence, is that it allows one to say things that otherwise would not be said at all: "what lies, unsaid, behind their [the writers] compulsion often using words to stand for objects, things, the concrete as in the inventory of found things Huck and Jim take from the house floating on the river" (Miller Amer. 237, 238). Miller later calls this a "transparent simplicity" of language and sentences (Miller Amer. 239).

Under this rubric, religion and sermonizing fare badly. Piety is satirized and churches become only signs of obligations and sometimes visited by hogs. "If you notice, most folks don't go to church only when they've got to; but a hog is different" is Huck's view discovering several hogs wandering around a church where he's gone to retrieve Miss Sophia's Bible.[24] The sermon and its message become sources of ridicule as seen in chapter 18, the men of the feuding families carrying their guns into the church, keeping them between their knees or leaning them against the wall. The sermon, Huck reports, was "pretty ornery preaching—all about brotherly love" "and such-like tiresomeness, but everybody said it was a good sermon" concentrating on "faith and preforeordestination and I don't know what all, that it did seem to me to be one of the roughest Sundays I had run across yet" (Twain 90). The ungrammatical account is appropriate for the youthful Huck and overall tone of the text.

The key to *Huckleberry Finn* (1884) is its orality which blends the delivery of a sermon with the character of the young narrator, engaged, repetitive, and using unpunctuated, misspelt language and vernacular diction. The vernacular is a noun and the substance, the colloquial an adjective and a manner of expression according to Richard Bridgman who further adds that the vernacular "is defined as a nation's common fund of language" or what others labeled "ordinary language."[25] But in Twain and in the sermon, the visual, the text on the page, and the oral intersect.

But if Twain's informal style charmed, it also had dangers. The colloquial encouraged vulgarity, obscenity, fragmentation, repetition, and an undermining of serious thought. But its informality ruled, breaking out of the straightjacket of a pseudo-British rhetoric and formal sentence structures that would have been incompatible with the character.

To recap: at the start of the American style, the sermon inherited a formal shape with the overall goal to claim God's promise in today's world, Puritan or modern, with rigor, solemnity, and rhetorical power. Often beginning with a biblical text, exegesis followed, the preacher outlining the content, intent, and argument of a passage. The goal was to explicate the meaning of the source then move to its application to the lives of the listeners. Three questions often shaped the structure: what does the passage mean, is it true and believable, and how is it applicable to our situation? The answer will decide the purpose of the sermon. But if sermons have formal characteristics, they have no set arrangement and can focus on a single verse or several passages. But the sermon is the core of worship. Instruction, exhortation, and spiritual liberation—they are the goals, a triangle of message, speaker, and audience. Homiletics, the art of preaching, sustained a population eager to be taught.

But if the form is generally recognized, the content shifted from exhortations of God and instructions for a holy life to a set of urgent topics from revolutionary war, slavery, and politics to relationships, redemption, and patriotism. But always with clarity: "Whatever ideas I consider, I shall endeavour to take them bare and naked into my view," Bishop George Berkeley's claim, became the watchword of the New England preachers (in Miller Nature 176).

The Puritan style gradually overrode the ornate, elaborate style and performance metrics of the preacher's art to present the tenets of faith expressed in common language and form appealing to an undereducated audience. A vernacular style replaced the effort at overused Latinate structures, Seneca instead of Cicero. The goal was to simplify language so that it could be understood, amplifying concepts in plain language. Tropes had to be understandable and it had to be personal, emotive, unlike the scientific style which sought to be impersonal and objective. Emotion brought conviction. Periodic sentences with dependent clauses and subordinating conjunctions, where the message of the sentence was suspended until the last clause were too difficult to follow. Preferable were loose sentences usually with coordinating clauses with "and" as the frequent conjunction or use of simple, brief statements strung together by colons and semicolons. They were easier to follow. A sermon by Henry Smith, popular London preacher of the Elizabethan period, is an example: "*It is said that drunken porters keep open gates; so when Noah was drunken, he set all open. As wine went in, so wit went out; as wit went out, so his clothes came off.*"[26] Repetition with variation of simple constructions lent force to the image.

Bishop Thomas Sprat in his history of the Royal Society explained that members sought to return "to the primitive purity and shortness, when men delivered so many *things* almost in an equal number of *words.*" The goal was to bring all things "as near the Mathematical plainness as they can."[27]

Utilitarian was the aim of the American plain style, plainness equated with truthfulness. For the Puritan preachers, it was in harmony with plain living in the wilderness. The Puritans, again, "identified simplicity of expression with authenticity, truth" (Kr 61). Thomas Hooker made this clear in his preface to *A Survey of the Summe of Church-Discipline* (1648). The discourse "*comes forth in such a homely dresse and course habit, the Reader must be desired to consider. It comes out of the wildernesses, here curiosity is not studied"* (Kr 61). Hooker made it clear that *"Plainnesse and perspicuity"* were his goals and in this way able to "make a hard point easy and familiar in explication" (Kr 62). "God's altar needs no polishing" (Kr 62)

But the concept of the plain style was not stable; by the mid-eighteenth century, it had lost its hegemony partly because of new ties with English literary life, growing wealth, and increased middle-class aspirations that wanted higher thoughts in higher language. Style came to be elaborate and complex.[28] *Stylus planus* faded but still had an impact on the American sentence. Cicero soon overshadowed Seneca.

ii

The sermon preceded the novel, not only chronologically but stylistically, becoming an essential channel of communication transferring ideas of right and wrong behavior, colony news, and the importance of holidays. Threats matched exhortations, the written supplementing the oral. The nature of the content determined the form of presentation, emotion, as well as thought, shaping the sentences. The goal of the American sermon was to make it alive which meant departing from traditional forms by inserting rhetorical questions, deliberate pauses, and even lapses of memory to enhance the speech dramatically. The speaker may also depart from the written text through spontaneous remarks or interpolations in the printed work. The order of syntax may shift from written to verbal delivery. Intensity is key, shaping the rhythm as the extemporaneous takes over. The stylistic impact altered the nature of the American Sentence.

The language and imagery were powerful and dominating as Emory Elliott outlines in *Power and the Pulpit in Puritan New England* (1975). Jonathan Mitchell's statement in *Nehemiah on the Wall in Troublesome Times* is representative:

> [T]he crown is fallen from our head; woe unto us that we have sinned. For this is our heart faint, for these things our eyes are dim .... *Let those dreadful Thunder-claps, which of late have broken over our heads, awake and call us up from the bed of Sloth.*[29]

Metaphor, fear, and a tone of prophetic warning rule over those lost in the wilderness, itself a metaphor of loss and emptiness within the self. The titles alone of the sermons generated fear: *God's Just Desertion of the Unjust* (1622) or *The Times of Man are in the Hands of God* (1675).

John Oxenbridge of the First Church of Boston was equally florid and elaborate in his titles, mixing chastisement with comfort: *A Quickening Word for Hastening a Sluggish Soul to a Seasonable Answer to the Divine Call* (1670). William Hubbard began to introduce new metaphors with more moderated and less biblical titles: *The Benefit of a Well-Ordered Conversation* (1684) or Thomas Thatcher's *A Fast of God's Choosing* (1674), where sensuous imagery replaced threats and warnings. There was no impulse to scold but to praise, or at least encourage, extended by Samuel Willard expressed in his collection of two hundred and fifty lecture/sermons, *A Complete Body of Divinity* with its goal of a covenant of redemption with metaphor replacing doctrine. There was also a shift to the "spiritual value of a man's earthly activities" partly expanded by Cotton Mather, son of Increase (Elliott 180). His sermons stressed assurance and renewal for "the *saved* Believer" expressed emotionally, metaphorically: "we were in a *Sea of fire* miserably scorched and scalded, and yet it was *mingled with Ice*" (Elliott 188, 190). Such dynamic language impacted the structure and control of the American Sentence.

But Emerson, also an ordained Unitarian minister who delivered 164 sermons, went further. His sermons began to project an autobiographical aura, more so after the death of his wife. The meaning of his homiletic narratives shifted as he reached higher levels of self-understanding until his religious reversal and decision to leave the church in 1832. This is part of a narrative that replaces doctrine with self, especially after a crisis in an effort to create a new man. The style of the sermons reflects this change adapting it to transmit a shift in beliefs and attitude expanding Luke 17:21: "The kingdom of God is within you." Self-reliance emerges with an authority now located in the self.[30] Self-representation derives from understanding and a recreation of the self transmitted through a natural and personal style generated rhetorically, not historically (Roberson 20–1). The "Divinity School Address" of July 1838 critiqued conventional forms of Christianity, calling for a new spirituality based on individual experience and personal insight. Self-discovery and self-reliance become the keynotes. The alteration of narrative and broadening of discourse, resulting in his personal transformation, remakes the sermon and impacts the style and the formation of the American Sentence. Acceptance of a more direct informal style prepared Americans for the curt, precise style influenced by a new technology: the telegraph.

In the aftermath of the Civil War, the Reconstructionist era saw the emergence of what Leo Marx called the machine in the garden. Technology challenged the pastoral as an American ideal. The shift heightened the need for a new style, a new form of expression to match the acceleration of speed in production and the transfer of information and goods. Signs of this conflict were evident but varied: Thoreau in *Walden Pond* (1854) records a train whistle suggesting technological imagery to introduce "a new mode of perception."[31] A more sensational example occurs at the end of chapter 1 of Frank Norris's *The Octopus* (1903). Walking through the lyrical landscape of the San Joaquin Valley, the protagonist witnesses a locomotive smash into a herd of sheep: "the iron monster had charged full into the midst, merciless, inexorable .... backs were snapped against the fence posts; brains knocked out. Caught in the barbs of the wire ... the bodies hung suspended." The engine became a

> galloping monster, the terror of steel and steam, with its single eye, cyclopean, red, shooting from horizon to horizon ... the symbol of a vast power, huge, terrible, flinging the echo of its thunder over all the reaches of the valley ... ; the leviathan, with tentacles of steel clutching into the soil, the soulless Force, the iron-hearted Power, the monster, the Colossus, the Octopus.[32]

Henry Adams would reflect his contrast between the pastoral and the technical in his two master symbols from *The Education of Henry Adams* (1905/6): the Virgin and the Dynamo. Earlier, as a sign of contrasting worlds, he had used a motor car to visit the medieval cathedrals of France presented in *Mont Saint Michel and Chartres* (1904). Two other motor car enthusiasts at this time were Proust and Gertrude Stein.

The contradictions between the technological and the pastoral formed the basis of Lionel Trilling's important essay "Reality in America" (1940) in which he showed that contradiction is the essence of the American culture. The power of America rests in paradox.

Challenges to the rhetorical formalities of the American Sentence resulted in what was a loosening of American syntax, a growing sense of familiarity complexly mixed with emotion countering rhetorical doctrine. Henry James's *The Portrait of a Lady* (1880–1) encapsulates the change with a youthful Isabella Archer confronting the social and rhetorical establishment of Europe. The conflict of voices is as powerful as the conflict of cultures. Following a disagreement with her aunt about being able to sit up alone with Lord Warburton at Gardencourt, is the following:

Ralph meanwhile handed Isabel her candlestick. He had been watching her; it had seemed to him her temper was involved—an accident that might be interesting. But if he had expected anything of a flare he was disappointed, for the girl simply laughed a little, nodded good-night and withdrew accompanied by her aunt. For himself he was annoyed at his mother, though he thought she was right. Above-stairs the two ladies separated at Mrs. Touchett's door. Isabel had said nothing on her way up.

"Of course you're vexed at my interfering with you," said Mrs. Touchett.

Isabel considered. "I'm not vexed, but I'm surprised—and a good deal mystified. Wasn't it proper I should remain in the drawing-room?"

"Not in the least. Young girls here—in decent houses—don't sit alone with the gentlemen late at night."

"You were very right to tell me then," said Isabel. "I don't understand it, but I'm very glad to know it."

"I shall always tell you," her aunt answered, "whenever I see you taking what seems to me too much liberty."

"Pray do; but I don't say I shall always think your remonstrance just."

"Very likely not. You're too fond of your own ways."

"Yes, I think I'm very fond of them. But I always want to know the things one shouldn't do."

"So as to do them?" asked her aunt.

"So as to choose," said Isabel.[33]

The notion of social and rhetorical independence is clear in the form of this curt and direct exchange. One might claim that Isabel alters the architecture of the American Sentence, reforming it in response to character and context with an American spirit confronting a European outlook. It also reveals a powerful self-reflexiveness. The development of the telegraph will further advance stylistic changes. It is no surprise that James's "In the Cage" (1898) is a novella focusing on a London telegraphist deciphering messages and gleaning meanings between Lady Bradeen and her lover, Captain Everard. James himself sent and received frequent telegrams.

In short, machine power, creating the demand for speed, found its way not only by image but method. There was no time for elaborate sentences; everyone rushed to the point intensified by the transformation of knowledge covering large distances; in short, the telegraph created what one critic has deemed "electric rhetoric."[34] Sentences with facts were now speedily transmitted; there was no time for theology or sin.

Notes

1. Increase Mather in *The Puritans*, eds. Perry Miller and Thomas H. Johnson. Rev. ed. (New York: Harper and Row, 1963) II: 494. Also useful is Charlotte Kretzoi, "Attitude and Form: Puritan Style in 17th Century American Prose," *Hungarian Studies in English* Vol.14 (1981): 57–68.
2. Perry Miller, "Declension in a Bible Commonwealth," *Nature's Nation* (Cambridge, MA: Belknap Press, 1967) 14. Hereafter Declension.
3. Sacvan Bercovitch, *The American Jeremiad* (Madison, WI: University of Wisconsin Press, 1978) xi.
4. See Richard Bushman, *From Puritan to Yankee: Character and the Social Order in Connecticut 1690–1765* (Cambridge, MA: Harvard University Press, 1967) 37, 288.
5. Robert Alter, *Pen of Iron, American Prose and the King James Bible* (Princeton: Princeton University Press, 2010) 3. Also useful is Nancy Ruttenburg, *Democratic Personality: Popular Voice and the Trial of American Authorship* (Stanford, CA: Stanford University Press, 1998). Alter is particularly helpful in distinguishing style from discourse (20–2).
6. The phrase "speaking intellect" appears in *Harper's Monthly*, 1856. See *A Companion to Mark Twain*, eds. Peter Messent and Louis J. Buddy (Malden, MA: Blackwell 2005) 211. Also helpful is Donald M. Scott, "Print

and the Public Lecture System, 1840–60," *Printing and Society in Early America*, ed. William L. Joyce, *et al* (Worcester, MA: American Antiquarian Society, 1983) 278–99.

7   See Walter J. Ong, *Orality and Literacy: The Technologizing of the Word* (London: Methuen, 1982) 152.

8   Both passages are from "The Character of Puritan Preaching, Part 4," Place for Truth, biblical doctrine from the Alliance of Confessing Evangelicals. https://www.placefortruth.org/blog/the-character-of-puritan-preaching-part-4.

9   Michael Warner, "Note on the Sermon Form," *American Sermons, The Pilgrims to Martin Luther King, Jr* (New York: Library of America 1999) 889.

10 On the importance of the Sunday sermons, see Harry S. Stout, *The New England Soul: Preaching and Religious Culture in Colonial New England* (Oxford: Oxford University Press, 1986). For a useful survey of Stout, see Sargent Bush, Jr. "Hearing the Word as Spoken: Five Generations of Sermons in New England," *Early American Literature* Vol.22 (1987): 133–43. One further resource is Robert Benton, "Annotated Check List of Puritan Sermons Published in America before 1700," *Bulletin of the New York Public Library* Vol.74 No.5 (May 1970): 286–337. The earliest is Richard Mather, "The Summe of Certain Sermons upon Genes [sic]:15.6," 1652. The latest is Henry Stubbe, "Conscience Is the Best Friend upon Earth," 1699.

11 See https://www.obbietylertodd.com/post/preach-like-a-puritan.

12 Leland Ryken, *Worldly Saints: The Puritans as They Really Were* (Grand Rapids MI: Zondervan, 1986) 15, 16. The trivium is also key: grammar, dialectic, and rhetoric: the grammar is learning the details of a subject; the dialect required mastery of the principles or interconnectedness among the basic facts to gain a whole picture. Rhetoric is the ability to express the totality of what has been learned. Helpfully surveying details of Puritan preaching is Joseph Steele, "A Classical Analysis of Puritan Preaching," *Reformation* 21 (August 23, 2010). https://www.reformation21.org/articles/a-classical-analysis-of-puritan-preaching.php.

13 See *Reformation* 21: https://www.reformation21.org/articles/a-classical-analysis-of-puritan-preaching.php.

14 On the tabulation of sermons, see Harry S. Stout, *The New England Soul: Preaching and Religious Culture in Colonial New England* (New York: Oxford University Press, 1986) 3–4. As Stout notes, there were few if any competing public speakers. For a lengthy and useful review by Sargent Bush, Jr, "Hearing the Word as Spoken: Five Generations of Sermons in New England," see *Early American Literature* Vol.22 No.1 (1987): 133–43.

15 On the matter of uniform type in the Colonial period, this paragraph from the Walden Font Co. is helpful:

 Virtually every printer seems to have used the same exact type. This goes so far that, unless the piece in question is printed in one of these few faces, we do not consider it "the real thing." To find the reason for this lack of variety, we have to go back in history. The place is England, the year, 1637. The Star Chamber just decreed that "there shall be four founders of letters for printing and no more." There are many reasons for this measure; most prominently the fear that too much printed material might educate the masses beyond the comfort level of the ruling class. In any case, the new restriction reduced the number of available type styles to a small, mediocre selection. While some printers resorted to importing superior type from Holland, many others looked for a "homegrown" solution to the problem. They found it in William Caslon (1692–1766), a renowned engraver and tool maker. Caslon was commissioned to cut punches for a number of distinguished presses in London. He based his new designs on the Dutch fonts of the time and achieved such marvelous results that his typefaces quickly became the standard for all kinds of printing, from fine books to the lowest of newspapers. Especially printers in the American colonies used the new type so extensively that no piece of eighteenth-century American printing looks "real" to us unless it is printed in Caslon. https://www.waldenfont.com/OnPrintinginAmerica.asp.

16 *An Arrow* 3. The Puritan Ministers went to court which fined the dancing master £100 and encouraged him to leave. The sermon/tract does not dispute the value of dancing, "a natural expression of joy," but questions the morality of "*Gynecandrical Dancing*," generally known as *Promiscuous Dancing* or dancing between men and women whether old or young (An Arrow 1–2: https://digitalcommons.unl.edu/cgi/viewcontent.cgi?article=1111&context=zeabook).

17 Abraham Joshua Heschel, "What We Might Do Together," *American Sermons, The Pilgrims to Martin Luther King, Jr.* (New York: Library of America, 1999) 865. Heschel delivered his remarks in 1967.

18 Mark Twain, "Autobiography" in Thomas D. Zlatic, "I don't know A from B": Mark Twain and Orality," *A Companion to Mark Twain*, eds. Peter Messent and Louis J. Buddy (Malden, MA: Blackwell, 2005) 222. Also see Twain, "A Memory of John Hay," *Autobiography*, Project Gutenberg, https://gutenberg.net.au/ebooks02/0200551h.html.

19 Benjamin Franklin, "Autobiography," *Autobiography, Poor Richard, and Later Writings*, ed. J. A. Leo Lemay (New York: Library of America, 1997) 580. Also see Howard Mumford Jones, "American Prose Style 1700–1770," *Huntington Library Bulletin* No.6 (Nov. 1934) 117. Full article: 115–51.

20 See Ezra Tawil, *Literature, American Style: The Originality of Imitation in the Early Republic* (Philadelphia: University of Pennsylvania Press, 2018).

21 Noah Webster in Gunnel Tottie, *An Introduction to American English* (Malden, MA: Blackwell, 2002) 9.
22 Noah Webster, *An American Dictionary of the English Language* (1828) Vol. 2 (539). There are over 70,000 entries. https://webstersdictionary1828.com/Dictionary/sentence.
23 Perry Miller, "An American Language," *Nature's Nation* (Cambridge, MA: Belknap, 1967) 234. Here after Miller Amer.
24 Samuel L. Clemens (Mark Twain), *Adventures of Huckleberry Finn*, 2nd ed., ed. Sculley Bradley, *et al* (New York: Norton, 1977) 91. Hereafter Twain.
25 Richard Bridgman, *The Colloquial Style in America* (New York: Oxford, 1966) 17, 19. Also see Sieglinde Lemke, *The Vernacular Matters of American Literature* (London: Palgrave/ Macmillan, 2009).
26 Henry Smith, "A Glass for Drunkards," *The Works of Henry Smith, including Sermons, Treatises, Prayers, and Poems*, Vol. I (Edinburgh: James Nichol, 1866) 304–5. https://dn790008.ca.archive.org/0/items/worksofhenrysmit01smit/worksofhenrysmit01smit.pdf.
27 Charlotte Kretzoi, "Attitude and Form: Puritan Style in 17th Century American Prose," *Hungarian Studies in English* Vol.14 (1981): 60. Hereafter Kr.
28 R.S. Carroll in an early thesis, *Studies in the Background and Practice of Prose Style in New England* (Cambridge, MA: Harvard University Press, 1951) suggests that "plain" has three levels of meaning: in 1640 it meant simple and homely; in 1680, it referred to something austere and chastened; but 1720 it meant natural and easy. See Kr 67 ftnt. 12.
29 Mitchell in Emory Elliott, *Power and the Pulpit in Puritan New England* (Princeton: Princeton University Press, 1975) 105–6.
30 Susan Roberson, *Emerson in His Sermons: A Man-made Self* (Columbia, MO: University of Missouri Press, 1995) 19. Hereafter Roberson.
31 Leo Marx, *The Machine in the Garden* (New York: Oxford University Press, 1964) 247. Henry Adams's *Mont St. Michel and Chartres* appeared privately in 1904, reprinted in 1913.
32 Frank Norris, *The Octopus, A Story of California* (Garden City, NY: Doubleday, Page & Co., 1903) 50–1.
33 Henry James, "The Portrait of a Lady," *Novels 1881–1886*, ed. William T. Stafford (New York: Library of America, 1985) 258–9. The passage is from Ch. VII, Vol. II.
34 See Kathleen Welch, *Electric Rhetoric, Classical Rhetoric, Oralism and a New Literacy* (Cambridge, MA: MIT Press, 1999).

Chapter 2
The Telegram: American Speed

our mountains, lakes and rivers are all a blaze of fire,
And we send our news by lightning, on the lively telegraphic wire.
"UNCLE SAM'S FARM," POPULAR SONG
BY JESSE HUTCHINSON, JR. C. 1850

A calculating engine is one of the most intricate forms of mechanism, a telegraph key one of the simplest. But compare their value.
GEORGE ILES, "JOTTINGS FROM A NOTEBOOK," 1918

i

Facilitating the drama of the American Sentence in its shift from the elaborate rhetorical and didactic forms of the Puritans and the emotive expressions of the Transcendentalists, to the brief and direct statements of twentieth-century Americans was the telegraph. This new method of communication meant a style of writing that eliminated extraneous words and phrases. They simply cost too much.

In 1843, the US government financed the first telegraphic communication line inaugurated in 1844 between Washington and Baltimore, the first message transmitted on May 24, 1844, by Samuel Morse. By 1866, the first transatlantic cable was laid and messages between Europe and North America began altering geopolitics, finance, journalism, and personal lives. News of Lincoln's assassination was sent by telegraphy and some suggest that Lincoln conducted the war only through telegrams. The telegram played pivotal roles in history: the Dreyfus Affair hinged on forged telegrams sent by Esterhazy, one of which accused Dreyfus as a German spy; the Zimmerman telegram of January 1917, sent by the Germans as a cipher text and intercepted by the British, outlined a proposed alliance between Germany, Mexico, and Japan if the United States declared war on Germany. The foreign secretary, Arthur Zimmerman, offered generous financial support and help in regaining the lost territory of Texas, New Mexico, and Arizona. He also noted that unrestricted submarine warfare would resume.[1]

Publication of the Zimmermann telegram galvanized American public opinion against Germany, even though three months earlier Woodrow Wilson won reelection with the promise to keep America neutral. Linked to Germany's resumption of submarine warfare, the Zimmerman telegram compelled the United States to join the war. The first line of the telegram is "130 13042 13401 8501 115 3528 416 17214 6491 11310." Decoded, it reads "we intend to begin on the first of February unrestricted submarine warfare."[2]

In wartime, a series of communication forms preceded the telegram: smoke signals, signal flags and the semaphore, a set of visual signals and rotating paddles whose position encoded the message. There were 556 semaphore towers throughout France in 1792 covering 3000 miles and used by the French military until the 1850s; wig wag, developed during the American Civil War, used flags and movement equivalent to the Morse code, although it might take five waves of the flag for a single letter. The US Navy used semaphore with flags or colored paddles to convey messages; an experienced operator could send twelve to fifteen words per minute. There was a limit, however, to the distance of communication, usually one mile for the naked eye. But the telegraph superseded all of these forms with the almost instantaneous transfer of information, news, and sometimes gossip. Americans alone did not invent the telegraph but they put it to exceptional use.[3]

How does it work? The electric telegraph

> sends an electric current to a receiving station. When the sender presses on the telegraph key he interrupts the current creating an

audible pulse that is heard at the receiving station. It cannot carry voice or other data, and relies only on pulses to communicate. The receiver on the other end decodes the pulses to decode the message.

In Morse code each letter "is represented by a unique series of short dots (dits) and longer dashes (dahs). The duration of a dash is three times the length of a dot. Each word is separated by silence, equivalent to one dash." Morse developed the code after observing the optical or semaphore telegraph in Europe.[4]

By 1890, the Atlantic cable could handle up to fifty words a minute. Before the First World War, Britain was connected with France by eight undersea telegraph cables, with Belgium by three, Holland by three, Germany by six, and Norway by two. The Atlantic was crossed by seventeen. By 1902, a Pacific cable was laid from Vancouver to New Zealand (Fleming, ETHA 78). The word telegraph means "far or distant writing." But cost limited word length, the average length in the 1900s in the United States was 11.93 words but more than half were ten words or fewer.[5] Use of the telegraph peaked in the 1920s: at its height in 1929, an estimated 200 million telegrams were sent.[6] In 2005, however, only 20,000 telegrams were sent at the cost of c. $10 a message; the last telegram was sent in January 2006 when Western Union discontinued the service.[7]

Importantly, following the start of the First World War, Britain cut Germany's undersea telegraph cables. It was left with just one but even that was under British control. Any message sent through it could be intercepted and read by Britain. Germany retaliated by attacking allied cables in the Pacific and Indian Oceans in late 1914. The attacks marked the start of the "cable wars."[8] During the First World War and afterward, the sight of telegram delivery boys were "heralds of doom" conveying news of injury or death. Ironically, today "Telegram" is the most used messaging app in the Ukraine/ Russia conflict even favored by President Zelensky of Ukraine. It is the most important social-media platform in the war, the center of the propaganda war allowing stories of Ukrainian resistance side by side with Russian disinformation.[9]

Beyond politics, the telegram became culturally significant. Ernest Hemingway learned of his Nobel Prize via a telegram dated December 28, 1954. In 1956, W.E.B. Du Bois, denied a passport to attend an African Congress of Black Writers and Artists in Paris, sent a telegram indicting the American institutions that blocked his travel.[10] When Steinbeck won his Nobel Prize in 1962, John O'Hara telegraphed, "Congratulations. I can think of only one other author I'd rather see get it." Beckett's telegram on being awarded the Nobel in 1969 was formal and sent to him c/o his publisher who, in turn, sent on a telegram to Beckett who was in Tunisia. It began with "In spite of everything, they have given you the Nobel Prize—I advise you to go into hiding." When soon called on the phone and told about it, he muttered that he was "damned to fame"; his wife declared it a "catastrophe."[11]

The telegram would dominate communication until the invention of the teletype and telephone. with sentences becoming concise, complete, direct, severe by necessity. And its impact has lasted: one of London's longest running papers—founded in 1855—is *The Daily Telegraph*.

Fascination with the telegraph soon made it a literary subject as in James's "In the Cage" (1898) preceded by Trollope's "The Telegraph Girl" (1877). Later authors repeatedly included telegrams in their plots from P.G. Woodhouse's *Right Ho, Jeeves*, to Evelyn Waugh's *Scoop* and Bulgakov's *Master and Margarita*. Joyce was beseeched by telegrams, beginning with the one his father sent to him in Paris when a student telling him his mother was dying and he should come home. Joyce, himself, received news of the publication of his *first* book via a telegram in Zurich in 1917. It started with a cablegram of two words from Ben Huebsch in New York to Harriet Shaw Weaver in London. It read "Published Huebsch." Weaver sent the news to Joyce in Zurich. In the "Proteus" section of *Ulysses*, Stephen recalls how his Paris stay was interrupted by the arrival of "a blue French telegram, curiosity to show: –Nother dying come home father" (Ulysses 3. 199–200).[12] The typo creates ambiguity: "another" person dying? Or is his mother dying? A second critical telegram is Bloom's speculating if "a private wireless telegraph which would transmit by dot and dash system" might be used to convey betting information (17. 1674)? A few lines earlier, Joyce had Bloom note the anticipation of "telegraphic code in ... cuneiform inscriptions" (17.773). Earlier still in *Ulysses*, Stephen sends Buck Mulligan a telegram canceling a meeting at the Ship, a Dublin public house.

Maurice Darantière, the printer of *Ulysses* in Dijon, sent Sylvia Beach a telegram the day before the book was to be shipped to Paris noting the scheduled arrival of the first two copies of the novel. Beach met the train and carefully carried the copies to Joyce's apartment on February 2, 1922, his fortieth birthday. It was also a Thursday, the same day of the week as in the novel.

ii

The development of the telegraph more or less began in 1800 when "current" electricity was born with the introduction of Volta's electrochemical battery which became a source of steady current. Another step was the discovery of a connection between electricity and magnetism in 1820. In 1831, Faraday discovered electromagnetic induction. Electrical signaling became the lynchpin of the telegraph. By 1837, an experimental railway telegraph was set up in London along a stretch of the London and Birmingham railway. Samuel Morse, an artist, not an inventor, began to experiment and demonstrated an early apparatus in 1837 and by 1844 he had a workable line forty miles long between Washington and Baltimore along the Baltimore and Ohio Railroad. Preceding all of this was an experiment held in Paris in 1746. The abbé Jean-Antoine Nollet, also a budding scientist, arranged approximately two hundred monks in a line over a mile long, each holding one end of a 25 ft iron wire in each hand. Once the monks were connected, the abbé went to a battery and sent a jarring electrical charge, shocking all the monks but also proving that electricity can be transmitted almost instantly through wires over a long distance.[13]

The art of the telegraph was underway; by 1851, there were more than fifty companies operating telegraph lines in the United States. By 1861, a transcontinental line was in place linking the Atlantic states with California. And by 1865, the International Telegraph Union formed; the following year, the first transatlantic telegraph cable was laid.[14] One of the early challenges was to increase the carrying capacity of the wires—and could operators at distance stations exchange messages simultaneously? A multiple-synchronous system then appeared, the wire able to carry two simultaneous transmission line in each direction at the same time (ETHA 146).

The fame of the telegraph soared in August 1844 when it was used to announce the birth of Queen Vitoria's second son, Alfred Ernest, at Windsor. The demand for rail travel further drove the establishment of telegraph networks, speed on rail initially competing with speed on wires. One complemented the other, although the telegraph "decoupled data transmission from transportation" overcoming limitations related to space.[15] Electronic messages outran horses, pigeons, and even trains. Yet a new fragmentation overtook exchanges. There was hardly any sense of grammatical or narrative continuity as the telegraphist in "In the Cage" discovers reading the telegrams of Lady Bradeen and Captain Everard. She, in fact, seeks to establish meaning through imagination, as much as missing detail. A syntactic discontinuity reigns creating confusions with the absence of conjunctions, coordination, or prepositions. Efficiency of expression meant eliminating connectives: bits and pieces (short and long dashes) disrupted syntax sacrificing coherence.

In *The Portrait of a Lady,* James reinforces this shift when Ralph Touchett tells Lord Warburton that his mother "chiefly communicates with us by means of telegrams, and her telegrams are rather inscrutable …. my mother has thoroughly mastered the art of condensation."[16] However, condensation can create confusion, as seen in the 1901 telegraphic report of the assassination of President McKinley. It read "McKinley shot Buffalo" interpreted by a Reuters subeditor in London as a report about the President's recent success at hunting (Menke 199).

To eliminate such mix-ups, codes and ciphers were used with specific definitions. The *Adams Cable Codex* (1894) was one reliable guide designed for travelers who have "investment interest at home about which they require information."[17] The secrecy of a code protects information and action. Someone in Paris about to leave for London replaces a sentence beginning with "Am going to" with "INGRATE, LONDON, TUESDAY." Instead of twenty words, three, although that could be reduced to two: "INTACT, LONDON" which would mean "leave here today for London, if anything new occurs, telegraph so as to reach me at that place" (Adams 2). A further code: "INSTITURO, INTOXICATE, BANKERS" asks "is everything all right at home"? Telegraph to me here c/o bankers. Other examples just from the letter A: "Abnormal: arrived—all well-address letters to care of—" (9). "Abstain: Call for letter (dated—) which I direct to you at general Post Office" (10). "Academic: Cannot prepay your passage" (11). "Accursed: Care of Baring Bros. & Co. London." "Alcoholic:—is seriously ill. We think you better return at once" (17). "Alcoholize:—Is much better. No need for you to come" (17). Several later examples: "Cigar: Have lost my code. Have sent for another." "Cigarette: Have lost my code. Where can I obtain another?" "Tobacco: You can obtain a copy of the Adams Cable Codex by applying to—" (162). "Lassitude: Think—is buying" (94). There was also a separate code table for dates, numerals, and fractions ("Percolate" equaled 4; "Perplexly," 9 ½. "Recurrence" meant 85,000 [149]). Codes also offered the hours of the day, the standing of firms, and accidents, as well as stocks and percentages. Life was fully encoded.

The Adams Code was invaluable, with the editors offering this advice: "[W]hen making up a message be sure *to write clearly and distinctly.*" It must be understood, especially in cipher; the telegraph operator "has to deal with *letters* and *not words*" (Adams 3). Furthermore, read your telegram carefully and recheck it "*to and from the code*"; "*an error may cost both the sender and the receiver a deal of trouble, worry and expense*" (Adams 3). The implications of this for style are clear. "Omit needless words" as Strunk and White would emphasize in *The Elements of Style.* All were encouraged to use code: it offered secrecy and reduced costs.

A 1928 handbook on how to write telegrams contained a section entitled "How to Save Words." It partly reads:

> If the telegram is packed full of unnecessary words, words which might be omitted without impairing the sense of the message, the sender has been guilty of economic waste. Not only has he failed to add anything to his message, but he has slowed it up by increasing the time necessary to transmit it. He added to the volume of traffic from a personal and financial point of view, he has been wasteful because he has spent more for his telegram than was necessary. In the other extreme, he may have omitted words necessary to the sense, thus sacrificing clearness in his eagerness to save a few cents.
>
> A man high in American business life has been quoted as remarking that elimination of the word "please" from all telegrams would save the American public millions of dollars annually.[18]

John Ambrose Fleming, a British developer, prepared the helpful *Wireless Telegraphist's Pocket Book of Notes, Formulae and Calculations I* (1915). Fleming makes no claim to completeness, referring to his work only as a "*Memoria Technica* of formulae, data and useful tables required in practical calculations connected with radiotelegraphy."[19] But telegraphy had become expensive, hence rarely used for anything but facts, information, and critical news, establishing a connection between technology and objectivity. Nevertheless, it found a place between the Pony Express and the telephone in the evolution of communication technology.

Telegraph companies, of course, charged by the word; to save money, one used fewer. They also had a maximum of fifteen characters per word for a plain language telegram and ten per word for one written in Morse code, Morse's invention assigning the shortest codes to the most frequently occurring letters. The letter "E" received the shortest, one dot, the letter "I" two. Numbers took on meaning: 1 meant "wait one," 73 meant "best regards." Language became frugal with economics shaping style. The goal was to convey information in as few characters as possible. Operators in the 1840s eliminated almost half the characters customers wrote down on message blanks (Hochfelder 75).

Shorter messages, sometimes altered by the operator who dropped words of low information content and abbreviated long words, meant reduced costs and higher profits. Speed was utmost. Customers during the Civil War period expected messages delivered not within a few hours but minutes. Over time an increased bandwidth and the use of automatic repeaters meant that messages could travel longer and even faster. The brevity, however, changed the production and consumption of information. What would become the Associated Press located their offices within the headquarters of Western Union in New York where, interestingly, Henry Miller worked for a while as an employment manager of messengers (although the telegraph style did not rub off on him). Access and distribution of the news became paramount. But the impact on style was at first negligible according to David Hochfelder:

> Because only a small minority of Americans used the telegraph to send or receive messages, telegraphy's effect upon written language was indirect and ambiguous at best.

Most Americans encountered the telegraph as a source of information in the pages of their daily newspapers. However, they did not usually read telegraphic dispatches directly—newspaper editors typically used these dispatches as raw material to write longer and more detailed stories.

(Hochfelder 74)

But this soon changed and the impact of brevity on commercial and then literary style grew, coinciding with changes in oratory, particularly political speeches. The so-called stump speech turned to idiom and the vernacular to keep listeners interested. Jargon, not etiquette or inflated speech, worked best. Using technical language was discouraged. People did not have the patience nor understanding. So, too, euphemism, eliminated by speakers and writers and certainly by telegraph operators. No more "limb" for "leg"; refined speech had no place in the speeded-up world of telegraphy. Plain speech was one product of telegraphic style (Cmiel Democratic 65–6). Rhetorical conventions were gone, repetition for emphasis eliminated, and stylistic flourishes erased. A new public idiom emerged.

But questions about the morality of style emerged in the 1830s and following, although the pace of information exchange made that concern moot. Overwhelming an initial middling style of the refined and vulgar was a drive to be direct and, if necessary, vulgar. The issue of morality receded; in a sense, there was no time to be "good." Speed overrode correctness.[20] But would informality and "roughness" encourage the violation of standards of personal conduct? Some thought that slang and informal speech polluted civil character; the *personal* substituting for the *ethical* was dangerous. Altered language in tone and expression implied the fall of civility; next would be the collapse of social order, all caused by language. Such a change would likely split the connection between manners and morality (Cmiel, Democratic 68–9). Instead of politeness, directness, instead of refinement, crudeness.

Because telegraph companies charged a fixed rate for the first ten words, and more for each subsequent word, most telegrams contained ten or fewer words. The sentence was redesigned and became incomplete, while the news took a different form: "[T]he matter-of-fact style and inverted-pyramid structure of the modern news story originated with telegraphic newsgathering," Hochfelder explains (Hochfelder 83).

But the speed of the telegraph also encouraged the frequent updating of stories. Expectations of timeliness grew and crowds formed at hotels, newspaper offices, and telegraph offices to learn the latest developments. There was also a change in the structure of news stories from chronological narratives to the inverted pyramid style. Get the facts up front in the fewest words and leave opinion and other matter behind. Don't personalize. Tone and structure shifted. Non-business people, however, did not use the telegraph often: expense held them back. They preferred the post for long-distance communication (Hochfelder 77–8). Additionally, most Americans understood a telegram as a sign of death or misfortune. In the First and Second World Wars, families received notice of casualties and death this way. The telegram was a sign of disaster.

Initially, the dot-dash code of Samuel Morse was to represent numbers that could be translated into words but it required its own alphabet. Originally formulated in 1838 and revised in 1844, the dots and dash registered on a tape matched to letters in English but first had to be deciphered. Soon, however, operators could determine letters by sound; they could send messages without looking at the tape.[21] Words became numbers with cost a continual factor. The telegraphist busies herself with counting out the sender's seventy words, not their meaning. They become only numbers, naked information commodified. One senses the creation of an "Electric Language," seemingly providing technological neutrality (Menke 95). As one journalist in 1894 pronounced, "[T]elegraphs are for facts; appreciation and political comment can come by post" (Menke 95–6). By May 1845, Morse and his associates formed the Magnet Telegraph Company to exploit their invention. By June 1846, they could exchange messages between New York and Washington.

There was also a new vocabulary. Rather than spell out every word letter-by-letter, conventions appeared by which telegraphers spoke to each other using short abbreviations, although there was no single standard. A list from 1859 included "1 1" (dot dot, dot dot) for "I AM READY"; "GA" (dash dash dot, dot dash) meant "GO AHEAD"; "SFD" meant "STOP FOR DINNER" (Standage 65). Numbers also functioned as abbreviations: I meant WAIT A MOMENT; 2 meant GET ANSWER IMMEDIATELY; 33, ANSWER PAID HERE (Standage 65). All telegraph offices on a branch line shared one writer, so several telegraphers listened in to wait for the line to become free.

Codes soon supplanted words and even numbers when telegraphing. Because private companies rather than the government controlled the telegraph network in the United States there were no rules banning the use of codes. As early as 1845, two public code books appeared to provide businesses with secret means to convey information. The title of one was *The Secret Corresponding Vocabulary Adapted for Use to Morse's Electro-Magnetic Telegraph.* The author was Francis O.J. Smith, a congressman (Standage 112). But because the codes were numbers, they were easily confused by telegraph clerks. Codes soon changed to code words to signify other words or even phrases. In 1854, one in eight telegrams between New York and New Orleans was sent in code (Standage 112). Words as a message go through several transformations: from language to electronic impulses (dots and dashes), to the sounds in the receiving operators earpiece and via code, to paper and then finally converted back to language. Mediating either end are operators who translate code. Simplified, the process is words/taps/electrons/taps/words. Discourse became code via electrical impulses.

Importantly, technology changed the grammatical content of messages, Western Union charging more for punctuation marks than a four-letter word with STOP the convention to indicate the end of a sentence. Punctuation also required a change of pace for the operator. STOP did not and was free; no charge. STOP was also favored by the military in the First World War to avoid any ambiguity with military messages. It signaled the end of a sentence. Morse code could not easily distinguish between upper and lower case letters.

Commercial codes became more prevalent. They also saved money: a code word would be a condensed message replacing several words but codes reduced revenue: fewer words were transmitted. But new rules by the International Telegraph Union (ITU) meant that messages in code would be treated like messages in plain text but no word could exceed seven syllables. Messages in cipher were charged on the basis that every five characters counted as one word (Standage 113). The ABC Code formed by a shipping manager was a popular commercial code which represented many common phrases using a single word, economical when sending expensive intercontinental telegrams. Ten words for £20 or $100 was standard. Nearly 90 percent of messages were business messages with 95 percent of them sent in code (Standage 114). But codes proliferated with odd and lengthy words; by 1875 the ITU attempted to regulate, imposing a fifteen-letter limit but a set of new codes suddenly appeared. By 1885, however, new regulations to limit words emerged: ten letters per word for telegrams in code and they had to be genuine words and the sending office could demand proof it was an actual word (Standage 115)! But code words were sensitive: a single misplaced letter in transmission could dramatically change meaning.

The impact of such restrictions on style, beginning with journalists was critical. Suddenly, a new, shortened style dominated: words were expensive. Authors would soon respond to this shift. Writing took on new urgency, intensity, and speed but expressions also needed control. By 1894, the ITU issued an official vocabulary of all permitted words. Any word not in the volume would be charged at the higher cipher rate. The first edition of the reference work had 256,740 words between five and ten letters drawn from eight permitted languages. But too many common words were omitted and the plan was soon scrapped (Standage 118).[22]

Speed became an important feature of the telegraphic style generated by commerce and soon war. The speed of information and news was crucial but increasingly rapid transmission became a technical challenge. Dispatches became delayed because of interference, electrical breakdowns, or lack of operator skill. An early solution was to increase the number of lines and the number of telegraphers. At one point, around 1890, Western Union had over 600 operators in one room in New York. The relay office in Chicago had space for 880 operators on a shift. However, the noise of the signals and typing competing with conveyor belts to dispatch the messages, with clerks shouting, was deafening (Coe 75–6). One of the fastest telegraphers, Thomas Edison, was taught Morse code as a teenager by a railway stationmaster. At one early stage, he could receive and decipher words at thirty-five words a minute (Standage 141). Other skilled operators could read incoming messages by listening to the clicking of the apparatus rather than reading the dots and dashes marked on a paper tape.[23] Andrew Carnegie was less skilled: he started out as telegraph messenger boy.

But the expense of sending remained high, although transmission was slowly increasing with new technology to expand capacity. But even with the development of multiplex transmitters, the best operator could hardly send on average more than 500 words per hour or twenty-five dispatches of twenty words, each of five letters. But the wire could soon transmit a larger number of signals with a system of perforated strips to allow for automatic transmission.[24] By 1879, the American Rapid Telegraph Company came into existence to mark the emphasis on speed. It advertised a new, automated system to send 2,000 words a minute instead of 1,000. But signal failures at one and two thousand words—promotion material had said 4,000 words—limited the success of these systems (Buckingham 156–7).

Simultaneous transmission became another new process, although only weak currents could be used on undersea lines. Heavier pulses would destroy the cable covering which would likely admit moisture which led to the destruction of insulation. Another challenge was sending telegraphs to moving trains which was achieved by having neighboring wires alongside the train. The speed of the train did not interfere with the communication. Yet, urgency defined the act of "writing," of message sending, and the faster the better because it was more effective and less costly. Telegraphic talent meant speed of transmission with various contests held nationally. Writing in dots and dashes became a contest reflected in a new, abbreviated, and curt writing style evoked with such newspapers named *The Toronto Daily Telegraph* of the *Sunday Telegraph*.

Interestingly, the *Daily Telegraph Style Book* (UK), focusing on grammar and style in 2018, emphasizes that adjectives "other than the purely and basically descriptive, have little place in news stories, and little more (other than occasionally for comic or ironic effect) in feature writing. Highly adjectival writing is a mainstay of tabloid journalism." Choosing the right word remained crucial: avoid the word "partner," for example, when used to denote an unmarried cohabitee unless absolutely necessary. "Use girlfriend, boyfriend, companion, lover, mistress, concubine, friend or any other apposite word." Banned words and phrases appear in the A-Z section.[25] Recent instructions for telegram writing have not changed: "Payment is made as per number of words used in the telegram"; "punctuation marks are not to be used. Write 'STOP' where a full stop has to be used"; "write the message briefly. Do not worry about grammatical errors." The source is a guide to telegraph writing in India.[26]

By 1880, Western Union controlled 80 percent of US telegraphic traffic. Headquartered at 195 Broadway, New York. The seventh floor had hundreds of telegraphers working in a room with chandeliers. Women were separated in the "Ladies' Department" earning 25 to 50 percent less than the men. Details, complaints, and criticism of Western Union began to appear in *The Operator*, a bi-weekly four-page paper with telegraph gossip, news, stories, and editorials beginning in late 1875. The literature of telegraphy ran from betrayals to mix ups, sometimes with gender. Rena poses as a man on the wire in "Playing with Fire" only to find that her supposed female sweetheart is a young gentleman. The hero in "Hamilton Doless" discovers that his intended is already engaged and dies of a broken heart. *Wired Love: A Romance of Dots and Dashes* by Ella Cheever Thayer (1879) describes a flirtation over the wire but awkwardness when they meet. "To speak over the wire was bliss, but to speak face to face, misery" is a line from another story.[27] Two other characters find it easier to continue their romance in dots and dashes and set up a private wire between their two rooms in the same lodging house. But the stories reflect not only romance but growing tensions between operators and Western Union, leading to a strike in 1883. One demand was equal pay for female operators.

iii

The speed of transferring data meant the reorganization of time and space. A more permeable space took over in business, politics, and even art. Maintaining a monumental center was less tenable as space became abstract, power delimited, and time annihilated. Slowness became "the new horror."[28] Impatience became the new anxiety, waiting an anathema. Modernism became the symbiosis between technology and identity: moving quickly, whether over the telegraph wire or in an auto, meant experiencing the energy of modernity, with speed and capital inextricably linked (SpHd 109). Western Union, whose controlling shares were owned by one of America's most disliked capitalist, the New York financier Jay Gould, became a near monopoly. Social as well as technical forces disrupted the nature of texts partly because the world (and its texts) became dynamic, generated and transmitted quickly. Telegraph messages, typed out superfast two-finger style on typewriters that had only capital letters and sent without punctuation marks, forced new constructions and formats (Coe 70).

Modernist texts soon reflected these shifts in sentence construction, duplicating speed on the page creating meta-fictional works (see John dos Passos, William Burroughs, Gilbert Sorrentino, Mark Danielewski). The characteristics of the telegram infiltrated the new writing taking over texts and images of modernism creating a "speed culture" (SpHd 10,55). Aldous Huxley summarized the excitement in 1931: "Speed, it seems to me, provides the one genuinely modern pleasure."[29]

But ironically, while literature often treated the telegraph as content, it was rarely written in the telegraph style. Dickens, as one example, never wrote the story he imagined to be told as a telegraph exchange. Nineteenth-century novels cited, but did not imitate, telegrams, although they incorporated them as part of the plot. Dickens's "The Signal Man," Trollope's "The Telegraph Girl," and Bronte's *Jane Eyre* are tales about information transmission via the telegraph exposing its workings and misunderstandings. *Telegraphic Secrets* (1867), a collection of short stories by Bracebridge Hemyng, emphasized telegraphic secrecy exposing the surprises and tensions expressed by telegraphs. And then there is Sherlock Holmes who repeatedly sends and receives telegrams. They have a crucial role in a set of stories including "The Sign of Three," "The Adventure of the Creeping Man," "The Adventure of the Copper Beeches," "The Adventure of the Naval Treaty," "The Adventures of the Blue Carbuncle," "The Adventures of the Second Stain," and *A Study in Scarlet*.[30] Plots and people are discovered, undone or solved via telegrams.

R.M. Ballantyne published two works focusing on the telegraph: *Post Haste: A Tale of Her Majesty's Mails* (1880) and *The Battery and Boiler; or, Adventures in the Laying of Submarine Electric Cables* (1883). *Post Haste* begins by tracing a telegram backward from its recipient in western Ireland to its sender in London. *The Battery and Boiler* focuses on a young protagonist's work on the *Great Eastern* in its effort to lay the Atlantic cable and includes a lecture on telegraphy. But none of these were in a telegraphic style. Telegraphic literature, that is written by and read by telegraph operators, concentrated on intrigue, romance, and adventure as its main themes. Flirting in Morse code repeatedly led to confusions as seen in the story "A Centennial-Telegraphic Romance," which appeared in an 1877 anthology, *Lightning Flashes and Electric Dashes* alongside short stories, poetry, and even plays written by, and for, operators in the 1870s and 1880s.[31]

iv

The telegraph rewrote the American Sentence having already impacted nineteenth-century Victorian fiction as a subject. New media and information systems "suggested new possibilities for representing the real." The telegraph altered the meaning of such older technologies as writing and print.[32] An extreme example is the apocryphal story about the briefest telegram message ever sent which may have been composed by Victor Hugo or perhaps Oscar Wilde. It was an inquiry about the sales of a new book and read: "?" The reply was just as succinct: "!".[33] Conceptually and stylistically, telegraphy meant more than writing at a distance. Fiction, itself, soon imagined itself as a "medium and information system in an age of new media" (Menke 3). Kipling expressed this less abstractly: "The best training you can get is in writing telegrams. Here a man realises more how far a word can go than in reading any of the famous authors. I am not in debt for style to anything or anybody but the telegraph system."[34] Kipling, conflating "the stylistic condensation of the message with the transmissive power of the medium," pinpoints the precision and value of the telegraphic method (Menke 218). But the syntactic and semantic compression requires readers to be active and fill-in-the gaps. The telegraph pressured language and self-expression. Style, not electricity, propelled the literary impact of the telegram.[35]

The mid-to-late nineteenth century was a period of rapid change with the development of the photograph, postage stamp, electric telegraph, electric lighting, telephone, typewriter, motion picture, and wireless telegraphy. New media technologies were everywhere, creating a media ecology generated by the rapid transmission of information, knowledge, and entertainment. Henry James sensed this in his reading of the opening installment of *Daniel Deronda*:

The threads of the narrative, as we gather them into our hands, are not of the usual commercial measurement, but long electric wires capable of transmitting messages from mysterious regions.[36]

Richard Menke calls this "telegraphic realism," although sometimes secrecy and the cryptic reign as in the coded telegram Lady Bradeen sends in chapter 13 of "In the Cage," which Captain Everard must recover in chapter 23 to determine its meaning. The message itself is divided into numbers and words decipherable only by the telegraphist. The key component of the message is a sequence of numbers (Cage 870–1, 906–9).

Telegraphy called attention to the limits of style and imposed a rewrite. In Wharton's *The Custom of the Country* (1913), Mabel Lipscomb makes signs across the auditorium of an opera house using her playbill as a fan: "No one else was wagging and waving in that way: a gestureless mute telegraphy seemed to pass between the other boxes."[37] And sometimes telegraphy brought comedy: *Love's Telegraph*, a play around 1846, also emphasized the movement of a woman's fan to which a man responds by twirling his glove. Earlier, in *Pickwick Papers*, Dickens has Sam Weller and his father exchange "a complete code of telegraphic nods and gestures" fulfilling the demands of what was once called optical telegraphy, the use of flags to signal letters.[38] What is important, as Menke argues, is that telegraphy offered novelists a method for thinking about the juncture of reality, materiality, and textuality (Menke 70). *The Electric Telegraph Popularised* (1855) by Dionysius Lardner was an encouraging response to the possibilities of new knowledge transfer decoupled from data and transportation. Electric telegraphy overcame geographic space. Traversing space was unnecessary; space itself was overcome, no longer an impediment. Words or letters as electrical signals were revolutionary, intellectually as well as scientifically and, of course, literarily. It was content without transporting its medium, transmission without physical movement or textual materiality.

Writers responded in kind, Dickens outlining a scheme of narration as a form of telegraphy around 1862:

> Open the story by bringing two strongly contrasted places and strongly contrasted sets of people, into connexion necessary for the

story, by means of an electric message. Describe the message—*be* the message—flashing along through space—over the earth, and under the sea.[39]

"*Be* the message." This is not far from Beckett on *Finnegans Wake*: the "writing is not *about* something; *it is that something itself.*"[40] The telegraph narrative unites the figures via unseen, electrical connections. The fragmented narrative creates a "remote intimacy" sharing knowledge and secrets.[41] Telegraphy offered maximum exposure *and* concealment simultaneously relying on words and codes. Separating public from private expression did not occur.

Understandably, the reliance of journalists in America and overseas on the telegram to file their stories caused their style to change. As early as 1848, an article speculated on the transformation the telegraph would bring to writing: in a word it would be "*brief* .... terse, condensed, expressive, sparing of expletives and utterly ignorant of synonyms." Its impact on American literature, adds the contributor, would be immediate and permanent but would it be better?[42] Conceding that it would alter the nature of written language did not mean improvement.

Appropriately, a young reporter at the *Kansas City Star*, Ernest Hemingway, found its style sheet helpful: "Use short sentences. Use short first paragraphs. Use vigorous English. Be positive, not negative."[43] The result was "linear, action-based American sentences" influenced by money, as much as writing practices (Hendrickson ix). Later, as a European cable correspondent for the *Toronto Star* in 1922, he favored "cablese," stripped down language for filing stories for overseas transmission. Two colleagues recalled how one night he came in and told Lincoln Steffens that his cable had "no fat, no adjectives, no adverbs—nothing but blood and bones and muscle. It's great. It's a new language" (Hochfelder 73).

Contrasting this approach was Henry Miller who could not release himself from the heavy style, weighted with images and adjectives. Flying across America, he writes:

> The stewardess, who has been trained to behave like a mother, a nurse, a mistress, a cook, a drudge, never to look untidy, never to lose her Marcel wave, never to show a sign of fatigue or disappointment or chagrin or loneliness, the stewardess puts her lily-white hand on

the brow of one of the paper-box salesman and in the voice of a ministering angel, says: "Do you feel tired this evening? Have you a headache? Would you like a little aspirin?"

This single sentence is replete with clauses that run-on to convey the sense of involvement. But this being Miller, he then writes: "When the plane lurches suddenly she falls and reveals a tempting pair of thighs."[44] Thomas Wolfe preceded this style with lengthy, rhetorically intense sentences exploring the themes of loneliness, family, time, and death; Norman Mailer followed with urgent, confrontational writing and forceful images dealing with identity and ambition.

V

But did the telegraph directly influence American prose style? Yes and no. The example of Hemingway is, perhaps overplayed. The number of journalists who became writers, inheriting the telegraph style, range from Mark Twain to Margaret Mitchell, Joan Didion, Maya Angelou, and Susan Sontag. But Hochfelder is hesitant to claim a direct influence pointing out that the relationship between technology, the telegram and literary style is interconnected but complex. The effect on prose style is evident but guided initially by economic concerns (words in telegrams were expensive). Supporting the adoption of the new style, however, were other social and cultural factors: the faster pace of American life after 1850, the spread of mechanization during and after the Civil War, the growing importance of newspapers under pressure to develop a sharper style, an expanding readership for popular writing (keep it simple) and an overall preference for the unpretentious. Get the story told and quickly was the new directive.

Even though few Americans outside of journalism or business sent or received telegrams, most had contact with the telegraphic style through the press which in many ways re-made language. Coincident with a speedier style was Franklin's folksy manner, Noah Webster's call for a national language, Emerson's cry for naturalness, what he identifies as "the language of the street," Thoreau's casual self-directedness reporting on Walden Pond and Twain's skill at storytelling through youthful, ungrammatical voices. Webster, for example, rejected the idea of imposed standards, preferring linguistic appropriateness. He defended rude speech and preferred simplified spelling linked to pronunciation (Cmiel 53). The creation of a democratic idiom created a willingness to accept the new, often the unproven, expressed tersely. Replacing decorum was drama generated by directness. Say it, don't spend time shaping it, which challenged the codified grammars and dictionaries of the eighteenth and nineteenth centuries. That American English emerged through the telegram may not be an overstatement as "visible speech"—letters that we see as well as sound in the composition of telegrams—began to dominate written expression in other texts.[45]

The telegraph represented immediacy, energy, importance, and speed, materially and linguistically. This became a metaphor of stylistic change itself involving intensity, exactness, and a vocabulary that was punchy, idiomatic, and curt. Emerson sensed this in a journal entry of late June 1840:

> [T]he language of the street is always strong. What can describe the folly & emptiness of scolding like the word jawing? … Cut the words of [a] trucker or teamster and they would bleed; they are vascular & alive; they walk & run …. it is a shower of bullets, whilst Cambridge men & Yale men correct themselves & begin again at every half sentence …. this profane swearing & bar-room wit has salt & fire in it …. Guts is a stronger word than intestines.[46]

In broader terms, the new American Sentence, expressed through telegraphic language, reinforced traits many wished to see in the American character. It blended technological mastery and democratic forms of expression in an effort to formulate an American identity (Hochfelder 99). Informality of speech leveled the language embodying a variety of democratic principles linked to the ideology of nationalism and the creation of a national identity.

Whitman played a critical role, urging Americans to enjoy unruly words: celebrate the everyday, the sensual, the crude. Liberate language to create American English described as adding new words to the language or adding new meanings to old words.[47] Visitors felt alienated. Frances Trollope reported that she rarely "heard a sentence … correctly pronounced from the lips of an American." The expression, the accent, jarred. After visiting Easton, PA, another British visitor claimed that "it would kill a grammatical purist to spend a week in that vicinity" (Cmiel, Broad 918). Regional dialects were the main culprits and for a short time it was believed that the United States and Great Britain would create entirely different languages.

Kenneth Cmiel states the change clearly:

> Everywhere, it seemed, wild, undisciplined language was erupting in the 1830s and 1840s. Linguistic extravagance appeared at every turn, the disciplined language of refinement ignored or laughed at. Tall talk, fantastic overstatement in the service of self-aggrandizement, burgeoned in popular literature.
>
> (Cmiel, Broad 920)

But Noah Webster and others sought a nationwide language. Americans had the right to invent their own idiom; a new language for new ideas, he claimed. Whitman, in fact, believed that the American experience required an immense number of new words (Cmiel, Broad 932).

Hemingway almost naturally gravitated to this free-ranging but exacting style. As a young foreign correspondent in Paris, he saw and used "cablese," telegraphic instructions more than a formality of the job but a means for stripping down language, creating verbal drama in a variety of pared-down texts. The language of strict denotation soon ruled, unadorned prose encouraging Hemingway to form a writing system he called "the iceberg theory": the facts "float above the water, the unneeded details and context remain below."[48] What is visible is enough to evoke a sense of the whole. Prose became lean and spare. Hemingway went on to rely on telegrams throughout his life sending them to friends, editors, lovers, fans, and wives. Appropriately, he learned of his Nobel Prize in 1954 by telegram.

The move to the Hemingway-styled sentence was a reaction to the intricate but established conventions of literary discourse emulating a stratified, pseudo-classical culture created by mid-to-late-nineteenth-century American writers emulating European and British styles. Instead of Ciceronian prose relying on balanced subordinate clauses establishing parallelism and antithesis and elaboration, supported by repetition, was that of Seneca, focusing on things, not words with purpose not rhetoric its goal. This led to the *stile coupe* or curt style with short clauses that could stand alone. Reflexive pronouns and connectives are often missing, as well as coordinating conjunctions. Asymmetry, the product of brevity, appears relying on parataxis, placing "side by side" in contrast to hypotaxis, subjection, when clauses or phrases are arranged so that they depend on each other for meaning.

Instead of Henry James or Edith Wharton, writers of disjointed or slimmed-down sentences emerged conveying energy, upheaval: Stein, Dos Passos, Cormac McCarthy, Lydia Davis. The sentence shifted away from a received and conventional form to a subversive art undermining the accepted belief that a sentence orders thought and language into logical structures. For American writers, especially after the Great War, there seemed to have been very little that was logical. Openings take odd shapes as seen on the first page of Cormac McCarthy's first novel, *The Orchard Keeper* (1965): "Far down the blazing strip of concrete a small shapeless mass had emerged and was struggling toward him." The object is unknown until it whips past: it's a pick-up trip that recedes "into the same liquid shape by which it came."[49] The cadence and vocabulary are natural but at times confusing, described in this sentence from DeLillo's *White Noise,* outlining a kind of modernist pattern:

> She uttered two clearly audible words, familiar and elusive at the same time, words that seemed to have a ritual meaning, part of a verbal spell or ecstatic chant.[50]

In its new form, the sentence became "familiar and elusive," a composition that did not always contain a complete thought matched by incomplete expression. But formulating such a rhetoric generated anxiety, hence the emergence of stylistic edges and hesitations, echoing Aristotle who believed that every sentence is a combination of elements where each part has an independent meaning. Or Stein, who later explained that once a sentence was part of a paragraph which was part of a chapter which was part of a book. But that dissolved so that "nothing now is really convincingly part of anything else."[51]

In numerous essays Stein grappled with the structure and meaning of the sentence which she loved to diagram. Employing an idiosyncratic style reflects her own syntactic rebellion and determination to write individualistically rejecting, for example, commas.[52] They become the slaves of the sentence but if a sentence can't make sense without multiple commas, rewrite it, she argued. A friend of Stein's later commented that Stein "regarded a corner as something to cut, and another car as something to pass, and she could scare the daylights out of all concerned."[53] For Stein, the normative sentence was an anathema, the conventional sentence understood as an authoritarian, closed form to be dismembered. Let disorder form freedom, replacing symmetry.

In *Lectures in America*, Stein celebrates the sentence, while expressing her pleasure in sentence hunting: "I really do not know that anything has ever been more exciting than diagramming sentences," she announces, adding that parsing sentences is "completely exciting and completely completing." Her chapter "Sentences," the longest in *How to Write,* works to subvert conventional sentence grammar developing an offshoot from the conventional map of the American Sentence identified as subject–verb–object. Sentence diagramming was actually an American invention, created by a teacher, S.W. Clark, in 1847.

The Second World War contributed to the new style preceded by the use of rudimentary war telegraphs in the Civil War (with mobile military telegraph wagons) and, of course, the First World War. Integrated with diplomacy, telegrams took on new import, the Earl of Clarendon, nineteenth-century British foreign secretary first appointed in 1853 and again in 1865 and 1868, noted that "a telegram is a condensed despatch; I have had more trouble ... in writing a telegram than I have in writing a despatch" (Nickles 81). But even telegrams took time: foreign minister's clerks manually coded and decoded important telegrams, a process that often delayed messages. Cipher coded messages clearly took time; for expediency, foreign ministries often sent uncoded messages disregarding secrecy.

Two significant telegrams relating to war are the Zimmerman (noted earlier) and that of the Japanese to US Secretary of State Cordell Hull. This message from December 1941, delivered late from the Japanese government, announced the cessation of negotiations between the two countries before the surprise Pearl Harbor attack. After the war, Japanese officials blamed the incompetence of the Japanese embassy in Washington for the unnecessary delay, but if it would have arrived earlier, it would have allowed America to prepare for hostilities. The delayed telegram arrived forty minutes after the attack on Pearl Harbor began (Nickles 82–3).

Before 1914, German officials actually anticipated the backlog of telegrams that would occur in the event of war; there would be increased traffic from governmental authorities plus an increase in censorship. Such pressures would disrupt the telegraph system. Officials discouraged the sending of unnecessary telegrams, reducing the length of necessary messages. In the diplomatic crisis of July 1914, a large number of telegrams arrived late or were garbled because of an overloaded system. There were similar challenges at the French foreign ministry. The need to decode the large volume of telegrams added to the delay.

The situation in Britain, two days before the declaration of war on Germany, saw telegraphic congestion at its worst. Confusion, anxiety, and excitement became common during war time, leading to an important blunder. Based on an intercepted message from the German government warning German ships that hostilities with Britain were imminent, British officials incorrectly interpreted the information as meaning that Germany had declared war. That was wrong but they went ahead and rewrote their own declaration of war. They soon learned of their error and recalled the first declaration of war for a softer statement on backing Belgium (Nickles 133).

Telegraphy at this level actually impeded decision-making; foreign ministries simply had too much information, while events seemingly outran telegraph messages. And when they did unravel the information, ministries often made rushed decisions. Costs added to complications since telegraph companies levied excessive rates for messages in code, twice the rate of regular texts. Britain and the United States used codes that converted plaintext into numbers. Telegraph companies penalized numerical codes by expressing all numbers as words and charged accordingly. But the United States, in particular, sought to cut costs; during the Civil War, the Secretary of State advised American diplomats "to use HALF sheets of paper" where it will suffice to contain the text of the note to be copied, reducing foreign postage costs (Nickles 177).

Another measure of the impact of the telegraph and rapid forms of communication were a set of returning soldier/writers: Norman Mailer, Joseph Heller, Herman Wouk, Irwin Shaw, J.D. Salinger, James Jones, and Leon Uris—who found the danger and intensity of narrating battle affected their prose: suddenly, short, emphatic, elliptical statements (often orders relying on military acronyms) redefined a sentence, undercutting any effort to embellish or elaborate the syntax or vocabulary.[54] Dialog in their books suddenly reflected the terse, direct exchanges on-and-off the battlefield. The collapse of the body's coherence from injury and harm created a parallel collapse of syntax and form. These writer/soldiers wrote with immediacy, intensity. Dispatches were always urgent; there was no time to be excessive. Uris, in fact, received an award as one of the fastest radio/telegraph operators in the Marine Corps after he enlisted. And sometimes, influence was direct: Salinger met Hemingway in Paris and they corresponded. One resut was Salinger's "For Esme—with Love and Squalor" (1950), narrated by a traumatized soldier emphasizing a sparse dialog which would also characterize Salinger's later work.

Coincident with the general emphasis on rapid language was a new "poetics of speed." The acceleration of life (and even death from the war and violence) meant faster, more compact syntax expressed by Langston Hughes:

Autos honked. Trees rustled. People passed.
Arnie went out.
"Poor Little Black Fellow"[55]

Sentence structures tightened, anticipated by William Carlos Williams. Seeking a kind of "rapid-transit poetics," Williams praised a "flash of insight with proof by performance."[56] He often reported that his prose pieces were written speedily, "on the spur of the moment," broken syntax the result of "the speed of the emotions." In his selected essays, he praises Pound's *Cantos* for being "swift with a movement of thought" and Duchamp's decision that "his composition for that day would be the first thing that struck his eye in the first hardware store he should enter."[57] He also admired Emily Dickinson for her "swiftness impaling beauty." Marianne Moore's disjunctions were similarly understood as forms of speed, moving rapidly from one thing to the next as in her poem "Marriage."

In his *Autobiography*, Williams urged writers (and readers) to "get on with it, keep moving, keep in speed, the nerves, their speed, the perceptions, theirs, the acts … keep it moving as fast as you can, citizen."[58] He even understood Shakespeare as a "switchboard … in reverse. The actions pressed the keys and recorded them on the page."

His analogy for the poet's mind is a "lightning calculator" in the head: "Watch it work, that's all there is to writing (if it works) .... let it turn itself into a codex on the page."[59] Williams emphasizes verbs, claiming that words in English are like Chinese Ideographs: they "carry in them a verbal idea of action" regardless of their conventional linguistic designation (Tichi 65–6). The job of the poet is not to describe a scene but to give it form and enact it. Williams's greatest example of idiomatic American speech is *In the American Grain* (1925) beginning with this declaration: "I have recognized new contours suggested by old words so that new names were constituted." Announcing a new American goal, he writes that he has sought to draw "from every source one thing, the strange phosphorus of the life, nameless under an old misappelation."[60]

Williams was not the first to remark on an American aesthetics of speed. In *The Education of Henry Adams* (1907; 1918), Adams commented on how "the typical American man had his hand on a lever and his eye on a curve in his road; his living depended on keeping up an average speed of forty miles an hour, tending always to become sixty, eighty, or a hundred."[61] The acceleration of American life, anticipated by the telegraph, confirmed by the automobile, found its way into its prose and poetry. Williams, finding pleasure in his aloneness in a car, noted that to rush simplifies but also complicates life. With his rapid movement, he attempts to take a "pad in the car with me and write while running."[62] One must always write while on the go.

The telegraph (and later telephone) challenged writers with conceptual and practical disruptions to literate communications. "The non-writerliness" of the telegraph in particular—beginning with limitations on proper syntax and word length, often substituting codes for words—led to the shortening and abbreviation of the American Sentence which became an accepted standard often experienced in modern communication, notably via the cell phone. Ali Smith's short story, "Being Quick," from *The Whole Story and other stories* (2003), displays this clearly. Disconnected mobile phones dominate; disruption undermines continuity. Messages often do not reach their destinations and when they do, reassembled, often jumbled letters substitute for sentences: "WHR R U? XXX" a character texts but without a reply.[63] Yet to message quickly becomes the keynote of the age.

The telegram ordered and disordered the idea of a text and, more importantly, the idea of a sentence which soon became a contested form. Certain writers believed a sentence commissioned and completed an idea; a set of new writers disagreed, becoming defiant and initiated an aggressive new style identified by compact, often incomplete sentences and thoughts. The omission of conjunctions (*asyndeton*), the elaboration of parataxis, the elimination of coordination, and the end of parallelism identified the style of rapidity: "They snipped the ribbon in 1915, they popped the cork, Miami Beach was born." Soon, semicolons, dashes, and colons operated as connectors to separate or connect paratactic constructions with abruptness the new practice: "She must rush, she must hurry, before it was too late."[64] Norman Mailer and Steinbeck are the sources, indirectly following William S. Burroughs and his cut-up technique with Stein in the background. As Joyce forecasted in 1926, we do not (and perhaps cannot) any longer express ourselves in "wideawake language, cutanddry grammar and goahead plot."[65]

Notes

1   David Paull Nickles, *Under the Wire, How the Telegraph Changed Diplomacy* (Cambridge, MA: Harvard University Press, 2003) 137ff. Nickles, on the creation of distant power via the telegraph, quotes Orwel who noted that telegraphy reduced "the one-time empire builders ... to the status of clerks, buried deeper and deeper under mounds of paper and red tape" (Nickles 34). It also promoted hierarchical structures. Foreign ministries, for example, controlled the flow of messages, often requiring approval from the head of mission or first secretary, the only officials allowed to handle the main codebook. In France the foreign minister asked heads of mission to provide written justification for each telegram sent (Nickles 35).

2   "Zimmermann telegram," National WWI Museum and Memorial, Kansas City, MO. https://www.theworldwar.org/learn/about-wwi/zimmermann-telegram. As narrated by the National WWI Museum and Memorial:

> The secret to the British interception began years earlier. In 1914, with war imminent, the British had quickly dispatched a ship to cut Germany's five trans-Atlantic cables and six underwater cables running between Britain and Germany. Soon after the war began, the British successfully tapped into overseas cable lines Germany borrowed from neutral countries to send communications. Britain began capturing large volumes of intelligence communications.
>
> In October 1914, the Russian admiralty gave British Naval Intelligence (known as Room 40) a copy of the German naval codebook removed

from a drowned German sailor's body from the cruiser SMS Magdeburg. Room 40 also received a copy of the German diplomatic code, stolen from a German diplomat's luggage in the Near East. By 1917, British Intelligence could decipher most German messages.

3   For details on the development and application of the telegraph, see the Museum of Global Communications, Porthcurno, Cornwall, where the first international undersea telegraph cable was brought ashore connecting Britain to India. The message transfer time was nine minutes instead of six weeks by ship. By the Second World War, fourteen cables came ashore at Porthcurno carrying some 70 percent of all war communications. Telegraph operations ended in 1970, one hundred years after it began. The telegraph code for the Porthcurno Telegraph Station was PK. https://pkporthcurno.com/.

4   Quoted material and details preceding it from "War Communication during WWI," National Museum of the Marine Corps, https://www.usmcmuseum.com/uploads/6/0/3/6/60364049/nmmc_wwi_military_communication_resource_packet.pdf.

Also useful is Andreas Marklund, "Communications Surveillance during World War I," EHNE, Digital Encyclopedia of European History. https://ehne.fr/en/encyclopedia/themes/material-civilization/between-control-and-liberty/communications-surveillance-during-world-war-i. Military censorship of telegrams in Europe is his subject.

5   David Hochfelder, *The Telegraph in America 1832–1920* (Baltimore: Johns Hopkins, 2012) 19. Hereafter Hochfelder.

6   Ronnie Phillips, "Digital Technology and Institutional Change ... The Impact of the Telegraph and the Internet," *Journal of Economic Issues* Vol.34 No.2 (2000): 267–89.

7   Karlis Kanderovskis, "Telegraph," University of Chicago Theories of Media, Keywords Glossary, 2007. https://csmt.uchicago.edu/glossary2004/telegraph.htm.

8   On this topic and the state of cable conflict during the First World War, see "From Australia to Zimmermann: A Brief History of Cable Telegraphy during WWI," part of "Innovating in Combat: Telecommunications and Intellectual Property in the First World War," https://blogs.mhs.ox.ac.uk/innovatingincombat/files/2013/03/Innovating-in-Combat-educational-resources-telegraph-cable-draft_FIN.pdf.

9   See Vera Bergengruen, "How Telegram Became the Digital Battlefield in the Russia-Ukraine War," *Time*. March 21, 2022. https://time.com/6158437/telegram-russia-ukraine-information-war/.

10 See Juliana Spahr, *Du Bois's Telegram* (Cambridge, MA: Harvard University Press, 2018) and Linda Rosenkrantz, *Telegram! Modern History as Told through more than 400 ... Telegrams* (New York: Henry Holt, 2003).

11 Hannah Simpson, "Samuel Beckett and the Nobel *Catastrophe*," *Samuel Beckett Today* Vol.30 No.2 (2018): 337–52.

12 James Joyce, *Ulysses*, ed. Hans Walter Gabler, *et al* (New York: Vintage Books, 1986) 3.199–200. Reference is to section number and line numbers.

13 Tom Standage, *The Victorian Internet* (New York: Walker and Company,1998) 1–2. Hereafter Standage.

14 Much of this information comes from *The Electric Telegraph, an Historical Anthology*, ed. George Shiers (New York: Arno Press, 1977). Hereafter ETHA. This is a collection of early and often technical articles on the electromagnetic telegraph. One valuable example is Charles Buckingham's "The Telegraphy of To-Day" rpt. from *Electricity in Daily Life* (New York, 1890). Buckingham notes that in the United States, Western Union had 600,000 miles of wire annually transmitting more than 50 million messages a year. Signals read by sound were thriving.

15 Richard Menke, *Telegraphic Realism* (Stanford, CA: Stanford University Press, 2008) 72. Hereafter Menke.

16 Henry James, "The Portrait of a Lady," *Novels 1881–1886*, ed. William T. Stafford (New York: Library of America, 1985) 201. See Ch. 1 of this study for a fuller discussion of the exchange.

17 "Preface," *The Adams Cable Codex*, 7th edition (Boston: E.A. Adams & Co., 1894) 2. Hereafter Adams. E.A. Adams & Co. were Ship Brokers, Steamship Agents and Commission Merchants in Boston.

18 Nelson E. Ross "How to Write Telegrams Properly," (1928) at "The Telegraph Office." https://web.archive.org/web/20170315175434fw_/http://www.telegraph-office.com/pages/telegram.html. "The Telegraph Office" is a web page by Neal McEwen with various information relating to Morse telegraphy. https://web.archive.org/web/20170311130840/http://www.telegraph-office.com/tel_off.html.

19 John Ambrose Fleming, *Wireless Telegraphist's Pocket Book of Notes, Formulae and Calculations* (Glasgow: Wireless Press, 1915) vii. He adds that the 347-page "pocket book" is for operators and students "out of reach of mathematical books, or who have allowed their knowledge to be come rusty" (vii).

20 Kenneth Cmiel, *Democratic Eloquence, The Fight over Popular Speech in Nineteenth-century America* (New York: William Morrow, 1990) 67. Hereafter Cmiel.

21 Lewis Coe, *The Telegraph* (Jefferson, NC: McFarland & Co., 1993) 66.

22 The next problematic area was money transfers and security with banks entirely relying on codes to confirm amounts and transfers. Manipulating the telegraph to transmit race results was also a profitable subterfuge (Standage 118–21). On the Dreyfus affair and coded incriminating telegrams, see Standage 121–6.

23 Sample Morse codes: . —A—... B... C—.. D.
24 Amédée Guillemin, "Telegraphic Apparatus for Rapid Transmission," ETHA 626.
25 "Grammar and Syntax," *Telegraph Style Guide*, January 23, 2018. https://www.telegraph.co.uk/style-book/grammar-and-syntax/.
26 "Telegram Writing," Pearson Longman Textbook for India and South Africa. See "Telegram Writing," https://www.scribd.com/document/191373376/Telegram-writing-1-pdf plus https://za.pearson.com/content/dam/region-growth/south-africa/pearson-south-africa/TeacherResourceMaterial/pea_9781447978671_m09_pep_lag_pr6_tg_eng_ng.pdf. Further instructions include the name of recipient written in one word; no numerals, only words. One mark would be reduced "if the student fails to copy the proper layout."
27 Britt Peterson, "The Golden Age of Telegraph Literature," *Slate* November 11, 2014. https://slate.com/technology/2014/11/telegraph-literature-from-19th-century-was-surprisingly-modern.html. Also helpful is Leslie Katz, "'At any time, day or night a telegram would bring me to your help': Sherlock Holmes and the Telegraph," SSRN (August 12, 2020; rev. March 8, 2022): https://ssrn.com/abstract=3666189 or http://dx.doi.org/10.2139/ssrn.3666189.
28 Enda Duffy, *The Speed Handbook, Velocity, Pleasure, Modernism* (Durham, NC: Duke University Press, 2009) 67. Hereafter SpHd.
29 Aldous Huxley, "Wanted, a New Pleasure," *Aldous Huxley: Complete Essays*, Vol. 3 eds. Robert S. Baker and James Sexton (Chicago: Ivan R. Dee, 2001) 263–4. Huxley believed that speed was the only new pleasure invented by modernity. On this topic and its psychological impact, see Theresa Brennan, *Exhausting Modernity* (2000) and *The Transmission of Affect* (2004).
30 A new title is Nicholas Meyer, *Sherlock Holmes and the Telegram from Hell* (New York: Penzler Publishers, 2024) involving Holmes and Watson in pursuit of a mysterious coded telegram requiring a journey to America.
31 The 1889 Cleveland Street scandal revealed that a male brothel in London supplied its upper-class customers with young telegraph boys.
32 Richard Menke 3. Menke concentrates on links between "imaginative writing and media innovation in nineteenth century Britain" (5). How real things became information tools becomes part of his argument that "realism and electric telegraphy" generated "intersubjectivity" (Menke 93).

On the issues of transposition of language into code and its digital nature, converting data-flow into a sequence of discrete functions, see David Trotter, "Telegraphy," *On Style in Victorian Fiction*, ed. Daniel Tyler (Cambridge: Cambridge University Press, 2021) 93–108. https://www.cambridge.org/core/books/on-style-in-victorian-fiction/telegraphy/0B64C7A74DB8087C7A00195BE50B1726#EN-fn-188.

33 Garson O'Toole, "Briefest Correspondence," *Quote Investigator*. June 14, 2014. https://quoteinvestigator.com/?s=Brief+correspondence. A variation is correspondence between an American merchant seeking news from his London agent. The exchange was "!" and the answer was "0." Ibid.

34 Rudyard Kipling, *Letters of Rudyard Kipling, Volume 3: 1900–1910* ed. Thomas Pinney (London: Palgrave Macmillan, 1995) 3: 329.

35 Kipling went on to write "Wireless" (1902), an early story of the next stage in modern information transmission, wireless telegraphy to be called "radio."

36 Henry James, "Daniel Deronda," *The Nation* February 24, 1876: 131.

37 Edith Wharton, "The Custom of the Country," *Novels*, ed. R. W. B. Lewis (New York: Library of America, 1985) 663.

38 Anon. "Theatres," *The Satirist or the Censor of the Times* September 13, 1846: 294; Dickens, *Pickwick Papers*, ed. Robert L. Patten (London: Penguin 1972) 700.

39 Dickens, *Charles Dickens's Book of Memoranda.* Transcribed and annotated by Fred Kaplan (New York: New York Public Library, 1981) 19.

40 Samuel Beckett, "Dante … Bruno. Vico… Joyce," *Our Exagmination Round His Factification for Incamination of Work in Progress* (1929; New York: New Directions, 1972) 14.

41 In "A Few Maxims for the Instructions of the Over-Educated" (1894), Oscar Wilde wrote that "the English are always degrading truths into facts. When a truth becomes a fact, it loses all its intellectual value." Wilde, *Oscar Wilde*, Oxford Authors Series (Oxford: Oxford University Press, 1989) 571–72.

   For "remote intimacy," see the Abstract to David Trotter, *The Literature of Connection* (Oxford: Oxford University Press, 2020). https://academic.oup.com/book/36855/chapter/322039275.

42 "Influence of the Telegraph upon Literature," *Democratic Review* Vol.22 (May 1848): 409–13.

43 Paul Hendrickson, *Hemingway at Eighteen* (Chicago: Chicago Review Press, 2018) xx; also see Peter Griffin, *Along with Youth, Hemingway, The Early Years* (Oxford: Oxford University Press, 1985) 38–55.

44 Henry Miller, *The Air-conditioned Nightmare in Norman Mailer, Genius and Lust, A Journey through the Major Writings of Henry Miller* (New York: Grove Press, 1976) 429.

45 The phrase "visible speech" originates with Alexander Melville Bell who prepared a universal alphabet in the 1860s. See Jill Lapore, A *is for American, Letters and Other Characters in the Newly United States* (New York: Knopf, 2002) 162–85.

Lapore is also useful in relating the importance of the first transatlantic cable, celebrated in New York in September 1858, and its potential to eliminate national boundaries and distinctions. One celebratory speaker noted that the world was no longer composed of competing hemispheres but one unified globe. She also notes the irony that the day New York celebrated the successful completion of the London—New York cable (September 1, 1858), it failed, and would not be successfully relaid with restored communication until 1866 (Lapore 140).

46 Ralph Waldo Emerson, *Journal*, June 1840 in Gay Wilson Allen, "Plain Talk from Ralph Waldo Emerson," *American Heritage* Vol.37 No.4 (June/July 1986). https://www.americanheritage.com/plain-talk-ralph-waldo-emerson. Also see *The Topical Notebooks of Ralph Waldo Emerson*, ed. Glen M. Johnson (Columbia, MI: University of Missouri Press, 1994) 3: 155.

47 Kenneth Cmiel, "Broad Fluid Language of Democracy: Discovering the American Idiom," *Journal of American History* Vol.79 (1992): 915 Hereafter Broad.

48 Andrew Yang "Words on the Wire," UX Collective (April 1, 2020). https://uxdesign.cc/words-on-the-wire-8ee91b75e894.

49 Cormac McCarthy, *The Orchard Keeper* (London: Andre Deutsch, 1966) 7.

50 Don DeLillo, *White Noise* (New York: Penguin, 1986) 155.

51 Stein in Donald Sutherland, "An Interview with Gertrude Stein," *Gertrude Stein: A Biography of Her Work* (New Haven: Yale University Press, 1951) 194.

For an attack on a return to pretentiousness in American literary prose and "verbal affectation," see B.R. Meyers, "A Reader's Manifesto," *Atlantic* July/August 2001. https://www.theatlantic.com/magazine/archive/2001/07/a-readers-manifesto/302270/. He also complains about the decline of the long sentence which has become only a list of attributes or images.

52 Theodore Adorno agreed. See his "Punctuation Marks," tr. Shierry Weber Nicholsen, *Antioch Review* Vol.48 No.3 (1990): 300–5. Punctuation marks are no more than traffic signals he writes, although "there is no element in which language resembles music more than in punctuation marks" (300).

53 Kay Armitage, "Gertrude Stein's Radical Grammar," *The Walrus* February 12, 2007. https://thewalrus.ca/2007-02-language/.

54 On the matter of censorship and the need to curb writing about the war by journalists, see Molly Guptill Manning, *The War of Words, How America's GI Journalists Battled Censorship and Propaganda to Help Win World War II* (Ashland, OR: Blackstone 2023). Control of the press was universal. In the United States, the American Secretary of the Navy

Frank Knox imposed stringent controls: newsrooms were not to publish information about US ship or troop movements, the development of weapons or the presence of British ships in American ports (Manning 12–13). Pearl Harbor intensified restrictions as censorship became widespread, impacting reporting and, of course, writing (Manning 14–15). Press releases misled and government reports even fictionalized events. A Code of Censorship prevented the reporting of facts. Only shortly before the first anniversary of Pearl Harbor did the navy release the number of Americans killed, wounded or missing, and the number of vessels lost and planes destroyed.

55 Langston Hughes, "Poor Little Black fellow," *The Ways of White Folks* (1934; New York: Knopf, 1969) 155.

56 William Carlos Williams, *Selected Essays* (1954; New York: New Directions, 1969) 213. On the general topic of rapid poetics, see Cecelia Tichi, "Twentieth Century Limited: William Carlos Williams' Poetics of High-speed America," *William Carlos Williams Review* Vol.9 No.1, 2 (Fall 1983): 49–73.

Tichi also points out the reaction of other authors to the "nervous, restless" American life, "a constant agitation, a violent moving … . Speed is the disease of Power which, having no present, feverishly strives to hurry to the future" wrote Waldo Frank in *The Rediscovery of America* (1929 in Tichi 53). Sinclair Lewis sensed this in his 1917 short story, "Speed."

However, American speed was in harmony with an age of high-powered machinery from trains and the telegraph to cars. In the mid-1920s, a social critique in the form of a Socratic dialog has Phaelon ask Socrates what, besides size, constitutes a test of American superiority? Socrates offers a one-word reply: "Speed." See Douglas Woodruff, *Plato's American Republic* (New York: Dutton, 1926) 32; Tichi, 50. Edna Ferber in the 1910s claimed that the twin condiments of the twentieth century were "pep and ginger" (in Tichi 51).

Speed meant vitality. The goal for Americans was acceleration; the country always seemed to be in a marathon. The historians Charles and Mary Beard wrote that the "brusque and breezy style" of contemporary American writing represented a transition "to a modern vernacular appropriate to the higher velocity of living" (in Tichi 54). Periodicals emerged for those in transit, while articles offered suggested reading times, duplicated by many online articles today.

Conveying speed on the page for Williams took the form of spacing, margins, divisions, type size, placement of punctuation, and ideograms. Unsurprisingly, perhaps, there is a Museum of American Speed in Lincoln, Nebraska, although its focus is automobiles, not literature.

57 William Carlos Williams, *Selected Essays* 213, 7, 14, 67.

58 William Carlos Williams, *Autobiography* (New York: New Directions, 1967) 330.
59 William Carlos Williams, *The Embodiment of Knowledge*, ed. Ron Loewinsohn (New York: New Directions, 1974) 13, 15; also see *Selected Essays* 268–9.
60 William Carlos Williams, *In the American Grain* (1925; New York: New Directions, 1956) [3].
61 Henry Adams, "The Education of Henry Adams," *Novels, Mont Saint Michel, The Education*, ed. Jane Samuels and Ernest Samuels (New York: Library of America, 1983) 1126.
62 William Carlos Williams, *Imaginations* (New York: New Directions, 1971) 290.
63 Ali Smith, "Being Quick," *The Whole Story and Other Stories* (London: Hamish Hamilton, 2003) 41.
64 Norman Mailer, *Miami and the Siege of Chicago* (1968; New York: New York Review Books, 2008) 11; John Steinbeck, *The Winter of Our Discontent* (New York: Viking, 1960) 198. One other Steinbeck example: from p. 258, "Yes, but hurry, hurry, hurry. News, news, news."
65 Joyce to Harriet Shaw Weaver, November 24, 1926. *Selected letters of James Joyce*, ed. Richard Ellmann (New York: Viking Press, 1975) 318.

Chapter 3
Criminal Sentences: The Press

"When in doubt, have a man come through the door with a gun in his hand."
 THOMAS WALSH, "DIAMONDS MEAN DEATH" (1936)

"This better be good."
 DIVISION CAPTAIN IN RICHARD PRICE, *LUSH LIFE* (2008)

i

American newspapers loved blood and scandal, sensationally presented in the curt telegraphic style. The popular press soon added marital infidelity and bizarre violence all expressed in a breezy tone often through slang. Circulation numbers rose, although some papers resisted the vulgar and maintained a usage book of unacceptable words. The *Chicago Tribune* avoided any rude terms and in 1852, *Arthurs's Home Gazette* promoted a paper free from "VULGARITY, LOW SLANG, PROFANITY, or anything that can corrupt or deprave the mind." The *Chicago Times*, however, dove in, abusing politicians, officials, and the well-to-do with style. New York's *Commercial Advertiser* promised a paper that was "NEWSY! SPICY!! SUCCESSFUL!!!"[1] Good taste battled coarseness with readership the prize. In the new spirit, *The New York Herald* soon referred to eternal punishment as "perpetual roasting" and "eternal basting" (Cmiel 63).

Newspapers renewed the American Sentence drawing heavily on the telegraphic style, the medium fashioning how the message was to be told, form shaping the expression of content. Journalism, especially when reporting on crime, revivified a syntax that was short, sharp, and swift. Headlines initiated the short-handed method focusing on speedy consumption and accelerated information, treated in the body of the story by telling the story quickly and dramatically. Expression trumped content, becoming itself the content.

Delivery was everything often expressed in fragments, increasingly a journalistic habit. Suddenly, subordinate clauses stood alone for emphasis, while words in lists broke up: "She told a grim story. A story with many twists. And turns."[2] The grammatical independence of what we might label the sentence unchained, often meant breaking grammatical rules for rhetorical effect. The ellipsis may reign yet the statement could still be understood. Sentences became stage directions with oral discourse replicated in informal media today such as texting. The phrase and the clause stand in for the complete (subject–predicate) sentence—as in posters, advertisements, news headlines, and weather reports confirm.

A "middling rhetoric" emerged in the early nineteenth century reflecting increased education and democratic sentiments, undermining the neoclassical tropes of earlier writers, and journalists. A populist poetics developed incorporating regional dialect. Vulgar demagoguery replaced Ciceronian oratory. Papers and speakers had to be *en rapport* with their audiences. The goal was not authority over audiences but sympathy, if not identity with them. That meant a level of diction equal to their understanding. Popular rhetoric, like the popular or plain style, took over, although certain papers felt the need to reclaim their moral refinement. In the spring of 1881, they reprinted the complete *Revised New Testament* when it first appeared. The entire work was telegraphed to both the *Chicago Times* and *Tribune* and it was published in their Sunday editions two days after the New York publication. Ninety-two compositors worked around the clock at the *Tribune* to set type (Cmiel 217).

Nevertheless, bluntness became the new standard called "plain speaking" rooted in Swift and Thomas Paine. Straightforward and rough, it emphasized truth, not politeness. The "hard form" meant deliberate insults relying on invective and *ad hominem* attacks. Civil discourse became heated and slanderous in some cases instigated by the press. Euphemisms (often used to hide sexual or sensual language) were gone as "seduced" replaced "betrayed." Instead of pomposity, there were direct, immediate, often inflammatory statements in a language understood by all. A new public idiom emerged.

There was also a reversal of sender and receiver, altering the telegraph model. Not the sender but the receiver, the reader, paid to read the words reversing the economic model of the telegraph. But with intriguing, lurid, or surprising stories, people eagerly paid. Costs ran from a few pennies to twenty-five cents. Within time, interest in sleaze became so popular that publishers and the press created the Nickel Weeklies and "dime novels," quickly written sensational stories with a focus on crime and its punishment. This would convert into the wildly popular pulp magazines with titles like *Detective Story Magazine*, *Dime Mystery Magazine*, *I Confess*, and *Black Mask*. By December 1933, the latter rose from 66,000 copies a week to over 103,000 copies a week, at .20c per issue. Two years later, with a change of editors, crime fighters replaced the action detective.[3]

Crime, of course, long fascinated the public with printers between 1674 and 1860 issuing hundreds of books, pamphlets, and broadsides relating to criminal activity. These included conversion narratives, execution sermons, trial reports, romantic biographies, and, finally, newspaper stories. By the first half of the nineteenth century, the "print culture of crime" became a competitive industry appealing to a mass readership stressing narratives of sex and violence with as many grim details as possible.[4] The cautionary impulse of early accounts gave way to vivid reporting including the number of gunshot wounds or what body parts were dismembered. Readership increased in a competitive drive for profits. This was not surprising, since public hangings in New England, running through the early eighteenth century, drew thousands, addressed by clergymen and eagerly recounted in printed execution sermons and broadsides. The crime narrative shifted, however, with a new emphasis on the criminal act rather than the execution of the accused.

Arrests, crimes, trials, escapes, chases, and executions became the new content. In the early press, actions against piracy and counterfeiters took precedence over burglary, robbery, rape, and murder—but that would quickly change as pirates died out (Cohen 15–16). Superseding redacted trial transcripts, including indictments, witness testimony, closing arguments, verdicts, and prison sentences, were dramatic accounts of criminal activities, often exaggerated. By the early nineteenth century, paid journalists were, for the first time, sent to police court or to attend major criminal trials (Cohen 31). More graphic sexual content also dominated.

Expanding the telegraphic style was a new emphasis on an intensified use of adjectives, adverbs, and sensationalist nouns. Beginning in the late 1800s with Joseph Pulitzer's *New York World*, reporting concentrated on violence, crime, and sex. He knew that a racy headline would sell papers. "Baptized in Blood" and "Little Lotta's Lovers" are two examples. Two more: "Severed Leg Hops to Hospital"; "Hubby's bad breath Kills His Wife." Hearst's *New York American* (morning paper) and his *New York Evening Journal* (afternoon paper) competed with equally lurid headlines which often took over the entire front page. Such style, labeled Yellow Journalism, became standard in the tabloids relying on oversized pictures and dominant graphics featuring sensational and/or salacious front-page stories. Anonymous sources were celebrated for giving an inside scoop. The impact on the form of the sentence was significant with half expressions, innuendos, and false claims dominating. Discarded were previously established journalistic standards.

A language of phrases replaced the conventional structure of the formal sentence; traditional and accepted syntactical hierarchies were outdated as Whitman showed. Superordinate or subordinate clauses disappeared. No phrase was grammatically superior to another as a lengthy passage from Whitman's 1855 Preface to *Leaves of Grass* illustrates. The lengthy passage of twenty-one prose lines is an extraordinary, unregulated "sentence" that appears to restart with each phrase separated by ellipses without any rhetorical need to stop. The topic is opposition to slavery "which shall never cease till it ceases or the speaking of tongues and the moving of lips cease. For such the expression of the American poet is to be transcendent and new." Only after repeating "cease" three times does the sentence seem, synthetically, to halt its various narratives and sub-narratives. The passage undermines any traditional sense of what a sentence might be, replacing any accumulation of references with emotional urgency leading to a significant end. There is a swirling, experiential submersion in a set of clauses supported by present participles that link the past and present with the "essences of real things."[5] In doing so, the passage remakes the concept of formal syntactic expression creating what one might legitimately call "the democratic sentence" with no part superior to another.

Dramatic headlines strengthened the appeal of criminal stories assisted by speedy prose, truncated facts, and minimal quotations by witnesses, authorities, or onlookers. Sharp and occasionally humorous, sensational headlines became expected:

"City Stripper to Wear the Evidence"
"Ghost Solved Crime"
"Dead in a Shoe Box"
"The Bobbed Hair Bandit"
"Last Chapter of Lurid Romance is Cell in Prison"
"Night-Long Jazz Orgy Delays Music Loving Killer"
"JERKED TO JESUS" (a Chicago hanging)
"Nottingham Child Rapist caught after officer noticed distinctive walk"
"Harlem man argues self-defense in cricket-bat killing"
"Arizona man gets life in prison for burying wife alive"
"Rapist-murderer on death row avoids lethal injection by claiming to be 'too fat'"
"'Killer' Librarian Retiring after 34 years"

This last is the most recent (August 8, 2024) with a catchy opening: "All summer long, Bev Wowak has been killing people—and she hasn't even been all that picky about choosing her victims. Still, it's a lot of work." According to the reporter, she had first to think of the people to kill and then the method. The perpetrator of this mayhem is a librarian on the North Shore of Long Island, noted for her monthly short stories and the careful selection of her victims: John Berendt, author of *Midnight in the Garden of Good and Evil,* must go for overusing the Oxford comma. She killed another with a lobster because he hated seafood. A fellow librarian practically begged her to be killed; she did so with a book cart.[6] The sensationalism of the headline slightly misleads, but not entirely.

The title of the pulps exceeded newspaper headlines for sensationalism:

    Bagby, George. *Give The Little Corpse a Great Big Hand*
    Shannon, Carl. *Lady, That's My Skull*
    Boucher, Anthony. *The Case of the Seven Sneezes*
    Spillane, Mickey. *Survival … Zero!*
    Chase, James Hadley, *You're Lonely when you're Dead*
    Chandler, Raymond. *Farewell, My Lovely*
    Bellem, Robert Leslie. *Serenade with Slugs*
    _____. *Slay it isn't so!*
    Taylor, Samuel W. *The Grinning Gismo*
    Phillips, Max. *Fade to Blonde*
    Kane, Frank. *Trigger Mortis*
    Thompson, Jim. *The Killer Inside Me*
    Walsh, Thomas. "Diamonds Mean Death"

Vicarious adventures in crime and punishment satisfied an increasing appetite for the sordid, the sexual, and the subversive. Trials became dramas described in detail with outcomes imagined, predicted, and confirmed. Crimefighting became a national pastime competing for popular attention with sports. The hard-boiled detective, an American invention, stepped forward from the pulp magazines and novels with their racy covers promising exposés, murders, and, if necessary, mutilation. Titillation was everywhere. All of this impacted the American Sentence which was becoming edgy, threatening, and exciting. Heroes carried "gats" and their girlfriends were drunks. And it started with the press.

ii

Numerous early and mid-twentieth century writers began as journalists and the experience encouraged them to respect fact, not to deal with it second-hand. The celebration of "concrete, commonplace American realities" originated in journalism just as the journalistic style, itself, originated in large part with the telegraph.[7] But having an angle was unavoidable, what Emily Dickinson recognized when she wrote that we cannot face the truth directly: "Tell all the truth but tell it slant—/ Success in Circuit lies/ Too bright for our infirm Delight [.]"[8] However, sensational crime reporting disregarded the warning. An immediate, direct style shaped the sentence and its content. No holding back. Reaffirmed was the primacy of experience as a cornerstone of an American aesthetic but without rhetorical excess or exaggeration as the telegraph enforced.

The workshop of the American Sentence began with dots and dashes, limiting any effort at verbal embroidery. Crime reporting and then pulp magazines would "double-down" on the style, where suspicions always ran high. Detective Flaherty, in Thomas Walsh's short story "Double Check" (1933), explains: "We haven't figured the thing right from the start. There's something in back of this we're not even sniffing. It don't hang together the way it is."[9] Doubts, uncertainties, and opinions replace objectivity and clear thinking. Your gut becomes your brain.

For the press, crime was designed for concise, if graphic, representation: sensational details were a part, but not too much a part, of the story. Yet information was and it had to be precise and clear for maximum impact: "How many bullets, what address, how many bodies?" was the guide. The opening of a story from the *New York Daily News* headlined "Young Bride becomes Instant Widow after Shooting an Abusive Bigamist Husband" begins romantically but then turns dramatic:

> Margaret Herlihy, 21, was a summer bride, married on the first day of the solstice, June 21, 1942. Two months later, the blue-eyed, titian haired beauty was a widow.
>
> (*New York Daily News*)

By omission, we fill-in the space between her marriage and her widowhood confirmed a few sentences later when we learn that she shot her violent husband in their bedroom after a vacation in Mexico. In the final paragraph, we read: "Thirty-seven minutes was all it took for the all-male jury, composed of miners and ranchers, to acquit her." Detail and abruptness unite.

Another headline, "NYC photographer fatally shoots wife amid nasty divorce," precisely condenses the story that begins with details about the successful photographer who captured movie stars, heads of state, and celebrities. He was known to build drama with artificial light "but when a scene of high drama—a love nest slaying—came straight to his doorstep, there were no special lighting and no camera in his hands. He was holding a gun."[10] The dramatic, reversal method substitutes a gun for a camera. Supplementing this style were often realistic photos of shootings, knifings, and poisonings with work by Weegee in New York perhaps the best-known.

Matching the terseness of the stories were intense passages from the now-popular pulp fictions:

> "She was standing in the doorway and she had the .45 automatic ... Carter whirled around like a dancer and jumped sidewise crouching. Marjorie Smith shot him.
>
> Marjorie Smith shot him again, deliberately, in the back. Carter collapsed weakly and slid down the stairs, bumping soddenly on each step ...." Norbert Davis, "The Red Goose," *Black Mask*, February 1934. The adverb "soddenly" intensifies the action.

****

> "You're the second guy I've met within hours who seems to think *a gat in the hand* means a world by the tail." Marlowe in Chandler, *The Big Sleep*. Dramatic clichés and gangster talk.

****

> "From the doorway a roscoe said 'Kachow!' and a slug creased my noggin." Robert Leslie Bellem, *Hollywood Detective* (Cheap Thrills 133). Slang rules: a "roscoe," not a gun, causes the damage.

****

> "Slug him again! said the punk as she flailed out with her slipper." "Murder Wears Makeup," *Hollywood Detective*, August 1950. Irony: a slipper as a weapon.

****

Mickey Spillane kept the deadbeat style going as in this opening sentence:

"The Belmont Hotel was really jumping. Everything had happened so fast. How could just one death raise such a commotion?"
Mickey Spillane, "A Bullet for Satisfaction," *The Last Stand*, c. 1952. Surprise and contrast between "jumping" and a dead body.

"Journalese" became the conventional style displayed in numerous true crime magazines, graduating to the authors of hard-boiled crime fiction with their unsentimental, realistic, naturalistic sentences. Raymond Chandler, Dashiell Hammett, James M. Cain, and Mickey Spillane all had a hand in remaking the American Sentence, neatly summarized by this moment in Chandler's "Red Wind": "I got a cigarette out without being shot at, lit it and went into my story. It wasn't all true, but some of it was."[11] The staccato style and tone, matched by incomplete, or interrupted, dialogue mirrored street talk, criminal life, and scattered but forceful action as in this passage also from "Red Wind":

The brunette hung around in the shadows and a bottle gurgled and her temple bells gonged in her ears.
"It's all right, honeybunch," the man said. "it's all under control. Somebody bumped somebody off and this lad thinks we're interested. Just sit down and relax."

(Wind 217)

But in a 1949 letter, Chandler was firm: serious literature does not exist and detective fiction could never be part of such a category if it did. The "survivals of Puritanism in the American mind make all but the most literate people incapable of thinking of literature without reference to what they call significance." Most of the so-called serious literature or fiction is "the most transient stuff in the world; the moment its message is dated, damn quick, it is dead stuff," adding that he gets "a lot of fun out of sticking pins in the popular balloons."[12] His negative view displays a cynical approach to taking literature too seriously, including his own work. He also rejects any attempt at elevated language in a detective story. "Certain writers," he claims, "are under a compulsion to write in recherché phrases as a compensation for a lack of some kind of natural animal emotion. They feel nothing, they are literary eunuchs, and therefore they fall back on an oblique terminology to prove their distinction" (Lett. 164).[13] One must *feel* to write halfway decent mysteries; they have to convince.

The urbanized environment of much of the writing meant a city-style of tough guys fighting for survival or even to smile. From Hammett's *The Glass Key* (1930): "He did not smile. 'I don't believe in anything, but I'm too much of a gambler not to be affected by a lot of things'."[14] Later, "His mouth twitched in a meagre smile. He did not say anything" (Key 99). And later still, "he moved his lips in a thin smile that his eyes had nothing to do with … " (Key 127). The image wonderfully emphasizes detachment and division. But Mickey Spillane was more direct. From *One Lonely Night* (1951):

> All right, you conniving little punks, I'll play ball, but I'm going to make up a lot of rules you never heard of. You think I'm cornered and it'll be a soft touch. Well, you won't be playing with a guy who's a hero. You'll be up against a guy with a mind gone rotten and a lust for killing! That's the way I was and that's the way I like it![15]

Colson Whitehead in his *Harlem Shuffle* (2021) carries on the tradition of the curt, pulp fiction style: "Five hundred dollars, onetime payment. As far as bribes and payoffs went, the onetime nature argued in its favour."[16] Whitehead doubles down on brevity, diction, imagery, and syntax as in this moment when Ray Carney reconsiders his options:

> Almas's proposal made sense, though nor for the reasons she gave. Carney had put his family in danger, and that's why he had cursed at her. Left a trail to his door for bad men to follow. One of the crew dead, two others missing …. Pepper was right. It was Miami Joe, no doubt.
> (Shuffle 94)

The style is abrupt, incomplete, but effective. It captures the broken thoughts, worries, and concerns of the character.

Even in description, matched by action, Whitehead breaks the sentences into discrete phrases:

> Like most Harlemites, Carney grew up with broken glass in the playground, the pageant of sidewalk cruelty whenever he stepped

outside, and the snap of gunfire. He recognized the sound. Carney crouched and zagged toward the aluminum garbage cans. When he looked back, there was Miami Joe and the zing as his second shot hit the lid of the can next to him. It wasn't too far to the corner—he sprinted for it.

New York was like that sometimes—you turn a corner and end up in an entirely different city, like magic.

(Shuffle 98)

The sentence and its syntax become active agents of the story.

Virginia Tufte's *Artful Sentences* (2006) makes the point that syntax gives relational power to words to create meaning. It offers value providing "direction, not just structure."[17] The clause is the basic unit often surrounded by modifiers, complements, or objects. Collectively, they generate verbal activity, fashioning sentences of impact and meaning as Whitehead shows, expressing character, situation, or location. Rhythm and cadence contribute, shaping style, with compactness adding emphasis, clarity, and drama. But although the short sentence dominated critical forms of prose writing from the essay to realistic fiction, especially detective stories with their intransitive form—"Somebody sighed, from the heart; he looked up; it was Hannah. They were looking downward and sidelong"—it did not rule.[18] Faulkner, Mailer, Pynchon, DeLillo, Capote, Vidal, Morrison, and the like resisted. Some blended the styles of clarity and elaboration as seen in Updike. Writing of Ted Williams's last at-bat on September 28, 1960, in Boston (a home run no less), Updike wrote that when Williams swung "it was in the books, while it was still in the sky." The sentence records a memorable act before its completion which holds the reader in suspense while the ball is in animated suspension. But in the same essay, he turns to elaboration and allusion, stating that Boston's Fenway Park "offers, as do most Boston artifacts, a compromise between man's Euclidean determinations and Nature's beguiling irregularities."[19]

iii

Journalists for the Chicago and New York papers, absorbing the telegraphic style, altered it to include lurid details with a sense of an exposé. But in Chicago, it seemed violence and drama imposed themselves on a now speeded-up prose style focusing on sensationalism and scandal. Or rather, the sensational events forced the prose into a high-octane style to keep up with events. The crimes were relentless, widespread, and led by mobsters such as Al Capone, Baby Face Nelson, and Bugs Moran. Examples include the dramatic Leopold/Loeb murder case of 1924—two privileged teenagers kidnapped and killed a fourteen-year-old neighbor but escaped the death penalty because of a psychiatric defense introduced by Clarence Darrow; and the March/April 1924 love murders committed by the attractive Beulah Annan and Belva Gaertner, a 38-year-old cabaret singer and "twice a divorcée of page one notoriety" who killed her 29-year-old lover.[20] Each glamorously and modestly posed at a police station, in jail and in court.

Their images, often of the two murderesses together, were printed across the country, intensifying the reputation of the city as crime central, while elaborating the salacious side of the press. One headline read "Chicago's Murderess Row, 1924," while another was more direct: "Demand Noose for 'Prettiest' Woman Slayer" referring to Beulah Annan, only twenty-three. The paper claimed she was "the prettiest woman ever accused of murder in Chicago—young, slender, with bobbed auburn hair; wide set, appealing blue eyes" and more.[21] She was acquitted, partly because of her dazzling beauty and Southern drawl wrote the *Chicago Tribune* overlooking her "glibness with the trigger finger."[22] The language and tone joined the tabloids with pulp magazines.[23]

Another crime cementing Chicago as the crime capital of the United States was the St. Valentine's Day Massacre of 1929. Seven members of Chicago's North Side gang were lined up against a wall in a Lincoln Park garage and shot with a machine gun and shotgun; it, too, made international headlines ranging from "Gang War Breaks Out Again as Mob Slays trapped Men" to "7 in Chicago Rum Gang Lined up, Shot to Death" and "Massacre 7 of Moran Gang." Two of the assailants were dressed as policemen and two as businessmen: one headline read "Murder Cops Hunted in Massacre." Al Capone likely ordered the hit to eliminate Bugs Moran's gang who was highjacking Capone's liquor shipments from Detroit.

In New York, it was the 1928 execution of the murderous Long Island housewife Ruth Snyder who, with her lover, killed her husband. Adding to the media frenzy was a photograph of her execution in an electric chair at Sing Sing taken by a photographer from the *New York Daily News* who had an ankle camera. Its publication resulted in the sale of 250,000 extra copies of the paper. Above the image was a one word headline: "DEAD!" Sensationalism ruled the press and press style with competitive mass communication on the rise, one paper trying to outdo the other. Sex and crime sold papers. And journalists, now writing in the short-burst style almost duplicating the firing of a submachine gun, treated crime as entertainment. But they resorted to bribes, disguises, and false information to elaborate "the news." Replacing the in-your-face reporting, just the facts, was an emphasis on drama and emotion It is Beulah Annan stepping "demurely from the witness stand with [the] settled complacency of a school girl who has said her piece."

iv

The new world of pulp magazines rapidly incorporated and adopted the sordid, lascivious and irresistible style of the Yellow Journalists. The two forms of media—the papers and the pulps—ignited a style that was unforgiving and unforgotten with a tough-guy tone summarized as "hard-boiled." Twisting and intensifying the telegraphic and journalistic style, sentences became punchy, jumpy, raucous, alive, and American. They had strength, kick, pizazz as seen in this opening by the journalist, later dramatist and screen writer, Ben Hecht, to his column "The Man Hunt":

> They were hunting him. Squads of coppers with rifles, detectives, stool pigeons were hunting him. And the people who had read the story in the newspapers and looked at his picture, they too, were hunting him.[24]

The diction, rhythm, and language are immediate and without confusion. Readers didn't need dictionaries; they only had to hang out on the street and pick up a copy of the *Chicago Daily News*.

"Man Hunt" was one of a set of daily columns by Hecht for the *Daily News*, each a different tale about the city, sixty-four of them published by Pascal Covici in book form. The style was an extension of the tabloids with extensive detail. At one point, the hunted Tommy O'Conner, looking out of a smeared window, watches "a drift of snow across the roofs. A scribble of snow over the pavement" (35). The scene continues with clipped sentences emphasizing the freedom of the hunted and his determination that he would not be caught and hanged:

> Scared? No. just waiting. Hunters winding in and out like the snow that was falling. People were funny. They got a big thrill out of hunting a live man who was free in the streets.
>
> (37)

He waited until dark and then wanted to go out and buy the papers and "give them a reading" (38). But he senses they are coming for him: "A gun crept out of Tommy O'Conner's pocket. He pressed himself carefully against the wall. He waited ..... black figures of men floating casually down the street. All right—let them come" (38).

The writing is crisp, dramatic, tense expressed through syntax that is limited and direct. Each of Hecht's stories was based on an actual incident "developed by a period of soaking in the peculiar chemicals of Ben's nature." They also introduced subjective journalism "lit with the moods of Ben himself, not of the things dramatized .... the writings of a reporter emancipated from the assignment book and the copy-desk."[25]

Crime reporting became glamorous with certain niche categories: Ione Quinby, was one of Chicago's first female reporters who specialized in female murderers, extortionists, adulteresses, and kidnappers. She interviewed many in their jail cells. She followed Colette who attended and wrote about a series of trials in Paris including that of a Mr. Weidman, the last man to be publicly guillotined in the county. She also wrote of the Landru trial, a murderer accused of killing a succession of wives.[26] The crime reporter soon became a detective story favorite. Thomas Polsky's *Curtains for the Editor* (1939), William P. McGivern's *Night Extra* (1957), Pete Hamill's *Dirty Laundry* (1978), and Max Byrd's *Paris Deadline* (2012), set in 1926 at the Paris office of the *Chicago Tribune*, are all examples.

Theoretically, murder lost its mayhem through a precise and specific manner of reporting generated by aggressive if not occasionally felonious actions. Chicago crime reporters often broke into courtrooms to get scoops, one hanging upside down from the eaves of a courthouse roof, fifty feet above the ground, to peer through the windows of the jury room. Crime reporters even acted as local law enforcement. In the 1890s, the sheriff's department swore in reporters as deputies and allowed them to make their own news by raiding gambling dens and brothels. Papers often supplied badges that reporters could flash to pass themselves off as detectives or assistant coroners (Notorious 19). By the 1920s, the police provided press cards with a note from the chief of police stating that journalists be extended all courtesies. Scandal was the goal reported in a breathtaking manner at breakneck speed heading toward drama without mystery.

Journalists parleyed their license for crime reporting into flamboyant headlines and stories. And no work captured this better than Ben Hecht and Charles MacArthur's *The Front Page*, a 1928 play that revealed the chicanery and deceit of journalists among each other, as well as the public. Set in the press room of the Chicago Criminal Courts Building, seven phones, representing seven papers, populate the landscape of desks, a table, cigarettes, and banter with poker the main action— until an escaped criminal appears through a window and, through the sympathy of a single reporter, is hidden in a large roll-top desk. Various shenanigans follow, the plot, such as it is, is fast, embodying the notions of American speed in action and dialog. Humor is not far away, with stage directions emphasizing that free telephoning and a constant poker game are the big draws, while the press room is a place where "they meet to gossip, play cards, sleep off jags and date up waitresses between such murders, fires, riots and other public events as concern them."[27] Hecht summarizes the reporters as "Katatonic, seedy Paul Reveres, full of strange oaths and a touch of childhood" (Front 3).

Chaos reigns, from awkward attempts at telephone interviews to frequent calls to police sergeants for news. Tough editors rule. When one reporter wanted to go to Hollywood, the managing editor of the *Examiner*, Walter Burns, had him thrown into jail for arson, changed by another reporter to forgery (Front 7). And when they phone-in a story, "Give me rewrite" is the frequent cry. While they await news from the police about the hanging of an Earl Williams, who supposedly shot a Black man, they complain it will probably be the last because "they're putting in an electric chair. Going to toast them like Lucky Strikes" Endicott of the *Post* announces (Front 12). Betting and reporting are simultaneous activities. Facts are casual. Asked to get a statement from the sheriff, Murphy tells his editor, "Quote him for anything you want— *he* can't read. *Hangs up. Bensinger's phone rings*" (Front 20).

Diamond Louie, former owner of a fruit stand and now a gangster with a gun, enters in his new role as a newspaper man but warned not to shoot anyone until after the election or he won't make the front page. He listens against the background of the whir and crash of the gallows in preparation for the hanging of Williams the next day. Hildy Johnson enters, a "*lusty, hoodlumesque half drunken caballero that was the newspaperman of our youth,*" claims the third person narrator (Front 31). "*Chicago,*" the narrator intones, "*is a sort of Yellowstone Park offering haven.*" For this rare, well-dressed type, "*a rowdy outburst succeeds his entrance*" (Front 31). And after a scene where Hildy tells off the editor Burns and quits, Hildy preens, celebrating a new future in advertising in New York with his soon-to-be bride.

A satire of New York journalists follows plus a further critique of Chicago reporters, "a lot of crumby hoboes, full of dandruff and bum gin" (Front 37). The satire broadens with Hildy declaring that journalists only peek through keyholes and wake people up "in the middle of the night to ask them what they think of Mussolini" (Front 40). He calls himself a "cross between a bootlegger and a whore" (Front 40). The writing becomes increasingly sharp. A tart, Mollie Malloy, enters, a "soiled and gaudy houri of the pavement" but the boys are glad to see her: "always glad to see whores" (Front 46). She responds with "if you was worth breaking my fingernails on, I'd tear your puss wide open." And she never had a "love nest" with the accused Williams causing Endicott, another reporter, to shout, "everybody knows you're his affinity!" a tremendous comic shift in tone based on one word (Front 47)! But a problem persists: can the hanging be moved up from 7am to 5am to make the City Edition? No go: "you can't hang a fella in his sleep, just to please a newspaper" the sheriff answers (Front 53). Ah, but you can issue reprieves three days before election in order to run on a law and order ticket with the backdrop of stopping Communism: Sheriff Hartman's new pledge is "to reform the Reds with a rope" (Front 57).

In this world of slang and lingo, a wife is "a ball and chain"; agitated, a character has "fish hooks in his pants"; a pair of gloves are "onions," while reporters are a "lot of lousy, daffy, buttinskis, swelling around with holes in their pants" repeatedly asking officials "what's the dope" (Front 58, 40, 65, 88)? And corruption is rampant, from politicians to policemen. Everyone is complicit.

Actual Chicago papers were models as the reporters use loud, rapid, coarse language often speaking over each other. The three-act structure shapes the drama with a final "dirty trick" at the end. Poker is their main activity interrupted by frequent calls to either other police stations for info or rewrite desks. A sample: McCue: into phone: "Hello, Sarge? McCue. Anything doing? ... Yeah? That's swell ... *The players pause.* A love triangle, huh? Did he kill her? ... Killed 'em *both*! Ah! ... Was she good looking? ... " (Front 6).

After the reporters rush out to cover a jail break with shots fired (some into the press room) and sirens wailing with Williams "on the lam," Hildy calls Walter Burns to reverse his departure and report the action. Act I ends; Act II opens with searchlights crisscrossing the room and broken glass everywhere. In the ensuing chaos, fabricated details about the escaped prisoner multiply while Hildy, in fractured speech, dictates a story to Walter Burns but he had to pay $260 for the exclusive, money he was to use for his honeymoon (Front 76–7). When his fiancée Peggy discovers Hildy spent their money, *"[H]er vocabulary is reduced to a coal of fire"* (Front 79).

In the midst of the manhunt, comedy erupts. The mayor suddenly appears, *"walking as if on snowshoes and carrying an unlighted cigar with which he gestures as if it were a wand. The events of the last hour have unhinged him"* (Front 86). Murphy then asks him, "Any truth in the report that you're on Trotsky's pay roll?" or that he sleeps in red underwear (Front 88)? The sheriff reports that he has hired four hundred deputies who now want supper: "Nothing doing!" the mayor shouts into a phone: "This is a man hunt—not a banquet" (Front 93)! A sudden reprieve from the governor conveniently gets misplaced; the hanging can go ahead and the mayor can count on the Black vote (since the white Williams supposedly shot a Black man). But with some of his missing money recovered via a loan from Diamond Louie, Hildy is about to leave when the escaped Earl Williams unexpectedly appears (Front 107). Comedy, tension, and action follow as Hildy hides

Williams in the oversized desk. Language games, insults, wild rumors, and an unexpected battle with Mollie, who jumps out of a window, take place—all this before the finale orchestrated by Walter Burns who suddenly appears, Hecht describing him *"in less hyperbolic language,"* as the embodiment of the "thoughtless" Boss Journalist, *"the licensed eavesdropper, trouble maker, bombinator and town Snitch, misnamed The Press"* (Front 129).

The critical tone of the dialog and mix of crime and the press may originate in Hecht's feeling that he was "a sort of pencil-outlaw," indirectly referencing his own interviews and reporting on Chicago criminals and then work on a biography of a Jewish gangster, Mickey Cohen. The provisional title of the book was to be *The Soul of a Gunman*.[28] The "outlaw" talk continues, Burns shouting to an assistant on the phone that "I want ten huskies from the circulation department to lam right over here" in preparation to move the desk with Williams in it (Front 135). The curtain falls as Peggy breaks up with Hildy who prefers his typewriter to her love.

Hildy begins to write his exclusive story on Williams at the opening of Act III following orders from Walter: "Lam into 'em, Hildy! Below the belt! Every punch!" (Front 141). "Stick on the wire!" (stay on the phone) is the order, while Hildy pounds out the lead, while Burns tries to get a story from a frazzled Diamond Louie telling him to "Take the mush out of our mouth!" (Front 154). "I'll butter this town with their brains!" shouts an angry Walter when his henchmen fail to show up (Front 158). "Take your paws off me," another screams (Front 161). The colloquial language and slang intensify, while the conniving goes on: in the final moments of the play, Walter gifts his watch to Hildy but tells his city editor (on the phone, of course) to have Hildy arrested in La Porte, Indiana, for stealing his timepiece. On that sour note, the play ends.

Throughout *The Front Page*, the writing is direct, comic, and exact. The press and the revised American Sentence join forces on stage; audiences understood every word. The popularity of *The Front Page* institutionalized the hard-boiled style soon to dominate the pulp fiction magazines dependent on a lurid style copied from the tabloids, once called "jazz journalism."[29] It would eventually lead to noir, a sinister style of immense appeal in the 1930s and 40s in books and film.

The play was made into a 1931 film starring Adolphe Menjou and Pat O'Brien; Howard Hughes produced, with the script by Hecht and MacArthur adapted by Bartlett Cormack and additional dialog by Charles Lederer and presented as a "screwball comedy." The talk was fast but not as quick as the revised, 1940 version, with major plot changes. This was the 1940s hit *His Girl Friday,* starring Cary Grant and Rosalind Russell, directed by Howard Hawks. As a result, the popularity of *The Front Page* soared. Hecht was an uncredited co-writer. The major change introduced by Hawks was that Hildy was a woman, now the ex-wife of Walter Burns. Ensemble scenes with spontaneous action backgrounded the plot with rapid, overlapping dialog. Hawks wanted to break the record for the fastest spoken dialog in film and used a sound mixer on set to increase the speed of dialog. The American Sentence raced across the screen.

V

Velocity increased the impact of the American Sentence, becoming, itself, an actual subject. In *Sleepers East*, a 1933 novel by Frederick Nebel, the speed of a train through a snowstorm is the cause of a fatal accident with the passengers commenting on how fast they were moving and how the train moaned and rocked on the tracks rushing through snowdrifts. Just before the accident and his own death, the engineer Magowan heard a noise like a spinning dynamo. He realizes it's speed itself: "Speed! That was it—that sound, growing, fast, faster. Speed!"[30] The almost maniacal devotion to speed causes the accident, acceleration the new focus, whether to get a job done or a story told.

Fast One (1933) by Paul Cain (aka George Sims) is an apt title. Some consider the story the hardest of the hard-boiled. Set in LA, it's a nihilist account of emotionless gangsters gunning each other down. The plot, as many in this genre, moves quickly, the story composed of linked episodes, sequences of action rather than an overarching narrative. *The New York Times* review described the book as a "ceaseless welter of bloodshed and frenzy, a sustained bedlam of killing and fiendishness, told in terse staccato style."[31] The protagonist, Gerry Kells, less than midway in the novel, explains that he's already been "mixed up in five shootings in the last thirty-two hours."[32] He went to LA from New York because "I happened to be too close to a couple front-page kills" (FO 40). But he murders without conscience and is seemingly amoral.

The story is about how Kells gets out of various frame-ups fashioned by a set of gangsters fighting for control of LA. The talk is curt and to the metaphorical point: "There's a lot of water been under the bridge since I seen you this afternoon" (153). *Fast One* packs lots of action into a very short time frame and ends with a dramatic car chase. Sample dialog:

> He glanced at the speedometer. "You'll have to do a little better. I think there's a fast one on our tail now."
> She said: "The curves ... "
> "I know, baby—you're doing beautifully. Only a little faster." He smiled. (*Fast One* 169)

Character is of no interest; it's only about the action, always corrupt. As Cain casually characterizes this world, "It was a little after six, full daylight, but the fog made it night" (FO 105).

But some writers parodied the need for speed in writing. Norman Mailer was one. In the first year of the *Village Voice,* he wrote seventeen pieces entitled "Quickly: A Column for Slow Readers" (January 11 – May 2, 1956), extending the appeal of speedy reading and narrative where events whizzed by, a technique for his treatment of controversial topics which generated immediate responses. Letters and even phone calls objected to his breezy manner with important topics which often relied on insults. "On Lies, Power, and Obscenity" opens with:

> [T]rue to my commitment to the *Voice*, I wrote it quickly. Because I do not want to lose all my readers at once, I suggest all but the slowest readers pass me by this time. If you are not in a mood to think, or if you have no interest in thinking, then let us ignore each other until the next column. And if you do go on from here, please have the courtesy to concentrate. The art of careful writing is beginning to disappear before the mental impotence of such lazy audiences as the present one.[33]

An insult was always a good ploy, especially in the cause of good writing. In his very first column, he told his readers he was writing it out of sheer egoism and insulted everyone by declaring Greenwich Village a province of undernourished snobs and critics. At the start of his second column, he noted that his lazy audience should read it with care and slowly. Readers responded by protesting his narcissism and condescension, adding that his novels weren't very good either—but he continued his combative tone and took pride in his speedy style of writing.

vi

The pace of pulp fiction, embodying the telegraphic style, is partly a result of their production. Deadlines and quick publication on cheap paper heavy with wood pulp meant writers had to write fast with little editing; producing content was the key. Speed partly reflected new technology and production methods. High turnover at lower prices led to profit, not the sale of fewer, if better written and produced magazines and books. With its terse dialogue and brief descriptions, pulp writing encouraged speedy reading, the stories anticipating the choppy, quick-cut style of film. Chapters were short with a great deal of action in a brief space reconceptualizing time. And murders constantly piled up, with Dashiell Hammett's *Red Harvest* (1929) a possible record: There are at least twenty-two, one couple done in with an ice pick, others killed with either bullets or poison. Matching the action is taciturn writing wasting no time: "Reno called him a lousy fish-eater and shot him four times in face and body."[34]

For the pulp fictionist, writing itself was quick: Jim Thompson wrote *The Killer Inside Me* (1952) in less than a month and produced twenty-one novels in twenty years. Agatha Christie supposedly wrote *The Mysterious Affair at Styles*, her first detective novel, in two weeks. Ed McBain wrote his 87th precinct novels in about a month each. Earl Stanley Gardner published four novels, eighteen novelettes, and two short stories in one year, 1939. Georges Simenon wrote ten novels in eleven months between May 1932 and April 1933. His aim was to write a novel in eleven days. Frederick C. Davis wrote a story a week for the pulps starting on a Sunday and mailing it off on the following Saturday—while in his first year at Dartmouth. Six years later in 1930, he was in New York writing 125,000 words a month. Robert Sidney Bowen averaged around 150 odd short stories and novelettes a year. His yearly "wordage average [was] four or five hundred thousand words."[35] Richard Deming reported that he likely appeared in fifty-five different pulp magazines. In 1950, he was earning $800 a month from his writing (Goulart 191).[36]

Dashiell Hammett was relatively speedy having worked as a messenger boy, a stockbroker, a timekeeper, and a special op for the Pinkerton Detective Agency which constantly demanded quick results. Hammett provided pithy and frequent operative reports transferred to his writing style. His first novel *Red Harvest* (1929) was lively with jumpy, slangy dialog pulled from the street. Pace was key, his Continental Op explaining that "I don't like eloquence. If it isn't effective enough to pierce your hide, it's tiresome, and if it is effective enough, it muddles your thoughts."[37] Hammett's first crime story, "The Road Home," appeared in the popular *Black Mask*, known for its racy (in both senses of the word) tales. Over an eight-year period of remarkable productivity at *Black Mask*, Hammett wrote the novella *The Big Knockover* and began and completed his ms. of what would become *Red Harvest*. *The Dain Curse* appeared the same year with *The Maltese Falcon* in 1930 and then *The Glass Key* (1931). He even had plans for a stream of consciousness detective novel, in further pursuit of speed anticipating what one critic has labeled "Electric Rhetoric."[38]

In the words of Raymond Chandler, Hammett "took murder out of the Venetian vase and dropped it into the alley .... He wrote at first (and almost to the end) for people with a sharp, aggressive attitude to life. They were not afraid of the seamy side of things; they lived there."[39] His sentences embodied this. Hammett had a style, Chandler writes, "but his audience did not know it .... they thought they were getting a good meaty melodrama written in the kind of lingo they imagined they spoke themselves." This was the "American language" which "had no overtones, left no echo, evoked no image beyond a distant hills .... he was spare, frugal, hardboiled .... he wrote scenes that seemed never to have been written before" (Chandler 989). The American Sentence hit the streets. This may be analogous to Barthes's "writing degree zero," an effective anti-style creating silent, transparent sentences.[40]

Such writing reflects disillusioned characters who see life darkly and are often caught in its pain unless they take action as Sam Spade does when he confronts the gun-totting Joel Cairo in *The Maltese Falcon*:

> Spade's elbow went on past the astonished dark face and straightened when Spade's hand struck down at the pistol. Cairo let

the pistol go the instant that Spade's fingers touched it .... Fist, wrist, forearm, crooked elbows and upper arm seemed all one rigid piece .... the fist struck Cairo's face.[41]

This is action presented with tight phrases and tart words joined by a constricted but effective cadence.[42]

Chandler, described in the *New York Herald Tribune* "as the pick of the hard-boiled mystery scribblers" with a style balanced "between the way most people talk and the kind of hardness that just makes you tired," outlines the drama of the American Sentence in its criminal guise, explaining that its energy comes not from brutality or flippant wit but from what the author "actually knows how to say" (Chandler 990).[43] He rejects the criticism that Hammett did not write detective stories, only presenting "hard-boiled chronicles of mean streets with a perfunctory mystery element dropped in like the olive in a martini" (Chandler 990). Murder is always an act of cruelty, even if the murderer occasionally looks like a playboy or college professor. The goal is to effect movement, intrigue while showing "cross-purposes and the gradual elucidation of character, which is all the detective story has any right to be about" (Chandler 991). We all live in a non-fragrant world and "certain writers with tough minds and a cool spirit of detachment can make very interesting and even amusing patterns out of it" (Chandler 991). Detachment is perhaps the clue and method of the obsession of crime writers with tough, short, realistic sentences to convey the action imitating the style of police crime reports. As Philip Marlowe ironically tells a saucy dame in Chandler's *The High Window*, "I'm not tough. Just virile."[44]

For Chandler, the classic detective story, invented by Poe and perfected by Conan Doyle and Agatha Christie, disappeared. Ordinary life, with its physicality and sensations, overtook recessive vicarage life upset only by an occasional murder. As Chandler explained, Hammett "gave murder back to the kind of people that commit it for reasons" (Chandler 989). But Chandler's style was itself critiqued. Ross Macdonald, author of the *Lew Archer* series, claimed that Chandler "wrote like a slumming angel, and invested the sun-blinded stress of Los Angeles with a romantic presence." Macdonald claimed to siphon off the romance to make room "for a completer social realism."[45]

Heir to this style is Richard Price, New York novelist, screenwriter, and author of *Clockers* (1992), inspiration for *The Wire*. His novel *Lush Life* (2008) opens in Chandleresque style:

> Restless, they finally pull out to honeycomb the narrow streets for an hour of endless tight right turns: falafel joint, jazz joint, gyro joint, corner. Schoolyard, crêperie, realtor, corner. Tenement, tenement, tenement museum, corner. Pink Pony, Blind Tiger, muffin boutique, corner. Sex shop, tea shop, synagogue, corner. Boulangerie, bar, hat boutique corner. Iglesia, gelateria, matzo shop, corner. Bollywood, Buddha, botanica, corner.[46]

Tone, alliteration, and detail present a showy but dark New York, consistent and surprising with dialog at the center of the novel making up nearly three quarters of the 455-page book. Street lingo dominates with neologisms, idioms, and surprising images everywhere. A blond girl on a bike stops in front of a now-empty murder scene, "the tattoo at the base of her spine drifting up from the ass of her jeans like blue smoke" (Lush 62).

The novel is compact, with characters talking over each other in an authentic way, often ending a statement in the middle of a sentence. A police interrogation lasts for pages but is never dull. One seems to eavesdrop through the laconic exchanges. Here, for example, is the answer of a cop when asked why his request can only be accommodated on Sunday night. His superior speaks: "Saturday's too soon. Monday I can't promise, Tuesday's unpredictable to the point of science fiction" (Lush 340). This is the American Sentence taken up several notches: it's slick, exact, staccato, and perfectly suited to the characters and their changing situations. And description, in its attenuated way, is poetic: the Lower East Side of New York has "canyonlike streets with their hanging garden of ancient fire escapes" (Lush 15); "The Clara E. Lemlich Houses were a grubby sprawl of 50-year-old high rises sandwiched between two centuries" (Lush 219). Price customizes clichés.[47]

And he doesn't hide the process, a passage early in the novel exposing almost all in a sentence that accumulates power and energy:

> Every cop on the scene, every Night Watch, every plainclothes and uniform, was either on a cell phone calling in, calling out, calling

up, or else feeding each other's steno pad; Matty always taken by that, how you could literally see the narrative building right before your eyes in a cross-chorus of data: names, times, actions, quotes, addresses, phone number, run numbers, shield numbers.

(Lush 43)

The narrative builds right before our eyes. Price, in the words of James Wood, offers "vital speech ... inventing a life for dialogue rather than just taking it from life."[48] This exchange shows how: confronting a gunman early one morning, a character, Isaac Marcus, refuses to give up his wallet. "Not tonight, my man," is his bold reply. But the gesture, an investigating policeman explains, is "[s]uicide by mouth .... Home run to the heart, the shooter and his partner book east on Delancey" (Lush 39). Life, or the end of life, occurs daily in the Lower East Side where early one morning, in a voice "like crusted glue," a weary division captain answers the phone with "This better be good" (Lush 60).

vii

"Action, action, action is the thing" wrote the crime and Western writer Max Brand (pseudonym of Frederick S. Faust) and this applies to the structure of pulp sentences as much as plot. As long as you keep your reader (and often your hero) "jumping through fiery hoops on every page, you're all right," Brand declared.[49] The method to maintain this was the jump-cut the sentence as if cutting from one scene to another in a film. But quick, syntactically undemanding prose statements appealed for its immediacy. Adopted by the press from the telegraph style but pushed further in the pulps and mystery stories, it became *de rigueur* with its emphasis on stylized, visual violence. Think Capote *In Cold Blood* (1966) or Mailer in *The Executioner's* Song (1979). But, of course, there was another stream of American writing originating in the rhetorically shaped American sermon absorbed and extended by Melville and then James, elaborated by Faulkner with the interior thoughts of his intense characters. Pynchon with his baroque style, DeLillo with his action sentences framed by history and context, and Toni Morrison and the urgent need of her characters to speak if not preach are further examples.

Melville, aided by the American sermon, may have instigated this style. He was particularly difficult to escape. In 1952, for example, while an undergraduate at Bucknell, Philip Roth disfigured his copy of *Moby Dick* with scansion marks to emphasize Melville's metered prose. The final paragraph of chapter 33, "The Specksynder" was one. It begins with "But Ahab, my Captain, still moves before me in all his Nantucket grimness and shagginess."[50] Roth also scanned passages in chapter 23, "The Lee Shore" (one of the shortest in the novel), starting with the first sentence: "Some chapters back, one Bulkington was spoken of, a tall, new-landed mariner, encountered in New Bedford at the inn" (Melville 906). Roth was discovering how Melville became a "sentence-maker" drawing on a mix of biblical and colloquial diction, sometimes in the same sentence.[51] The pellucid, elliptical style is evident in the opening of chapter 41: "Ishmael, was one of that crew; my shouts had gone up with the rest; my oath had been welded with theirs; and stronger I shouted and more did I hammer and clinch my oath, because of the dread in my soul" (Melville 983). The monosyllabic confronts the polysyllabic. Melville's diction and syntax soon permeated such later writers not only in the prophetic style of Faulkner but the expressive as in Hemingway.[52]

In *Moby Dick,* the rhetorically energetic takes a long and short form, often colliding and interacting to enact a chemistry textbook of the American Sentence with formulas, thermodynamic laws, and examples of chemical bonding. It structures the experience of the sentence, offering its own phenomenology. The energetic prose of the biblical is constantly mixing with the nautical, creating repeated intersections between the religious and everyday. The contradictions of the American sermon (high rhetoric and direct address) transform themselves into the American character, infusing competing values in the American Adam who, like Ishmael, loves "to sail forbidden seas, and land on barbarous coasts," the end of chapter 1 (Melville 800).

Father Mapple's sermon in chapter 9 demonstrates the blend, through nautical metaphors of sin and repentance regarding the fate of Jonah expressed in language direct and specific: he travels, for example, with "no baggage, not a hat-box, valise, or carpet-bag" (Melville 839). Disobedience is error as the sermon propels its narrative forward leading to this admonition:

Woe to him whom this world charms from Gospel duty! Woe to him who seeks to pour oil upon the waters when God has brewed them into a gale! .... Woe to hm whose good name is more to him than goodness!

(Melville 845)

To be a castaway from God is to fall but "on the starboard hand of every woe, there is a sure delight" (Melville 845). Melville re-purposes the American sermon as a nautical adventure, delivered from a pulpit in the shape of a ship's bow and offered by a former harpooner entering the chapel in a storm with almost no protection, seeming more like a creature from the sea than a man, declaiming sentences that clash with the lore and idiom of the sea. Appropriately, he rises to his pulpit on a side ladder "like those used in mounting a ship from a boat at sea" (Melville 834). He "mounted the steps as if ascending the main-top of his vessel." After pulling the stairs up after him, he was "on board," "impregnable in his little Quebec" (Melville 835). For Melville, the pulpit becomes the prow of the ship of the world (Melville 836). The vividness of the sermon originates in its merger of God and the sea.

Epitomizing the seemingly contradictory union of the sacred and profane is Ahab's advice passing round the pewter mug of grog in a ceremony dedicating the three harpooners to his cause: "Short draughts—long swallows," almost a summary of the impact of the short sentence. He goes on to counsel that "'Tis hot as Satan's hoof" and then warns, "it spiralizes in ye; forks out at the serpent-snapping eye" (Melville 968). Two worlds intersect with an unusual neologism igniting the center, while creating a poetic cadence that yet sounds like everyday speech. Before Melville broke stylistic molds in *Moby Dick*, American diction emulated British models but the hybridity of Melville's novel, through its original and consistently powerful sentences mixing the modern and archaic, makes it an "American synthesis ... creatively indecorous." He had a new and effective formula, a discovery in textual chemistry.[53]

Essayists, poets, and novelists, not just pulp writers or journalists, favored the terse, direct style of the revised American sentence—"omit needless words" was Strunk and White's mantra in *The Elements of Style* of (1918)—offering syntactic drama as much as punch. Examples can be found in Mailer, Didion, or Elizabeth Hardwick who begins her lengthy essay on Russian literary women in this fashion:

> The famous carry about with them a great weight of patriarchal baggage—the footnotes of their lives. Footnotes worry a lot. They, loved or unloved, seem to feel the winds of the future always at their back. The graves of the greatly known ones are a challenge to private history; the silence is filled with riddles and arcane messages.[54]

The prose is lucid, dramatic, developing select metaphors to convey in short-hand what a compound sentence would take time to accumulate. Single words substitute for phrases and impregnate the reader: "silence," "riddles," and "arcane messages" pierce the curtain a reader may have dropped. Commenting on the frenzy of Sofia Tolstoy, who copied *War and Peace* seven times, and her exclusion from the dying Tolstoy at the provincial train station of Astapovo, Hardwick writes that "with her mangled intelligence, her operatic, intolerable frenzies of distress, she comes forth still with an almost menacing aliveness, saying it all like a bell always on the alert" (Hardw. 275–6). Here, the build-up of clauses in apposition, each a new thought and expression, leads to a climax both unexpected and effective. The importance of the shortened American Sentence, reflecting speeded up experiences, may be what the artist David Salle conveyed to Janet Malcolm. Of his art he insisted that one must go against literalism and *"live the life of the imagination* …. I want to have and to give *access to feeling.* That is the riskiest and only important way to connect art to the world—to make it alive."[55]

Lydia Davis, Annie Dillard, Laurie Moore, Cormac McCarthy, or Anne Carson, through their elliptical styles, constantly seek to give "access to feeling." For Lydia Davis, this occurs through the truncated style of her stories, some no more than one or two sentences (see "Bloomington" or "Judgment" from *Can't and Won't,* 2014). One well-known example is "A DOUBLE NEGATIVE" from *Samuel Johnson Is Indignant* (2001):

> At a certain point in her life, she realizes it is not so much that she wants to have a child as that she does not want not have a child, or not to have had a child.[56]

The one sentence story is itself an example of a double negative. It is the thing it describes.

A number of her stories are about the making of stories. In "Can't and Won't," the narrator explains that she was denied a writing prize because she used too many contractions. She would not "write out in full the words cannot and will not, but instead contracted them to *can't* and *won't*."[57] "Local Obits" consists of one sentence obituaries, concisely summarizing lives. In "Writing," the narrator decides to stop writing and "pay more attention to life" (Can't 252).

Earlier, in "We Miss You," Davis actually discusses the nature of sentences and their form. The story consists of get-well letters from a class of fourth graders. The short story, "Suddenly Afraid," in its entirety reads

> Suddenly Afraid
> Because she couldn't write the name of what she was: a wa wam owm owamn womn[58]

The aesthetic is precise and economical, a charged encounter with narrators reaching for conclusions that yet avoid them. Words and sentences become their own subject as in "THEY TAKE TURNS USING/ A WORD THEY LIKE":

> "It's *extraordinary*," says one woman.
> "It *is* extraordinary," says the other.[59]

Ironically, it was translating Proust that prompted Davis to create the one-sentence story. Working with *Swann's Way*, she reacted to Proust's lengthy sentences. The length of a thought in his sentences made her "want to see how short a piece of fiction could be that would still have a point" (Davis in Faulkner, Brevity 128). In short, her tactic is, as she states in the title of her 1986 volume, *Break It Down*. And in all of her works, Davis seems to be aware of Picasso's definition of style: "Style is the difference between a circle and the way you draw it," the focus on method and compression."[60]

Annie Dillard similarly writes boldly with short sentences and sharp images. The critic Sam Anderson neatly states Dillard's mission: "to crowbar surprise, sentence by sentence, into all the tiny gaps of our ordinary experience." In her work, the unusual becomes the familiar, calling for "fireworks, with only a ballpoint pen" ("Recalling Niels Borhr!"). Compression brings power to her surprises.

Dillard's advice on writing is equally unorthodox:

> Write as if you were dying. At the same time, assume you write for an audience consisting solely of terminal patients. That is, after all, the case. What would you begin writing if you knew you would die soon? What could you say to a dying person that would not enrage by its triviality?[61]

The sentences are brief and short but the ideas are big, filled with meaning. There is no meandering or digression. Repetition reinforces the impact of the statements, while contradictions are part of the meaning: "Write about winter in the summer. Describe Norway as Ibsen did, from a desk in Italy; describe Dublin as James Joyce did, from a desk in Paris" (Abundance 106).

The writer, she goes on to say, "plays the edges. That's where the exhilaration is: He hits up the line. He pushes the edges" (Abundance 107). And her sentences embody the form even if the reader recoils: "Reason balks, poetry snaps, some madness enters, or strain" (Abundance 107). Noun verb, noun verb, adjective, noun, verb verb. Simple but impactful.

Susan Howe is parallel. The New England poet known for her layered and allusive work expressed in original texts that remake the page through typography and explore the visuality of language, also draws on the brief, precise, and pointed. She often prints lines upside down or with cross outs. Words often overlap each other on the page obscuring a text; reading becomes an act of deciphering. To emphasize brevity, there are large gaps between words, white spaces contributing to the reading by stressing the words individually. The isolation deconstructs the words into morphemes, phonemes, and graphemes. A line of prose or poetry is not only a line of representation but a verbal space whose separateness defines its meaning. We don't read the words as much as see and parse them.

The variety of her work, marked by the range of titles (*Chanting at the Crystal Sea*, *My Emily Dickinson*, or *A Bibliography of the King's Book*), draws on history and the past. Prose is often her source and in "Articulation of Sound Forms in Time" she employs the diaries of a New

England minister lost in the wilderness, a theme continued in a collection of her essays, *The Birth-Mark: Unsettling the Wilderness in American Literary History* (1993). *Pierce-Arrow* focuses on the American logician/philosopher Charles Sanders Peirce and involves three long sequences. The intriguing *Spontaneous Particulars: The Telepathy of Archives* (2014) addresses records of the past and her belief that one can apprehend the past through slighted voices and anonymous histories, what she calls "factual telepathy" creating what she labels "Frame Structures," and the title of an essay from *The Quarry* and title of a collection from 1995. Her poem, "SECRET HISTORY OF THE DIVIDING LINE," begins with the title printed left to right and then upside down and reversed reading from right to left with a dividing line in the middle.[62]

Illustrating the brevity of her writing, using the brief sentence as a form of primacy in her search for causes, is this excerpt from *My Emily Dickinson* expressed in prose:

> When I love a thing I want it and I try to get it. Abstraction of the particular from the universal is the entrance into evil. Love, a binding force, is both envy and emulation. HE (the Puritan God) is a realm of mystery and will always remain unknowable, authoritarian, unpredictable. Between revealed will and secret will Love has been torn in two.

And a few lines later:

> What *is* the communal vision of poetry if you are curved, odd, indefinite, irregular, feminine. I go in disguise. Soul under stress, thread of connection broken, fusion of love and knowledge broken, visionary energy lost, Dickinson means this to be an ugly verse. First I find myself a Slave, next I understand my slavery, finally I re-discover myself at liberty inside the confines of known necessity. Gun goes on thinking of the violence done to meaning. Gun watches herself watching.[63]

Gun is the name of the female poet created by Dickinson and a play on her poem, "My life had stood—a Loaded Gun/In Corners—till a day/The Owner passed—identified—/ And carried Me away/And now We roam in Sovereign Woods" (My 34). Howe even includes a dictionary definition of a gun from Webster's, intensifying the presence of her prose (My 118). But Dillard, always clear, declared: "[I]t is no less difficult to write sentences in a recipe than sentences in *Moby-Dick*. So you might as well write *Moby-Dick*."[64] She also declared: "Push it. Examine all things intensely and relentlessly. Probe and search each object in a piece of art .... follow it down until you see it in the mystery of its own specific and strength" (Wr. Life 114). Writing for Howe is physical and is always an analytical act: "Real events that are Facts, are interconnected by ties and links to a deep inner theme of composition as *conflict.*"[65] She extends this in "The Disappearance Approach" from *Quarry* again using fragments to build short sections into architectural referencing and structures.

The elliptical style of Anne Carson extends the work of Annie Dillard and Susan Howe but without the typographical experimentation. It is, nonetheless, intriguing, its fragmented forms absorbing and challenging. *Decreation* (2005) is a key example with her prose poem "Seated Figure with Red Angle (1988) by Betty Goodwin" composed of seventy truncated conditionals—not sentences—a model. The unfinished nature of the work is the point:

> If red is the color of italics.
> If italics are a lure of thought.
> If Freud says the relation between a gaze and what one wishes to see involves allure.
> If you cannot remember what word you wrote.[66]

The reader literally fills in the blanks. Or as Carson writes in "The Anthropology of Water," "I watch the sentence come clawing into me like a lost tribe" (Plainwater 120).

Preceding this method was her 1992 volume *Short Talks*, a series of prose statements on a multitude of topics:

> Short Talk on Gertrude Stein/ About 9.30
> How curious. I had no idea! Today
> Has ended.
>
> Short talk on Disappointments / In Music
> Prokofiev was ill and could not attend

The performance of his first Piano
Sonata played by somebody else. He
Listened to it on the telephone.[67]

In this volume, she surprises as in one of two poems about Kafka "Short Talk on Rectification" which lists some of Kafka's habits, including setting his watch an hour-and-half fast. His hesitant relationship with Felice—it lasted five years—and ended with him in a sanatorium where "he left glass sentences all over the floor" (ST 32). The image is telling, the sentences of glass fragile, reflective, and transparent. And clarifying: "It is as if we have all been lowered into an atmosphere of glass," she writes in her poem, "The Glass Essay" developing ideas of transparency.[68] Fragments are Carson's favorite poetic form from which she creates and occasionally imitates.

In Carson there is a constant play of words as in the title of her most recent book, *Wrong Norma* (2024). Norma is not the name of a woman, but, in Latin, it is a set square establishing the correct right-angled relation between vertical and horizontal axes. It's an ordering device to counter the sharpness of Carson's prose, each sentence an arrow aimed at a target. Decreation may be apt—she decreates to make the form and meaning new, revising or fragmenting sentences to their essence which may be syntactically challenging. But what does it mean to move to the fragment? Deracination? Recreation? Her pull is to the economy of words, to intensify the language, echoing Susan Sontag who declared, "Words mean. Words point. They are arrows. Arrows stuck in the rough hide of reality." Collette also understood: "You become a great writer as much through what you refuse your pen as through what you grant it."[69] All of these writers display calculated restraint soon to be challenged by a new writing medium, the screen.

HARD-BOILED   A SAMPLER: OPENERS:

"I growled: 'Hey, what the hell—!' And raised my bedroom window, peered out into the foggy midnight. Whereupon a tall and much too handsome bozo on the fire escape fetched me a vicious clout over the thatch with a set of brass knuckles." Robert Leslie Bellem, *Hollywood Detective Magazine, c*. 1940s.

> "This is how it is when you wake up in the morning of the morning you have waited a life time for; there is no waking state. You are all at once wide awake …." Horace McCoy, *Kiss Tomorrow Goodbye,* 1948.

> "The morning sun struggled through the cobweb-covered window. The sickly yellow oblong that fell upon the bare floor was a jaundiced imitation of sunlight." Earl Stanley Gardner, "Hell's Kettle," *Black Mask*, 1930.

> "When Ethel's Mama blew up, she shook the earth in more ways than one." Lester Dent, *The Deadly Dwarf* (orig. title *Repel*), 1937.

> "They were going to kill Dopey Dilldocks at midnight the day after tomorrow." Mickey Spillane and Max Allan Collins, "The Big Switch," *The Strand*, 2008.

> "The first time I laid eyes on Terry Lennox he was drunk in a Rolls-Royce Silver Wraith outside the terrace of The Dancers …. There was a girl beside him." Raymond Chandler, *The Long Goodbye, 1953.*

Brrrrrrriiiiiiiiiiiiiiiiiiiiiiiinng!

An alarm clock clanged in the dark and silent room. A bed spring creaked. A woman's voice sang out impatiently:

> "Bigger, shut that thing off!"

Richard Wright, Native Son, 1940

"No one wanted to say it to me, that the girls were dead. But I knew." Rod Reynolds, *Cold Desert Sky*, 2018

MIDDLES:

> Twenty-four hours a day somebody is running, somebody else is trying to catch him. Raymond Chandler, *The Long Goodbye,* 1953 (232–3?).

> See why I don't like Freud? Get him into a case and right away you've got a headache. Everything a guy does gets explained ….
>
> William P. McGivern, But Death Runs Faster, 1948.

> I said: "Baby, this is going to hurt a little!" Then I pasted her across the face with the flat of my hand. Robert Leslie Bellem, *Hollywood Detective Magazine.*

I stepped quickly over to the girl and reached into my pocket and took out the small fancy .25 automatic and laid it down on her knee.

"Ever see this before?" Raymond Chandler "Trouble is my Business," 1939

CLOSERS (final sentences):

"What do you know, that punk that did the phone work on you tried to take me for a fifty cut on that C-note you tucked in my vest. I had to twist the sucker plenty."

Raymond Chandler, "Pearls are a Nuisance"

"I was glad when she left—even though she didn't bother to tell me good-bye."

Raymond Chandler, "Trouble is My Business"

I locked an arm around his neck and dragged him halfway across the counter. I slugged him so hard it made my wrist ache.

I let go of him. He slid down behind the counter, and I ran.

Jim Thompson, *After Dark, My Sweet*

Lee Server: How are you doing?

Abe Polonsky: This is too early for me. I've been lying in bed and wondering whether it's worth it to take another breath.

Abe Polonsky, screenwriter *Force of Evil*

Notes

1. See Kenneth Cmiel, *Democratic Eloquence, The Fight over Popular Speech in Nineteenth-century America* (New York: William Morrow and Co., 1990) 61. Hereafter Cmiel.
2. In Jan Mieszkowski, *Crises of the Sentence* (Chicago: University of Chicago Press, 2019) 16.
3. Millie, "Black Mask Magazine," Dark and Stormy Night Mysteries, May 14, 2014. https://darkandstormynightmysteries.com/wordpress/?p=838. Also helpful is the Pulp Magazines Project at the Univ. of Pittsburgh. https://www.pulpmags.org/magazines.html.

4   Daniel A. Cohen, *Pillars of Salt, Monuments of Grace, New England Crime Literature and the Origins of American Popular Culture, 1674–1860* (New York: Oxford University Press, 1993) ix. Cohen points out that booksellers, ministers, printers, criminals, lawyers, and journalists all "influenced the tone and content of New England's crime publications" (ix). That later changed as newspapers gained great independence from such "forces."

5   Walt Whitman, "Preface" 1855 Edition, *Leaves of Grass* (Brooklyn, New York, 1855) iv. Whitman Archive, ed. Ed Folsom and Kenneth M. Price: iv. http://whitmanarchive.org/published/LG/1855/whole.html. The ellipses in the text are in the original.

6   Chris Francescani, "Killer Librarian retiring after 34 Years," *Suffolk Times*, August 8, 2024: 1.

7   Shelley Fisher Fishkin, *From Fact to Fiction, Journalism & Imaginative Writing in America* (Baltimore: Johns Hopkins University Press, 1985) 4.

8   Emily Dickinson, "Tell all the truth," Poetry Foundation. https://www.poetryfoundation.org/poems/56824/tell-all-the-truth-but-tell-it-slant-1263.

9   Thomas Walsh, "Double Check," *Pulp Fiction, The Crimefighters*, ed. Otto Penzler. Intro. Harlan Coben (London: Quercus 2006) 151. Walsh published the successful *Nightmare in Manhattan* in 1950.

10 Mara Bovsun, "NYC photographer fatally shoots wife," *New York Daily News* July 28, 2024.

11 Raymond Chandler, "Red Wind," *Pulp Fiction, The Crimefighters*, ed. Otto Penzler, Intr. Harlan Coben (London: Quercus 2006) 217. Hereafter Wind.

12 Raymond Chandler, *Selected Letters of Raymond Chandler*, ed. Frank MacShane (New York: Columbia University Press, 1981) 159–60.

13 Chandler extends his critique with a sharp criticism of Hemingway: "Ninety percent of [his writing] is the goddamndest self-imitation. He never really wrote but one story. All the rest is the same thing in different pants—or without different pants" (Lett 72). In a later letter, he justifies his rugged diction and vernacular: "When I split an infinitive, God damn it, I split it so it will stay split …" (Lett 86).

14 Dashiell Hammett, *The Glass Key* (London: Orion Books, 2002) 175. Hereafter Key.

15 Mickey Spillane, "One Lonely Night," *The Hammer Strikes Again*, ed. Mickey Spillane (New York: Avenel Books, 1989) 154.

16 Colson Whitehead, *Harlem Shuffle* (New York: Bond Street Books, 2021) 107. Hereafter Shuffle.

17 Virginia Tufte, *Artful Sentences, Syntax as Style* (Cheshire, CT: Graphics Press, 2006) 6. This is a fundamental text on the construction of sentences and how their form shapes meaning. Examples are varied and numerous. Sections include "short sentences," "free modifiers,"

"parallelism," and "Syntactic symbolism," the last section focusing on cadence. Helpful in grasping Tufte's approach is Peter Wayne Moe, "Virginia Tufte's Sentences," *Style* Vol.52 No.4 (2018): 385–403. The form of a sentence can be aggressive or not.

Among websites devoted to sentences is Ben Dolnick's "One Sentence," which explains and identifies "great sentences from books." Examples include nonfiction as well as fiction. https://bendolnick.substack.com/?sort=community. Also useful is "Brevity," an online journal of "Concise Literary Nonfiction" at https://brevitymag.com/. Lee Martin's "Talk Big" from issue 41(January 2013) is one concise example.

18 James Agee, *A Death in the Family* (New York: Avon, 1966) 150. Useful is this comment by Mary Ellen Chase from *The Bible and the Common Reader*: "In Hebrew poetry the number of syllables is nothing; the accented words are everything. They alone supply the rhythm, and they alone give the effect" (London: Palgrave Macmillan, 1948) 79.

19 John Updike, "Hub Fans Bid Kid Adieu," *New Yorker* October 22, 1960. Equally powerful is the sentence "Gods do not answer letters" to describe Williams's refusal to step out of the dug out to acknowledge the screaming crowd. https://www.newyorker.com/magazine/1960/10/22/hub-fans-bid-kid-adieu.

For a parallel moment, see the end of Philip Roth's *Nemesis* describing Bucky Cantor tossing a javelin before a group of astonished high school students: "Running with the javelin aloft," his throwing arm stretched behind him, he releases "the javelin high over his shoulder—and releasing it then like an explosion—he seemed to us invincible" (Roth, *Nemesis* [Boston: Houghton Mifflin, 2010]) 280.

20 "Hold Divorcee as Slayer of Auto Salesman," *Chicago Tribune* June 6, 1924. https://chicagology.com/notorious-chicago/beaulahandbelva/.

21 Maurine Watkins, "Demand Noose for 'Prettiest' Woman Slayer," *Chicago Tribune* April 4, 1924. https://chicagology.com/notorious-chicago/beaulahandbelva/. In court, when the murder scene was described, "she cupped her chin in a slim white hand, with its orange blossom ring, and didn't blanch as the state read her answer to the question," why didn't he (her drunken lover) get the gun, lying on the bed, first? "Darned good reason: I shot him" she casually replied. Ibid.

22 https://chicagology.com/notorious-chicago/beaulahandbelva/.

23 For a new account of tabloid journalism in the UK, see Terry Kirby, *The Newsmongers, a History of Tabloid Journalism* (London: Reaktion, 2024). He notes, among numerous texts, Ben Jonson's *The Staple of News*, a satire from 1625. He also notes that starting in the nineteenth century, the struggle for mass circulation meant a new concentration on crime, society scandals, and political campaigns.

24 Ben Hecht, "Man Hunt," *A Thousand and One Afternoons in Chicago* (Chicago: Covici Friede, 1927) 35.

25 Henry Justin Smith, "Preface," *A Thousand and One Afternoons in Chicago* (Chicago: Covici Friede, 1927) 3,5.

26 Robert Phelps, *Belles Saisons, A Colette Scrapbook* (New York: Farrar Straus and Giroux, 1978) 147.

27 Ben Hecht, Charles McArthur, *The Front Page* (Chicago: Covici Friede, 1928) 1. Hereafter Front.

28 Hecht in Adina Hoffman, *Ben Hecht, Fighting Words, Moving Pictures* (New Haven, CT: Yale University Press, 2019) 184. For the provisional title of the Cohen work, see Julian Gorbach, *Notorious Ben Hecht* (West Lafayette, IN: Purdue University Press, 2019) 254. Hereafter Notor.

29 Notor 37. On the overall world of pulp magazines, see the Pulp Magazine Project at the University of Pittsburgh, a colorful website with pulp covers, essays, excerpts, and bibliography. Https://www.pulpmags.lorg/index.htm.

30 Nebel in Erin A. Smith, *Hard Boiled, Working Class Readers and Pulp Magazines* (Philadelphia: Temple University Press, 2000) 92.

31 "Review, Paul Cain, *Fast One*," *The New York Times* (October 19, 1933).

32 Paul Cain, *Fast One* (London: No Exit Press, 1989) 67. Hereafter FO.

33 Norman Mailer, "On Lies, Power, and Obscenity," *Mind of an Outlaw, Selected Essays*, ed. Phillip Sipiora. Intr. Jonathan Lethem (New York: Random House, 2013) 28.

34 Dashiell Hammett, *Red Harvest* (New York: Vintage Books, 1972) 182.

35 Frederick C. Davis, Robert Sidney Bowen, "Memoirs," *Cheap Thrills, An Informal History of the Pulp Magazines*, ed. Ron Goulart (New Rochelle, NY: Arlington House, 1972) 190. Hereafter Cheap.

36 Other writers also worked quickly: Steinbeck wrote *The Grapes of Wrath* in five and half months; Melville took only six months to write *Moby-Dick*. Noël Coward took six days to write *Blithe Spirit*. Robert Louie Stevenson supposedly wrote *Dr Jekyll and Mr Hyde* in three days. Speed was everywhere. Raymond Chandler reported that Earl Stanley Gardner could easily write an entire book in a week or ten days (Lett. 162).

37 Hammett in Anne Diebel, "Dashiell Hammett's Strange Career," *Paris Review* September 14, 2018. https://www.theparisreview.org/blog/2018/09/14/dashiell-hammetts-strange-career/.

38 Kathleen Welch, *Electric Rhetoric, Classical Rhetoric, Oralism, and a New Literacy* (Cambridge, MA: MIT Press, 1999). Equally emphasizing speed and crime is *Snap* by Belinda Bauer, longlisted for the Booker Prize in 2018.

39 Raymond Chandler, "The Simple Art of Murder," *Later Novels and Other Writings* (New York: Library of America, 1995) 989.

40 The phrase "writing degree zero" is, of course, Barthes and suggests "a colourless writing, freed from all bondage to a pre-ordained state of language." Barthes, "Writing Degree Zero," *Writing Degree Zero and Elements of Semiology*, Preface by Susan Sontag (Boston: Beacon Press, 1970) 76. Barthes credits Camus with initiating this "transparent form of speech" (Barthes 77). Raymond Queneau also gets credit.

41 Hammett, *The Maltese Falcon* (New York: Vintage Books, 1992) 46.

42 Interestingly, Chandler claimed that the American style lacked cadence but without it there could be no harmonics: "It is like a flute playing solo, an incomplete thing." Chandler, "On English and American Style," *Later Novels and Other Writings* 1014.

43 *New York Herald Tribune Books* August 23, 1942: 17 in a review of Chandler's *The High Window*.

44 Raymond Chandler, *The High Window* (New York: Vintage Books, 1976) 16.

45 Ross Macdonald, *Self-Portrait* (Santa Barbara: Capra Press, 1981) 27–8.

46 Richard Price, *Lush Life* (New York: Farrar, Straus and Giroux, 2008) 3–4. Hereafter Lush.

47 Sam Anderson in *New York Magazine* claimed that Price "may be the best writer of dialogue since Plato." Anderson, "Stalking the Gramno," *New York Magazine*, February 27, 2008. https://nymag.com/arts/books/reviews/44616/.

48 James Wood, "Say What?" *New Yorker* March 31, 2008. https://www.newyorker.com/magazine/2008/04/07/say-what. Wood also refers to Henry Green's novel *Loving* as "perhaps the greatest English novel of Dialogue" told almost entirely in the speech of Cockney Servants.

49 Max Brand as Frederick Faust, *The Notebooks and Poems of Max Brand*, ed. John Schoolcraft (New York: Dodd, Mead, 1957) 39.

50 Melville, "Moby Dick," *Redburn, White-Jacket, Moby Dick*, ed. G. Thomas Tanselle (New York: Library of America, 1983) 949.

51 The writer Samuel Graham-Felsen, historian of the Philip Roth Personal Library and who first showed me Roth's scansion marks, is the source of the phrase "sentence-maker."

52 Robert Alter, *Pen of Iron, American Prose and the King James Bible* (Princeton: Princeton University Press, 2010) 48. Alter is also clear on the shifts in the Melvillian sentence between the paratactic and parallel (48–50). Hereafter, Alter.

53 Alter 74; reference to Bonnie Garmus's novel, *Lessons in Chemistry* (New York: Doubleday, 2022) is intentional.

54 Elizabeth Hardwick, "Wives and Mistresses," *Collected Essays of Elizabeth Hardwick*, Sel. Darryl Pinckney (New York: New York Review of Books, 2017) 74. Hereafter Hardw.
55 David Salle in Janet Malcolm, "Forty-One False Starts," *Forty-One False Starts, Essays on Artists and Writers* (New York: Farrar, Straus and Giroux, 2013) 37.
56 Lydia Davis, "A DOUBLE NEGATIVE," *Samuel Johnson is Indignant* (Brooklyn: McSweeney's Books, 2001) 66.
57 Lydia Davis, *Can't and Won't* (New York: Farrar, Straus and Giroux, 2014) 46. In some ways, Davis is heir to Felix Fenelon and his *Novels in Three Lines*, tr. Luc Sante (New York: New York Review Books, 2007). These short items appeared in 1906 in *Le Matin*. Two examples: "Fencing master Pictori was wounded, perhaps fatally, by the thrust of an amateur, M. Breugnot"; "Mignon, of Bagnolet, reprimanded by the inflexible Barot, his concierge, quieted him with two blows of his knife" (22, 112).
58 Lydia Davis "Suddenly Afraid," *Varieties of Disturbance* (New York: Farrar Straus Giroux, 2007) 189.
59 Lydia Davis, *Samuel Johnson Is Indignant*, Stories (Brooklyn: McSweeney's Books, 2001) 98.
60 Picasso in Grant Faulkner, *The Art of Brevity* (Albuquerque, NM: University of New Mexico Press, 2023) 170.
61 Annie Dillard, *The Abundance, Narrative Essays Old and New*, Forward Geoff Dyer (New York: Ecco/Harper Collins, 2016) 106.
62 Howe, "Secret History of the Dividing Line," *Frame Structures, Early Poems 1974–1979* (New York: New Directions, 1996) 94.
63 Susan Howe, *My Emily Dickinson* (Berkeley, CA: North Atlantic Books, 1985) 117–18. Hereafter My.
64 Annie Dillard, "The Writing Life" in *The Abundance* 110. Hereafter WrL.
65 Susan Howe, "Where Should the Commander Be?," *Writing* 19 (Vancouver) (November 1987: 3–20). Rpt. *The Quarry: Essays* (New York: New Directions, 2015).
66 Anne Carson, "Seated Figure with Red Angle (1988) by Betty Goodwin," *Decreation, Poetry Essays, Opera* (New York: Knopf, 2005) 100.
67 Anne Carson, *Short Talks* (Kingston, ON: Brick Books, 1992) 17, 20. Hereafter ST.
68 Carson, "The Glass Essay," The Poetry Foundation. https://www.poetryfoundation.org/poems/48636/the-glass-essay.

69 Susan Sontag, "The Conscience of Words," *At the Same Time, Essays and Speeches,* ed. Paolo Dilonardo and Anne Jump, Foreword by David Rieff (New York: Farrar Straus Giroux, 2007) 145.

In the words of a recent translator, Rachel Careau, Collette had a "seemingly effortless economy: it contains no excess, no ornament … . Her sentences can feel skeletal, the flesh carved away to convey their meaning with the fewest possible words. A master of concision, subtraction, condensation, renunciation, she is always trying to do more with less. 'You become a great writer', she states, 'as much through what you refuse your pen as through what you grant it'." This can apply to Carson. Collette was also fond of ellipses and selected words carefully. See Careau in Joseph Schreiber, "You who have loved me: *Chéeri* and *The End of Chéri*," *Rough Ghosts*, June 9, 2022. https://roughghosts.com/2022/06/09/you-who-have-loved-me-cheri-and-the-end-of-cheri-by-colette-a-new-translation-by-rachel-careau/.

Chapter 4
American Pieces: The Screen

"A sentence thinks loudly."

                    GERTRUDE STEIN, "MORE GRAMMAR FOR A SENTENCE" (1930)

The American Sentence has come full circle: from dots and dashes with the Morse code to bits and bytes with computer code. Enabling the change was the screen, moving from the movie screen to the computer screen to the smartphone. Words became numbers translated into pixels, essentially to abstractions. Print was unable to contain the forms and content of the remade sentence.

The screen sharpened the shape and delivery of the sentence initiated by the visualized dialog of the movies. Verbalizing words into images provided the sentence with a new elasticity pitched to the eye and ear. Overshadowing the words of a sentence were action and delivery. A sentence lost its authority in print, while its miniaturization or the computer screen or smartphone allowed changes and manipulation. Where did this lead? In many ways, to the posthuman where the technological substitutes for the human in making decisions and judgments. "The electrification of existence," a short-handed definition of the posthuman condition, has taken over. The individual has been removed from any "privileged position in relation to matters of meaning, information, and cognition."[1] The forces of technology, whether AI or future computing possibilities, have altered the significance of words by decentering the individual. Words have become numbers, the original intent of Samuel Morse when fashioning the Morse code. The conditions of representation have altered, with the value of humans measured largely by their function, their role in a system. One consequence is the redefined nature of the sentence.

The shift from print to the screen is not a new story but its impact on style is. The tension began in the medieval period as the conflict between a text and its illustration emerged. Illustrated manuscripts were important for the many who could not read Latin or, later, English. Alberto Manguel's *History of Reading* (1996) ties together many of the elements, from the development of silent reading, possibly initiated by St. Ambrose in Milan, departing from the normal practice of reading aloud, to the writing of forbidden books.[2] If the populace was unable to read, it should at least be able to hear, not just see, the text. Public readings were common; the development of punctuation helped, conveying signs of where to breathe and pause (Manguel 47–8). But by the ninth century, scribes in scriptoria had to be quiet while copying; until then, they worked by dictation or by reading to themselves out loud. But some disliked silent reading believing it led to daydreaming and the sin of idleness. It also escaped public censure; dangerously, the reader could silently make up his own mind or even story (Manguel 50).

Books soon took on another role: as aids to memory and learning. Conversation was the previous knowledge system with oral masters but books gradually supplanted them. The open codex was the key to information, history, ideas, with memorization acting as an intermediate process. Not everyone had constant access to a book. Aquinas, in fact, elaborated a set of memory rules for readers, leading to Renaissance scholars employing architectural models to place what they wanted to remember. Frances A. Yates's *The Art of Memory* (1966) is the classic study of the technique. Soon, printed conversations took place in the text, allowing questions and answers, likely drawn from classical drama and identified as dialog which gave sentences a natural form. The imaginary exchange between Petrarch and Augustine, the *Secretum meum* (fourteenth century) is an early example (Manguel 55; 62–4).

Following the model of Latin schools of the fifteenth century, education in reading became widespread, partly the result of Charlemagne's ninth-century order that all cathedrals and churches provide schools for the training of clerics in the arts of reading, writing, chanting, and calculus (Manguel 75). This quickly became an emphasis on the *trivium*: grammar, rhetoric, and dialectics. To follow were endless commentaries, highlighted by the Midrash, a collection of scholarly investigations into the meanings, or possible meanings, of sacred texts, notably the Torah, itself a mix of written text and oral commentary. The creation of a double text—the written work and a reader's gloss printed on the same page—revised the act of reading into a contested site of textual interpretation and dialog (Manguel 89; 62–3).[3]

From this brief account of reading, it is a short step to the illustrated book, originating in paintings on church walls to pictorial windows and carved columns all of biblical iconography. The images moved from plaster to stained glass, wood, stone, and eventually the page—but often in tension with the word (Manguel 101–2). Illustrated Bibles of the fourteenth century were on display in churches for the illiterate to admire. The iconography of the text was immediate and visually understood. But reading aloud continued with the idea of the *lector* established in Cuba in the 1860s to distract cigar workers from boredom while they worked. But the practice had been initiated thirteen centuries earlier by St. Benedict when he read a spiritual exercise out loud for the benefit of others (Manguel 114–15). As early as the sixth century AD, he set out rules for reading aloud in cloisters. In the Roman period, being read to at dinner was a new pleasure; by the eleventh century, *joglars* appeared in Europe, performers who would recite verses and occasionally texts with the emphasis on performance (Manguel 116–17). By the fourteenth and fifteenth centuries, informal readings at the homes of the educated became common; by the nineteenth century, it was almost an everyday event as Jane Austen and many others confirmed (Manguel 121). Betty Higden in Dickens's *Our Mutual Friend* (1865) remarks on Sloppy's ability to "do the Police in different voices" when reading the London crime reports out loud from the newspaper.[4]

But if the practice of reading (oral and silent) had been established and the shape of conventional sentences more or less determined, how did the screen transform the sentence? Speed is, again, the answer. The emergence of film, following the telegraph, demanded rapid composition, quick delivery, and even quicker expression. The movies contributed by their visual and oral treatment of a written script followed by television. In both, the immediacy of exchange between characters emphasized literal movement. It took little time for the sentence as a text to transfer to the computer and smart phone screen. But the screen has its own syntax with alters the form of the sentence. It also forms its own language.[5] Alarmed by the sudden transference from the page to the pixel, critics saw danger summarized by Jason Merkoski's *Burning the Page, the eBook Revolution and the Future of Reading* (2013). And yet, studies repeatedly show that learning from a printed text outshines learning from an eBook.[6]

The screenwriter became a transformative figure in the remodeling of the sentence initially with silent films where action needed terse statements in-between scenes and then with the introduction of "talkies." But after the introduction of sound in 1929, the screenwriter quickly realized that characters had little time to talk and often spoke over one another. Dialog had to be snappy, curt, and yet convincing to keep the viewer involved. Dialog competed with plot; it could not be slow or meandering, whether in comedy, drama or crime stories. Early screenwriting was, in fact, merely adaptations of existing plays. With sound, however, the need for detailed scripts with exact lines of speech became essential. Herman J. Mankiewicz and Ben Hecht were two early and successful figures producing quick-fire dialog to offset the reasonably slow and limited camerawork. The new concern was continuity, verisimilitude, narrative clarity, and then spectacle. In the early days, camerawork relied on wide shots: close ups were not yet technically manageable.

Scripts had to accommodate technical limitations, early cameras unable to run more than fifty feet of film at one time meaning a film of approximately one minute. By 1910, screenwriting formally began with scenarios that included shot numbers, cast, character locations, and a synopsis.[7] It gave directors a proper structure and they could now shoot scenes out of order. Rearranging the filmed sequences in post-production established continuity with a solid narrative structure arranged by the editor aligning the shooting script with the narrative. But increasingly, outside writers were needed to link the shooting script with the narrative movement. These outsiders, however, did not know the format or technical nature of filming. The studio had to often take over the detailed scenarios, reshaping them into proper screenplays. From outline to scenario to a continuity script infused with dialog was a common practice.[8]

The theater was the initial source of screenwriters, their skill at dialog, timing, rhythm, pace, and delivery essential for film. Among them were Ben Hecht, Preston Sturges, George S. Kaufman, Noël Coward, and such contemporaries as Arthur Miller, Harold Pinter, Tom Stoppard, and David Mamet. They may not have understood what was a fade-out or a dissolve, but they quickly grasped master scene, cut to or close shot. But in the 1930s and 1940s, the cadre of writers was large. The screenwriter Julius Epstein reported that each studio had 75 to 100 writers working on 50 to 60 pictures a year. But collectively, the credits had the same names of about 150 to 200 writers. You were given assignments and the ratio was 3 to 1, three written scripts for every one that was made. And generally, the studios treated writers poorly, although at 20th Century Fox "the script was king" because they had no stars.[9] Nevertheless, writers had little control over their scripts and faced daily rewrites. Or as Norman Krasna reported, "You can live a whole life as a writer in Hollywood without ever having *written* a movie, and you can still be considered one of the great ones" (McGilligan). Craftsmen not artists found success.

One example of the craft at work and where the sentence triumphed was *The Philadelphia Story* (1940) directed by George Cukor with Cary Grant, Katherine Hepburn, and James Stewart. Repartee reigned, short bursts that mixed rhythm, pace, and exact words. Divorcee Hepburn and ex-husband Grant constantly jab each other until their coexistence means remarrying despite interference from Jimmy Stewart. Written by Donald Ogden Stewart and an uncredited Waldo Salt, the film appeared when the Production Code prevented the depiction of extramarital affairs but divorced couples reconnecting was "Ok." The work was originally a play starring Hepburn who acquired the film rights with the assistance of Howard Hughes but she soon sold them to Louis B Mayer at MGM. Nominated for six Academy Awards, the film won two: Jimmy Stewart for Best Actor and Donald Ogden Stewart for Best Adapted Screenplay. To sustain the pace, Stewart (writer) wrote the filmscript while listening to a taping of a live performance of the play.

The comedy opens with comic plays on language and carries on throughout the film. The opening:

Tracy!

Tracy!

Tracy!

-How do you spell "omelet"?
-Oh, you.

Ninety-four for the ceremony
and ? for the reception.

I don't know where we'll put them if it rains.

It won't rain.
Tracy won't stand for it.

-Mother, how do you spell "omelet"?
-O-M-M-E-L-E-T.

-I thought there was another "L."
-An omelet's a funny wedding present.

The script relies on misunderstanding and a comic sense of propriety:

This stinks.

Don't say "stinks," darling.

If absolutely necessary, "smells."

These cards have
been changed again.

There must be a ghost in the house,
the ghost of bridegroom number one.

Don't talk about Dexter
as though he were dead.[10]

An important practitioner of contemporary screenplays was Robert Towne (1934–2024). Towne understood the strategy of the abrupt, repetitive sentence style demanded by film throughout his work with *Chinatown* a highlight. At the opening of the film—winner of the 1974 Oscar for Best Screenplay and named # 3 in the Writers' Guild of America's 101 Best Screenplays—this exchange takes place between a distraught client named Curly (Burt Young) and the detective, Jake Gittes (Jack Nicholson). Gittes has just seen photos of Curly's double-dealing wife:

Curly (*drinking, relaxing a little*)
She's just no good.

Gittes What can I tell you, Kid?
You're right. When you're right,
You're right, and you're right.

Curly Ain't worth thinking about.

Gittes *leaves the bottle with* **Curly**.

Gittes You're absolutely right, I wouldn't
give her another thought.

But then, this exchange:

Curly Thanks. You know something, Jake?

Gittes What's that, Curly?

Curly I think I'll kill her.

The statement rattles Gittes and the audience. It's unexpected. The scene then cuts to the exterior office with Duffy and Walsh, two associates of Gittes, questioning a nervous, "well-groomed, dark-haired woman."[11] The scene and dialog are quick, powerful, effective, yet mysterious: who is she? What does she want? It also illustrates how the medium shapes the dialog: there is no time for explanations summarized by the famous final line of the movie. Distraught over the body of Evelyn just shot by the police, Gittes's partner, Walsh, tries to drag Jake away, ironically consoling him with these simple words: "Forget it, Jake. It's Chinatown." Understanding the meaning requires no explanation. The action has offered that. This is the American Sentence at its clearest; no exposition necessary. The entire film has prepared us for the moment. The irony is clear.

Quentin Tarantino's *Pulp Fiction* (1994; with Roger Avery) is similar. It also opens with attention to language: a definition on screen from the *American Heritage Dictionary*: "PULP (pulp) n. 1. A soft, moist, shapeless mass of matter. 2. A magazine or book containing lurid subject matter and being characteristically printed on rough, unfinished paper." Next is a cut to an *in medius res* conversation between two small-time crooks in a coffee shop/restaurant, the language precise but repetitive, and at first confusing for the viewer.[12] Tarantino uses staccato lines to emphasize the beats to gain tension in what he labels the "Prologue," anticipating the forthcoming violence:

> **Young Man** No, forget it, it's too risky. I'm through doin' that shit.
>
> **Young Woman** You always say that, the same thing every time: never again, I'm through, too dangerous.
>
> **Young Man** I know that's what I always say. I'm always right too, but—
>
> **Young Woman** —but you forget about it in a day or two
>
> **Young Man** —yeah, well, the days of me forgittin' are over, and the days of me rememberin' have just begun.
>
> **Young Woman** When you go on like this, you know what you sound like?
>
> **Young Man** I sound like a sensible fucking man, is what I sound like.
>
> **Young Woman** You sound like a duck.
> > (imitates a duck)
> > Quack, quack, quack, quack, quack, quack, Quack … (Pulp 1–2)

Redundancy reinforces the emotional dynamic of the exchange between the two petty criminals harboring big ambitions. A few moments later, the young man reverses himself, hatching a plan to rob the diner/restaurant:

> **Young Man** See, I got the idea last liquor store we stuck up. 'Member all those customers kept comin' in?
>
> **Young Woman** Yeah.
>
> **Young Man** Then you got the idea to take everybody's wallet.
>
> **Young Woman** Uh-huh.
>
> **Young Man** That was a good idea.

Young Woman Thanks.

Young Man We made more from the wallets then we did the register.

Young Woman Yes we did.

Young Man A lot of people go to restaurants.

Young Woman A lot of wallets.

Young Man Pretty smart, huh?

Young Woman Pretty smart.
(into it)
I'm ready, let's go, right here, right now.

And with that, Pumpkin and Honey Bunny (their nicknames) grab their weapons, standup, and rob the restaurant. Pumpkin's robber persona is that of the in-control professional. Honey Bunny's is that of the psychopathic, hair-triggered loose cannon (Pulp 5–6).

Just before this exchange, there is another discussion over words, specifically "garçon," misused by the young man. The waitress, coming over with more coffee, tells him in a snotty manner that "'Garçon' means boy." Throughout the script words are defined, parsed, redefined—the Quarter Pounder with Cheese becomes a "Royale with Cheese" in Paris—the attention to words equal to the attention to violence.

In reversing gender roles, Honey Bunny pursues power and is the threatening one; the Young Man is hesitant and uncertain. From this scene, Tarantino cuts to the title and credit sequence, the movie formally beginning with Vincent (John Travolta) and Jules (Samuel L. Jackson) driving down a deserted LA street in a '74 Chevy Malibu on their way to murder a set of drug-dealing college students who seem to have double-crossed Marsellus Wallace, the drug dealer. The writing is again pointed but also comical:

Vincent In Paris, you can buy beer at MacDonald's. Also, you know what they call a Quarter Pounder with Cheese in Paris?

Jules They don't call it a Quarter Pounder with Cheese?

Vincent No, they got the metric system there, they wouldn't know what the fuck a Quarter Pounder is.

Jules What'd they call it?

Vincent Royale with Cheese.

Jules *(repeating)* Royale with Cheese. What'd they call a Big Mac?

Vincent Big Mac's a Big Mac, but they call it Le Big Mac.

Jules Le Big Mac. What do they call a Whopper?

Vincent I dunno, I didn't go into a Burger King.
But you know what they put on french fries in Holland instead of ketchup?

Jules What?

Vincent Mayonnaise.

Jules Goddamn!

Next is a dialog about what guns they should use to knock off the students. They have .45s but Vincent suggests shotguns would be better. As they approach an apartment house, the dialog gets shorter, as Vincent tells Jules he's about to look after Marsellus's girlfriend for the evening and asks:
How did Marsellus and her meet?

Jules I dunno, however people meet people. She usta be an actress.

Vincent She ever do anything I woulda saw?

Jules I think her biggest deal was she starred in a pilot.

Vincent What's a pilot?

(Pulp 11)

Again, words, often misunderstood, take precedent. When Vincent tells Jules he has to "take care" of Mia while Marsellus is out of town, Jules thinks it's to knock her off. Vincent immediately corrects him. "Not that! Take her out. Show her a good time. Don't let her get lonely" (Pulp

16). Language and the literary are evident throughout the film. During the final scene, a robbery back at the opening restaurant, Vincent is actually in the bathroom reading "MODESTY BLAISE" (Pulp 150). Even at this moment, Jules provides a critique of the Ezekiel passage he repeatedly recites. Literature and criticism end the film, although the final action of the two characters walking out of the coffee shop is done in silence (Pulp 157–8).

Throughout *Pulp Fiction*, the writing is direct and sharp. No digressions as psychology and action play out. The most rhetorical moments are when Jules quotes Ezekiel 25:17 which begins with "The path of the righteous man is beset on all sides by the inequities of the selfish and the tyranny of evil men." Jules first declaims this when shooting the students; the next is at the end of the film when he tries to redeem himself by acting sympathetically toward the two young robbers in the coffee shop and gives them his money before letting them escape. At that moment, Jules and Vincent silently leave the restaurant; the film ends, words incapable of interpreting the action.

All of these adjustments on the screen reshape the sentence, de-emphasizing cohesion and coordination. The pattern and dynamic of the sentence change as intransitive verbs upend the transitive. Sentences now cut, turn, and shift unexpectedly, embodying the nervousness of the film. Instead of linking verbs, there is the dramatic intransitive which always has impact, especially embedded or at the end of a paragraph. Early in his novel *Washington, D.C.*, Gore Vidal has a character stand in the rain who may, or may not, be witnessing or dreaming of two lovers: "But the cold rain was real; and so was the sudden soft moan from the pool house. *He fled.*"[13] The last two words dramatize the moment.

When a text moves from the page to the screen, it becomes unfixed and interactive. Short, concentrated expressions of language are favored, becoming quasi aphoristic, not periodic. A printed book often requires periodic rhetoric, one of subordination and transitions; reading is linear. Electronic writing or writing for the internet does not. A hypertext, with its electronic structure, ignores the rules of print. There is no single reading order; the reader has a choice of paths to follow. The "written space" is redefined. Printed books pretend to be closed and complete. An electronic text is constantly open and linked to other works. It is not, in the strictest sense, original nor composed by a single author.[14] But it is visual as well as impermanent and changeable.

Reducing the distance between the author and the reader occurs by turning the reader into his own author capable of altering, if only by font size and layout, the primary text.

The digital sentence is vertical, the non-digital horizontal. In some ways, it is the icon vs. the alphabet, the vertical linked to orality, the horizontal to the codex, the former connected with the expressive, the latter with the authoritative. Supporting the vertical are hyperlinks, codes, abbreviations, and incompleteness, operating through connections, allusions, and memory. It branches upward and outward; the print form branches horizontally, moving across sequences, phrases, and clauses. Image shapes the first, syntax the second. The column is often the visual shape of the vertical sentence, the paragraph the print. Compare Anne Carson's form for *Red Doc>* (2013) versus Colson Whitehead's in *The Underground Railroad* (2016). The first moves upward and downward (literally), the second spools horizontally across time, the land, and the page.

Carson:
He paddled the
Blues of Knossos during the
soup course then turned
with the haddock to the best
part of ballooning is
watching your own shadow
race over the ground below.

Whitehead:
Mable had packed for the adventure. A machete. Flint and tinder. She stole a cabin mate's shoes, which were in better shape. For weeks, the empty garden testified to her miracle. Before she lit out she dug up every yam from their plot .... the lumps and burrows in the dirt were a reminder to all who walked by. Then one morning they were all smoothed over. Cora got on her knees and planted anew. It was her inheritance.[15]

This is history moving backward and forward on a plane, almost simultaneously.

The visual rhetoric of the electronic text turns a printed text into pixels with different demands and expectations. Remediation summarizes the change, while "convergence," once the buzz word of the era and meaning the elimination of boundaries between new media forms, takes over. Replacing subject/verb/ predicate as the determinants of the sentence are text/ audio/ video or the competing mantra of clarity/ brevity/ sincerity.[16] Today, texts must be aware of their new obligations both in their form of composition and dissemination. Storytelling occurs on multi-platforms and in various shapes. New terms like content management, collaborative writing, and "structured authoring" come forward to influence the shape of the sentence where the reader becomes a controller.[17] Technologizing the text transforms the way readers experience the word (Wr. Inter 181).

"Structured authoring" is the most intriguing. As reading becomes an active exchange with the text, the traditional audience, once respectful of the author, disappears. Authors become their own content creators realizing that the establishment of an interactive text is a collaborative venture and one requiring "structured authorship." But what does it mean? In slightly redundant terms, structured authoring is an approach that "supports effective content management." It involves the development of organized frameworks used to categorize and structure information resources so they can be "used and reused most effectively" (Wr. Inter 115). Another, simplified, if paradoxical, definition reads: structured authoring divorces "the content from the formatting so you can focus on writing."[18]

To do this requires specifications for information models, types, units, metadata, templates, and the separation of presentation from content. Writing, in fact, becomes only a matter of presentation. Guidelines "dictate" the styles, length, order, and display of each content unit (Wr. Inter 115). These quickly become content templates easily transferable to blogs, wikis, chatbots, and additional data-base driven systems as well as mark-up languages.

Structuring content is essential for internet readers: as with print-based readers, when they "learn the structure of content and see patterns in how content is organized and accessed," they become "more proficient" in searching a text or a site (Wr. Inter 115). The process redefines the term "reading" becoming an act of remediation and adaptation with "less structured legacy content" (Wr. Inter 115). Other benefits include hierarchical navigation and site maps, reinforcing the organization of the work and contributing to more efficient absorption. The screen provides new reading systems that mean adjustment and change to one's reading and certainly writing practice. With a hypertext, one might be able to read a line of Milton or Joyce, while also linking to the historical meaning of a term, while seeing a reference image. Such hypertexts create a dynamic work that presents itself with visual and cognitive energy. In a sense, the reading never stops; there are always new links and possibilities.[19]

The computer offers a new writing surface with conventions different from those of the printed page; Bolter suggests that the page, in fact, is no longer a meaningful unit of electronic writing; it cannot contain its content in conventional form (Bolter 3). He also notes how electronic writing is both radical and traditional: "It is mechanical and precise like printing, organic and evolutionary like handwriting" but also "visually eclectic." However, electronic writing is also fluid and dynamic (Bolter 4) satisfying St. Teresa's desire: "I only wish I could write with both hands so as not to forget one thing while I am saying another."[20] The computer makes that possible (Bolter 4, 21).

Bolter also notes that an index shifts a book from a tree with branches to a network, unlike the table of contents which defines a hierarchy with chapters and sections. Indices record associate lines of thought throughout the text (Bolter 22). An index shows the same word or concept throughout the text. Widely separated passages come together. And an index shows another book that might be constructed from the material at hand.[21] Of course, all these elements affect the nature of writing and specifically the sentence which must, because of the medium, take on other properties.

Because the author of a work is no longer in control, the authoritative, fixed text becomes unregulated. This altering of the text, typographically and substantively, changes its meaning as "structured authoring" takes over. Marinetti and the Futurists may have initiated this sense of freedom. In one manifesto, they claimed that the conventional book, linear and inelastic, is outdated and destined to disappear. It was static and unresponsive to change in contrast to cinema. The transparent typographical surface of a book must be undone. Marinetti and the electronic text seem united, making every reader aware of the inherent expressivity of a text via its forms of presentation. A new phase would emphasize layout, radical fonts, color, illustrations, and revisions. Down with the trinity of clarity, brevity, and sincerity; up with energetic expression, radical forms and the foregrounding of image over the word. In short, the Dadaists. Lanham calls this the struggle between "icon and alphabet," which began with the emergence of the illuminated ms. and the tension between the transparent alphabetic information and opaque images (Lanham 34). But font size, typeface, and sequentiality transform the text into something opaque as seen in *House of Leaves* (2000) by Mark Danielewski, a work that forces the reader to see and respond to the printed text as an unorthodox material object. As it were, type is "poured" onto the page, itself a form of meaning.[22]

Text, theme, and significance become visual as one moves from book to screen. Digital aesthetics knows few limits, changing not only the experience of "reading" a text but creating a new one. Writing one, in the conventional sense, no longer applies. The freedom of style and form alters the nature of the sentence simultaneously propelling it forward in new shapes and size and backward, recalling an earlier, stable but seemingly outmoded form. Computer fonts, data banks, and AI-generated sentences lose human individuality and scale. Texts become "painted" by algorithms. The canonical has been erased in pursuit of the interactive. Writing is with a virtual paintbrush, not words. A text is a performance.

What does an electronic structure mean for the originality of literature and, more specifically, the sentence with the unequal distribution of the symbolic and the linguistic, or the pictorial and the phonetic? Can an algorithm write like Dr. Johnson, Norman Mailer, Lydia Davis, or Zayde Smith? Or will everyone be able to write like them with AI? Has the literary sentence lost its uniqueness? Can the screen provide any genuine cultural capital or has that also become fleeting, changeable, fluid? Will anything be excluded from the "canon"? If, as John Guillory argues in *Cultural Capital,* that canon formation is the result of the social function and the institutional aims of a "school," what happens if no "school" exists, no unified center? Has "school" become universal? If so, what has been lost?

Does every text, by virtue of its posting, become canonical? Do any texts have privilege to reimagine the exchange between cultural and material life?

One aim of the screen is to encourage individual acts of creativity and evaluation merging with revised socio-institutional conditions. But is it possible while still maintaining the integrity of a text? What is a text becomes, itself, a critical question. The upside of the screen is its accessibility but the down is the loss of the printed page. Access has diminished the "discourse of value."[23] But this may be a good thing, eliminating a somewhat misconceived conspiracy of judgment connected with privileged academics and professional critics. But no single paradigm exists and the social function of a canon has been undone by access. The multiplicity of readers and texts in their varied forms, shaped by the medium of the internet and screen, have altered the structural arrangement of reader and text and its principal constituent, the sentence.

Initially undermining texts as traditionally presented, the screen has superseded them, replacing the page with the electronic images shaped into words and, generating a new reading style: one swipes rather than turns a page. Literary language literally took a new form supported not by language but numbers referred to as code. Reading becomes a function of electronic impulses turning it into a technical science (Emre xx). Literature has taken the form of a memo, according to John Guillory, one that can be corrected, altered, and replaced. The febrile status of text, easily and often manipulated, is one of Guillory's concerns in *Cultural Capital*.[24] In his words, it might be time to "reconceptualize the object of literary study," not brought about by threats to the canon and its formation but by the screen having already forced the reconfiguration of text to meet the demands of the new media altering the process of sentence-making (CCapital 265).

A new class of cultural producers or influencers has become enmeshed in the making of literature and transforming it into a commodity. As Emre explains in her lengthy introduction to the 2023 edition of *Cultural Capital*, moral philosophers of an earlier period aspired to discipline taste so that production could exist in proportion to consumption: "the one balanced against the other just as, in a beautiful work of art, the parts exist harmoniously within the whole."

She continues:

> [T]he analogy between the aesthetic and the social led to the earliest stirrings of a theory of taste, which was trained on the thriving market for goods. The preliminary step in this training was the categorization of objects, with the creation of a distinct name, "the Fine Arts," for commodities that appeared to encourage the virtuous contemplation of beauty exclusive of mere sensual gratification.
>
> (Emre xxiv–xxv)

Emre further adds:

> From this history, we may see how a rich and variegated continuum became a tidy dichotomy, "the double discourse of value" that distinguishes objects by utility versus contemplation (CCapital 308). If they are directed to the end of use, then they are commodities, objects of craft; if they are directed to the end of cogitation or perhaps even reverie, then they are works of art.
>
> (Emre xxvi)

The purpose of these quotes is to underscore the cultural shift from continuity to division affecting conceptions of writing and reading literature, filtered down to the creation and maintenance of the sentence. Textual instability undermines the authority of the sentence.

John Guillory labels the current situation regarding style and writing as the "Post-rhetorical condition," the period following the demise of the classical curriculum and attention to the fearsome ability of language to persuade, anger, or comfort. In the post-Renaissance, the cultural system no longer sustained rhetoric, defined as the "array of pedagogic techniques for raising language to the level of a formal practice."[25] In simpler terms, it meant learning how to use language well, including speaking, reading translating, writing, commenting, or interpreting (G 128).

Today, literacy has replaced rhetoric as a form of "linguistic competence" creating the disappearance of rhetoric which has meant the loss of speaking and writing skills. Learning to read is now paramount, not eloquence or speaking well. This did not happen overnight. The "vernacularization" of the literate culture, according to

Barthes, took some three hundred years.[26] The main impact of the vernacular was on translation with the parallel elimination of the classical curriculum in universities and schools, replaced by an emphasis on technical disciplines and vernacular language study (G 133, 135–6).[27] This first occurred almost one hundred and fifty years ago when Harvard eliminated Greek and Latin as entrance requirements in 1869. A vernacular revolution occurred which prepared writers and readers for the revolution of the sentence which the internet has accelerated. But preference for the plain style started in the late seventeenth century when Joseph Glanville claimed that "[p]lainness is for ever the best eloquence, and 'tis the most forcible."[28]

Reinforcing the shift from rhetoric to literacy was the information age which filtered down to the structure and value of the sentence which began principally as a conveyer of specific forms of knowledge (which is not the accumulation of information). James Gleick, in *The Information, A History, A Theory, A Flood* (2011), charts the formal and informal history of information. Opening in 1948 with the invention of the semiconductor, to be named the transistor, Gleick then notes that in the same year was the invention of the bit as a unit for measuring information. Claude Shannon, an engineer/mathematician at Bell Labs, wrote the initial paper describing a bit and postulating a theory of information which soon led to information processing, information storage, and information retrieval.[29] Language, then a computer structured experience, needed to assemble complete thoughts, otherwise known as sentences.

Sentence comes from the Latin *sententia*, a way of thinking or opinion, originally from *sentiens*, the present participle of *sentio,* to feel, or think. In a sense, a sentence is a form of data compression (Gleick 344–6). Or as Hilary Mantel imagined, echoing the theme of Borges's "Library of Babel" (1941), an endless repository of information down to each letter:

> Suppose within every book there is another book, and within every letter on every page another volume constantly unfolding; but these volumes take no space on the desk. Suppose knowledge could be reduced to a quintessence, held with a picture, a sign, held within a place which is no place.[30]

Sentences can be condensed but not erased.

Information ages began with the invention of writing and gradually moved to employ literacy and numeracy as information technologies.[31] Today, information takes encoded forms, and allows for its transmission and management through texting, email, social media, or blogging (G 155). Technology differentiates composing sentences in the past from the present. There is now an implicit collaboration between writer and reader but also a new and sometimes disrupting sociability with one result the creation of the "paraliterary." This is when literary commentary appears outside the academy, a free-floating set of remarks and readings of various texts found through the internet.[32]

The issue becomes the relationship between writing and "the social forms of modernity" (G 300). Guillory seeks a sociology of writing, analyzing the memorandum which he curiously believes to be "the principal genre of writing in modernity" (G 300).[33] It is, itself, collaborative, summarized in the title of Lisa Ede and Andrea Lunsford's *Singular Texts/Plural Authors* (1990) which concentrates on the nature of collaborative writing and teaching practices; in publishing, this extends to the input of acquisition editors, outside readers, copyeditors, indexers, production coordinators, marketers, advertisers, and even influencers. Dal Yong Jin's *Artificial Intelligence in Cultural Production, Critical Perspectives on Digital Platforms* (Routledge, 2021) goes further, analyzing the convergence of AI writing, digital platforms, and popular culture. The impact of AI on cultural production and consumption is his concern and ends with the complex question of whether it is possible to sustain creative culture.

The worry is the saturation of AI in popular culture, replacing human originality. We live in "a new cultural world of technological innovation that AI and digital platforms create and develop."[34] The irony is that the "swelling use of AI in media and culture," in tandem with digital media platforms, came unplanned. This is both exciting and dangerous. AI is enmeshed with Google, Facebook, YouTube, Netflix, smartphones, and more, forcing a paradigm shift between digital media and popular culture. Machine Learning, a subset of AI, with synthetic data (information artificially generated rather than produced by actual events) on the horizon, dominates (Liu 4). Cultural production means not the actual production of cultural content but, through "structured authoring," the overall process, including production distribution, exhibition, and consumption of culture now embedded in AI use (5).

According to Foucault, social structures generate discursive practice, of which the sentence is part. This often occurs through grammar which is, itself, a social formation codifying usage.[35] But if Latin was the source of the formal tradition initially followed in the syntax and vocabulary of English, other social forces such as commerce and science, began to challenge its hegemony.

The social influence on language is strongly evident in the early American grammars, beginning with the clergyman and educator Rev. Dr. Samuel Johnson's *An English grammar; the first easy Rudiments of Grammar Applied to the English Tongue* (1765). This is generally accepted as the first English grammar prepared by an American and published in the United States. Noah Webster's first grammar, *A grammatical institute of the English language* and designed for schools, appeared in 1804; his second, *A Philosophical and Practical Grammar of the English Language* was published in 1822. Earlier, in the Renaissance, even the playwright Ben Jonson prepared a grammar entitled "The English grammar: Made by Ben Jonson for the benefit of all strangers, out of his observation of the English language now spoken and in use."[36] Studying a grammar aided the advancement of the poor, the undereducated, and the ambitious.[37]

Although she resisted the conventions of the normative sentence, Gertrude Stein loved grammar variously defining it in works like "Arthur A Grammar," "More Grammar for a Sentence," and "A Grammarian." As she once wrote, "It makes me smile to be a grammarian and I am"; "I am a grammarian I do not hesitate but I rearrange prepositions" she added.[38] But grammar for Stein was anything but rigid; it represented sign posts which one could, or could not, follow. She also loved diagramming and, despite her disregard of grammatical completeness, recognized how a grammar is the starting point of her own experiments partially summarized in her "Poetry and Grammar." Grammar may regulate the free flow of language through hierarchy and subordination but the ideal sentence is transparent, effacing grammatical operations.

One needs a grammar to begin if only to write its opposite, understanding how the "internal history of a country always affects its use of writing. It makes a difference in the expression, in the vocabulary even in the handling of grammar."[39] One of her most compelling essays is "More Grammar for a Sentence," even though she worked to subvert it. Her ideal sentence, as she explains in "Lecture 2" of *Narration*, was "the physical joining of words in space." She also admitted that in a sentence "there is no element of completion, it is a thing that exists by internal balancing that is what a sentence is."[40] Her remarks on what *is* a sentence anticipate what the internet demonstrates:

> A sentence is inside itself by its internal balancing, think how a sentence is made by its parts of speech and you will see that it is not dependent upon a beginning a middle and an ending but by each part needing its own places to make its own balancing, and because of this in a sentence there is no emotion
> (Narration 22–3)

The sentence becomes an object, an act of integration joining phrases, phrases forming into sentences, with or without punctuation. But the sentence also becomes a site of tension, embodying, through its construction, contradiction, and confusion: "If a sentence is choosing. They make it in little pieces. / I have practiced" (H to W 108).

Adding to the remaking (or if you prefer, unmaking) of the American Sentence is the realization that every sentence is a performance— by language, the author, and the page. It constantly reshapes its appearance and through its presentation, its meaning, as Susan Howe showed and as Mark Danielewski confirms in his novel *House of Leaves* (2000), which is a text that treats sentences as physical dramas: in one instance, a sentence becomes a descending series of individual words to match the trajectory of a bullet fired down a basement stairwell with individual pages devoted to separate words partly to convey the movement and sound of the bullet and its power,

though

                                    not

                                                  powerful

enough

                        to do more

than

                                                splinter

        a

                    panel

The visual and the textual unite.[41]

    Another semi-sentence of five words appears on two pages:

                  the
                  room

        saturated   in   silence

(H of L 237–8)

What's especially telling in these passages is the spacing, the use of the blank, and the line to enhance the impact of the sentence. The conceptual sense of the blank for the presentation of sentences, whether through margins, sidebars, or headers, plus font size and justification, resonates in the reading of the text. Every page has boundaries. Voids and gaps are telling, as Dos Passos earlier showed in the use of spacing in the "Newsreel" and "Camera Eye" sections of his novel *1919*. There, space and blanks offer, through absence, meaning as seen in "The Camera Eye (28)":

[W]hen the telegram came that she was dying (the streetcarwheels screeched round the bellglass like all the pencils on all the slates in all the schools) walking around Fresh Pond the smell of puddlewater willowbuds in the raw wind shrieking streetcarwheels rattling on loose trucks through Boston suburbs grief isnt a uniform.[42]

In *House of Leaves,* typeface is another physical way of presenting meaning. It runs the gamut from Courier to Times New Roman, Bookman, and Dante. Additional fonts are used intermittently: Janson for film intertitles and Book Antiqua for a letter written by Navidson. Layout incorporates columns, text running across the page without margins, footnotes (also in different type), italics, foreign languages, and several pages where the text runs in the gutter (473–4). One page is an inverted, upside-down text printed as a delta in the lower right-hand corner of the page (475). Page 481 is the upside-down phrase "Don't be" (481). In addition to the different typefaces throughout the novel, there are pages over-typed making the text identifiable but unreadable (624–7). Some pages are printed upside down or on a slant. No sentence section looks the same while passages in Greek, Latin, Italian, Russian, German, and English appear at the end of the novel. Illustrations and an index complete the 709-page text. Danielewski's visual writing refashions our conception of the sentence and what it might be as it also refashions the novel about a home bigger on the inside than the out.[43]

One additional example is Helen DeWitt's *The Last Samurai* (2000), also textually and typographically adventurous appearing the same year as *House of Leaves*. It is about language acquisition and reading, the young prodigy/protagonist Ludo learning Greek at six and declaring, "I would like to strike a style to amaze."[44] A long paragraph discussing a blend of languages follows: Latin across the top of a page (or perhaps German) followed by a solid mass of small type "describing Carling Black Label the beer" (Last 33). Ampersands are everywhere and punctuation reigns freely reflecting the rhythm of speech not traditional grammar. Blocks of text appear from *Gesenius' Hebrew Grammar* and a book on aerodynamics (Last 78–80; 269–70, 291, 295, 313, 314). Pages of equations and general math are frequent (see 219–27, 353). A Japanese Pictorial dictionary competes with Fraser's *Ptolemaic Alexandria* and *Njal's Saga.*

Erudite discussions of texts are repeatedly demonstrated in the novel with reference to Armenian, Czech, Chinese, Icelandic, and Finnish.

Printed passages in Greek, Japanese, and numbers inventively mesh with the arching narrative. It is intertextual and enjoys its own the textual repartee. It also plays with font size to emphasize voice. At one point, the mother, who is trying to apply Arnold Schoenberg's twelve-tone compositional method to literature, tells her son Ludo that Glenn Gould said of "The Well-Tempered Clavier" that the preludes

OKTOKAIENENEKONTASYLLABIC

were merely prefatory

ENNEAKAIENENEKONTASYLLABIC

and of no

HEKATONTASYLLABIC

Real musical interest (Last 33, 40).

    Fragmented and episodic, the novel challenges grammatical, rhetorical, and even typographical expectations often providing its own self-commentary as when the narrator provides a set of her own Greek translations and explanations, a challenge to any typesetter as are the pages reprinted from *Let's Learn Kana* (Last 136–7, 156–7). The novel encompasses film history, language education, probability analysis, music theory, and a type of Scheherazadean storytelling. It becomes an allegory of its own creation through a tart tone and brisk, if scholarly, style. Language fascinates her: in her new story "Entourage," a character becomes so obsessed with the oddities of different languages in new countries he visits, he returns with a suitcase full of books written in the native tongue choosing texts by their unusual letters. But his collection grows so large he has to hire an entourage of translators. He also fixates on certain letters: the frequency of z, w, and y in Polish, the dotless "I" in Turkish.[45] But this is not far from Ludo, the child of Sibylla in *The Last Samurai,* reading the *Odyssey* in Greek in his stroller on the Circle Line. But then his mother easily shifts from revealing parts of her past to Ernest Renan's position on verb conjugation in Aryan languages.

The internet's impact on the sentence has taken numerous forms, from a greater use of visual structuring to the idea that we no longer read but map a sentence, occasionally in the form of a diagram. It is format, rather than content, that matters: looking at, not through, the form of a sentence. A fluid interface operates today between composition and expression bypassing the stumbling blocks of print or at least stepping around them. "Reading" becomes as creative a process as writing enhanced by the screen. Communication becomes constructive, with digitally interactive designs of text leading to discoveries and new means of understanding. A text may become little more than an ecosystem, a social machine. Sentences have become tech-mediated interfaces that no longer rely on a single generative system of construction whether syntactic or metalinguistic. A sentence becomes a dialogic space, socially collaborative. Every sentence has, and originates, in a community.[46]

Speed may be the determining factor of this shift, the speed of composing and sending messages recognized in sentence form. These operating systems require new methods of writing with code at the heart of the new discipline operating under Moore's law: "[E]verything digital gets faster, cheaper and smaller at an exponential rate."[47] And originality has been distributed: it is everywhere whether through structured authorship or content providers. Asymmetry has taken over, partly because the social utility of rhetoric has faded. Creating new, complex systems in which there is no time for correctness and perhaps little time for accuracy, has dominated. But speed has always been an issue, appearing as a challenge with the introduction of the printing press. During the late seventeenth century, Marshall McLuhan argued, print itself called for a stylistic revolution: slow things down. "The speeding eye of the new reader favoured, not shifting tones," he explained, "but a steadily maintained tone, page by page, throughout the volume."[48]

John Guillory notes this in his *Professing Criticism* (2022) which shows how a new approach to literary study is needed, partly the result of the digital environment where digital composition is understood as a multimedia platform: films combine with photographs, video, animation, sound, music, and text. It is collaborative, again altering the nature of sentence composition, now by numerous voices and rewriting hands. Stories are not so much written as mapped out and then uploaded rather than published in any conventional sense. One views rather than reads a sentence.

Technological change has revised the concept of what a sentence is or might be. Synchronicity controls as the language processes images, words, sound, and movement within texts which can occur simultaneously via technology. This is not the death of the sentence but its remaking. It is not the crisis of the sentence as Mieszkowski claims but its reestablishment in a new form from screen-based texts to sound generated writing emerging not in print-based texts but on screen. The screen has become our pen, the tablet or the computer whiteboard the new blackboard. But with this advance, the cultural capital of literature as it was once celebrated has been depleted by the variety, multiplicity and dismissal of originality and imagination on one hand and the demands of the new writing implements. The professionalization of literary studies at the start of the twentieth century has worked against its own agency, part of Guillory's overall argument. Everyone is an author, everyone is a critic.

This new, ultra-public sphere of writing and criticism on the web undercuts the profession of literary studies. Reading and writing are directed outward—to an online readership only partially acquainted with literary theory but with no professional investment in it. The online magazine and the blog have overtaken any effort at professionalized criticism, now an interconnected phenomena. Online cultural commentators write with seeming authority. Writing takes place in a new, hybrid space.

A recent course description confirms the change:

> **Composing** is not just about crafting traditional essays by typing into a word-processing program. Today writers compose by using a variety of platforms to produce different forms. We compose slide shows, videos, audio documentaries, brochures, Tweets, Web sites, and much more. If we want to be effective composers in our complex, global world, we have to learn how to compose using these different platforms, and we have to understand what such forms allow, disallow, and require. We need both technical skill and critical understanding.[49]

The drive to be an "effective composer" overtakes all efforts at being an author, at learning to write and deciding what will be a sentence and how it will be understood rather than "read." This is the new condition of the American Sentence, coming full circle from the abstract dots and dashes of Samuel Morse to the bits and bytes of digital composition. A writer no longer needs a pen and a desk but a keyboard and a screen. "To be a writer in the 21st century means that you are a digital composer," announces a website related to Rhetoric Matters, a new, 2024 guide to university writing.[50] The distance traveled from the medieval scribe copying Latin texts has been vast yet the result, although not the practice, is similar.

What has, finally, been the impact of technology and the screen on the American Sentence? What is the role of AI in composing sentences, American or otherwise? What will be the future of the sentence under the threat of singularity, the idea that there is a constant acceleration in the progress of technology which will outstrip human talent fashioning intelligences greater than our own? A new super intelligence might repeatedly make upgrades for itself. This point of singularity occurs when a function takes on a progressive infinite value (Whiplash 243).[51] Will the line between human and machine become indistinguishable reaching the state of the transhuman or posthuman (Whiplash 243)? Should we herald the warnings but also welcome what Leopold Aschenbrenner outlines in his 165-page paper, "Situational Awareness: The Decade Ahead" (2024)? Will Large Language Models (LLM) provide the sometimes cumbersome answers?

Could we be at the final stage of the American Sentence, replacing complete statements with only machine-generated fragments, incomplete thoughts? Instead of a subject/predicate arrangement will there be only pieces of prose anticipated by such writers as Anne Carson? Her "Seated figure with Red Angle" is a series of more than seventy truncated conditionals, "if" clauses without a following main clause.[52] Her *Red Doc>* (2013), a sequel to *Autobiography of Red* (1998), is printed in narrow columns projecting the interface between prose and poetry as in "Love's Long Lost" with the lines

        Your taxi is
here. Who says this. Your
Redletter brain as you
Struggle and sift longlost
puns comes a torrent of

> noise each cell shimmying
> on its little mitochondrial
> hilt. Pure energy there.
> Memory is exhausting.[53]

Whether on one's phone, laptop, or even movie screen, sentences lose their balance. A bystander in the noir film *Shockproof* (1949), reacting to a newspaper headline, exclaims out loud, "Put a slug right through him!" Later, a hoodlum in a freight car tells the husband of a couple on the lam, she's a "smart looking tomato." Such abbreviated language based on slang says everything without saying much. The American Sentence accelerated in the internet age in its streamlined but incomplete form.

The stress on the visual overshadows the verbal necessitating abrupt and curtailed exchanges, limiting vocabulary while rupturing speech as code substitutes for words. In Text-speak, abbreviations rule, although they are sometimes ambiguous: "LOL" (Lots of Laughs or Love) or "LMK" (let me know). Texting has created a fresh vocabulary, technically, social media acronyms. A selection:

> AMA (Ask me anything), ASL (age, sex, location), BRB (be right back), BSAAW (Big smile and a wink), BTW (By the way), CPC (Cost per click), DYK (did you know?), FF (Follow Friday), FOMO (fear of missing out), FTW (for the win), GR (Got to run), IANAL (I am not a lawyer), ILY (I love you), IRL (In real life), JK (Just kidding), LOL (Laughing out loud), LMK (Let me Know), MFW (My face when), NVM (Never mind), OMW (On my way), POTD (Photo of the day), PPC (Pay per click), NP (no Problem), ROFL (Rolling on the floor laughing), RT (retweet).[54]

In film today, robots and action heroes do most of the talking (when it does occur), in-between chases, escapes, entrapments, and explosions. AI has a taken over many verbal transactions, aspects of the remade American Sentence. This is reaching macabre proportions with the proposal from ElevenLabs to use the voices of deceased figures such as James Dean, Judy Garland, or Burt Reynolds to narrate audio books, digitally produced celebrity voice-overs. Others have turned ChatGPT into virtual boyfriends.[55]

A further step is an AI program entitled "Scheherazade" where students can speak directly with well-known literary figures such as Socrates, Shakespeare, Montaigne, and Scheherazade. The aim is to bring great writers to life explained its creator, Martin Puchner now working on a writing course using "reverse outlining": turning paragraphs into phrases to make sense of a draft.[56] And if that is not enough, AI researchers at OpenAI are working on building AI that can perform human-like reasoning. This is an advanced use of LLM which can now excel at generating text and images with the hope that it can understand and make useful decisions. The label is AGI or Artificial General Intelligence.[57]

It is no surprise, however, that AI is generating a counter reaction. Titles such as *Moral AI*, *The AI Mirror*, and *The Atomic Human* are now appearing.[58] The dangers of machine intelligence are palpable. Fear is that a machine might be a conscious agent, aware of its own existence. Could thinking machines eclipse humans and creative expression in literature, music, art? The emerging consensus is that the hazards of AI must be contained partly because it contains undiagnosed biases in data sets and is harvesting personal information without consent. There are clear moral, social, and philosophical challenges. Responses in say ChatGPT are built statistically via algorithms not "thinking" in any sense. Conceptual understanding is largely absent. But more and more people are relying on AI for answers, accepting the concept of machines mimicking humans. For some a containment strategy is a requirement; for others a limitation.

Similarly, cyberattacks are becoming regular, threatening concerns as the October 2023 attack on the British Library, which affected all technology systems, or the July 2024 IT outage that disrupted airline and hospital operations worldwide, caused by a faulty software update, or the July 2024 Chinese cyberattack on Germany's Federal Office for Cartography and Geodesy which occurred in 2021, has shown.[59] The University of Edinburgh sponsors a Centre for Technomoral Futures. E.M. Forster's "The Machine Stops" (1909) anticipated many of these issues. In the story, one's well-being is totally dependent on a great machine. When it breaks down, chaos. But experience is showing that AI cannot provide technofixes; technology cannot substitute for human relations. AGI, conveyed to us on screens, is a threat as much as an aide, even as it lacks empathy, intuition, or a general sense of culture. Computational narratives are never complete successes.

Digital technology, especially for the computer and smartphone, goes beyond film projectors or even the movie screen in generating unimagined images, language, and sound. It allows one to be in two places at once by extending one's voice and senses over vast distances. It also allows one to interact with a vast storehouse of knowledge through the internet, updating one's knowledge and communicating with others, often done with AI agents such as "Hey, Google," or "Siri." One is today no longer a pure biological being; part of oneself runs on software, with user agreements, licenses, and copyrights. One does not own oneself because part has been created and is controlled by Samsung or Apple. These entities can and do update their own operating systems even without our knowledge.

An analogy to the web is the Renaissance Book Wheel, a sixteenth-century device to cope with the information explosion. Like a five-foot-high Ferris wheel, the book wheel held several books vertically on different shelves and could be spun to make different texts accessible, a form of predigital hyper-reading.[60] But reading on the web impacts writing on the web, specifically writing sentences on the web where reading and writing are multi-textual affairs. Fluid and flexible readers must respond to texts as those who write them: expansive and supple, receptive to unorthodox forms and expression. Digital narratives are by definition intertextual. One must construct sentences that are elastic which means through visualization, simulation, storyboarding, and even game design as partly outlined by Alan Liu in his digital programs. Digital media shapes the new sentence. In particular, Liu at Santa Barbara has established a set of programs that manifest technology and the digital humanities.

Machine-generated writing is a site of the unknown with the challenge how to determine if a sentence has actually been written by an individual or ChatGPT. Aschenbrenner's "Situational Awareness" (June 14, 2024) is helpful, Aschenbrenner is one of the founders of OpenAI. The essay, freely available on the web, predicts exponential developments in the application of AI, noting that "AI progress won't stop at the human-level."[61] Algorithmic progress will rapidly advance and the growth of superintelligence will be dramatic, anticipated by the gathering of vast databanks and funding for AI projects, including power build-outs and datacenters. Security, however, remains an issue plus the ethical issue that we "have machines now that we can basically talk to like humans" (Asch 10). Who will control them?

New terms and new approaches have appeared: cultural analytics, literary data mining plus quantitative formalism, computational textual analysis, algorithmic literary studies, computational literary studies. Marking some of these developments and the future of the sentence is the Electronic Literature Program; the Stanford Literary Lab; the "WhatEvery1Says," the humanities project at Santa Barbara initiated by Alan Liu. This program uses digital humanities methods to study media discourse about the humanities at large data scales. A further suggestive program is the FrameWorks Institute. Using framing theory, their work also attempts to strategize with sentences and their impact beginning with metaphor.[62]

But how has the sentence responded to the revolution in media communications and information technology? Context and history may help. Its resilience after its presentation in the sermon, the telegraph, the press, and the screen is remarkable. Adaptability is in its genes, articulating human thought, aided by the variability and responsiveness of language to new demands on expression. The creation of new sentence forms beyond traditional structures is consistent with the history and treatment of the sentence and its responsiveness. The environment of complexly hybrid material, virtual infrastructures, both micro and macro, means the reception of new, meta forms. Electronic rhetoric may be one answer, applying rhetorical principles to the new media while originating and accepting new ways of writing, from hybrid forms of expression to code, abbreviations, and even pictographs with implications for research, archiving knowledge, and plotting the future.[63]

The sentence is not a closed loop but an open form and the challenge is how to expand not contract its forms. The sentence no longer contains standard structures as it struggles to break free of obsolescence. Novelty and invention are its challenges in a world where programming languages have eroded the monopoly of ordinary language creating a new pyramid of expression. In this novel world, codes have become linguistic extensions of words. Grammar and syntax are being reassembled, while the language of metrics becomes a guide asking how many syllables, how many vowels, what is stressed and unstressed? One is back to counting words as with the telegram. Closure may be a fiction, the vital surpassing the grammatical. The situation remains complex as the poet Donald Justice wrote:

> We stand, now at the threshold
> Peering in, but the passage,
> For us, remains obscure; the
> Corridors are still bloody.[64]

Every new sentence today must be written strategically. Every statement is mediated, becoming a *daedalion* (in Greek, something curved or a deviation from a straight line).[65] The new sentence creates a unique, special montage fulfilling Lev Manovich's wish in *The Language of New Media* (2002) to create more cross-domain material; *corpora* should be untidy, mixing formats, metadata structures in a syntactic remix. As Robert Frost remarked, "[A]ll writing is only as good as it is dramatic."[66]

The notebook may, in fact, be the dominant metaphor of textual expression (rather than Guillory's memorandum) on the net, its discursive entries of no particular order or system. It is a network of random ideas and moments. It permits, if not encourages, lapses in narrative, non-verbal lines, and linked illustrations shaping semiotic spaces. Inversions and disruptions become conventions. Hierarchy is itself overturned by internal and other textual contradictions resulting from semiotic dislocations. In *How We Became Posthuman,* N. Katherine Hayles actually titles her chapter on these developments "From Hyphen to Splice: Cybernetic Syntax in *Limbo,*" referring to a 1952 dystopian novel by Bernard Wolfe. The trope of *Limbo* is the notebooks of Dr. Martine, a neurosurgeon. We quickly sense the flexibility and viability of the notebook as an early "word processor."

As Roland Allen outlines in his recent history, the notebook as a form more or less started with the availably of paper notebooks in thirteenth-century Florence which facilitated book-keeping.[67] Sketchbooks soon became had a role in the daily studios of artists like Cimabue and Leonardo. Sixteenth-century children keep commonplace books, collections of miscellaneous quotations including excerpts from classical authors. Hamlet cries out for his "tables" in Act I. v. 105–10, exclaiming "Meet it is I set it down, that a man may smile and smile and be a villain" (I. v. 105–10). "Meet it is": I shall absorb the tale and its duplicity told to me by the ghost and write it down in my "tables," his "table-books," an Elizabethan type of commonplace book. While saying the words, he takes out his notebook and scribbles.

There is, of course, no single explanation for the importance of a notebook which might be to record or remember. But for da Vinci, Coleridge, Henry James, Proust, Kafka, Virginia Woolf, Paul Valéry, Leonard Cohen, or Paul Theroux, notebooks were essential workshops or laboratories testing ideas. But thoughts in a notebook enter randomly and read nonlinearly, anticipating the access and reading system of the Web offering non-linear access with a few clicks. No reading necessary. Lydia Davis makes this clear in her short essay "Revising One Sentence," although she does point out the importance of revising her notebook sentences because "it is hard for me to let a sentence stand if I see something wrong with it." Revising may also inspire a new sentence in new story.[68]

Novels often told their stories through notebooks, journals, or diaries, including Anne Bronte's *Tenant of Wildfell Hall*, Bram Stoker's *Dracula,* Doris Lessing's, *The Golden Notebook* in addition to Toni Morrison's *The Color Purple*, Nicholas Sparks's *The Notebook* (1996), James A. Levine's *The Blue Notebook* (2009), and Antoine Laurain's *The Red Notebook* (2015), topped by a section of Hernan Diaz's *Trust* (2022) told in journal and note form. Joan Didion summarizes much of this absorption in her essay "On Keeping a Notebook" from 1966 reprinted in *Slouching towards Bethlehem*. A notebook for her is how an experience, a thought, or an idea *"felt to me"* at the time she jotted it down. They always "give us away" despite our best efforts to record only what we see.[69] It is a random record, a holding place for fragments of memory and experience.

In the universe of AI, the sentence may have become redundant. Undisciplined creativity is the new practice; word clusters replace traditional sentence structure with the goal the quick absorption of a statement or idea. Holding the reader's attention is the new metric with swiping, instead of reading, the new exercise. The impact on the position and posture of a word is intense and often isolates it from any syntactic order. Words are not written but presented. Indeed, to "write" for

Reddit, Facebook, X, WhatsApp, or other messaging platforms seems to mean only to illustrate or list. There is no time to write normally, only time for visuals, abbreviations, bullet points, or customization. There is a rush to compose, to comment, to criticize. Sentences have become unnecessary. Why write when you can show?

The sentence, one could argue, is no longer needed. It has dissolved into incomplete statements or code; it has melted into numbers. The irony, however, is that machines are writing better, more effective sentences than humans, sentences tailored to individual situations. Creatively, they even write better stories, although substantively they are weaker, lacking the human dynamic. Artificially constructed through Generative AI via platforms like ChatGPT, Copilot, LaMDA, or Gemini, these systems often create synthetic data while redesigning the sentence. And programs now stretch further, Meta releasing an AI model, ImageBind, that combines data from text, images, video, 3D data, audio, and motion: the result is more immersive generative content. OpenAI Codex trains LLMs in programming language allowing them to fashion their own source code for new computer programs. The sentence, as a form of human expression, is no more, anticipated by the first chapter of Ron Silliman's *The New Sentence,* published nearly forty years ago: "Disappearance of the Word, Appearance of the World." Henry Miller had also sensed the threat, although he still defended the need for books:

> I believe that today more than ever a book should be sought after even if it has only *one* great page in it: we must search for fragments, splinters, toe-nails, anything that has ore in it, anything that is capable of resuscitating the body and soul.

But he also admitted that "We write, knowing we are licked before we start."[70] Agency is no longer part of the power of the sentence.

While sentences have been socially constructed and collaborative, the process has altered, having forfeited control to the screen and AI. One in fact views rather than reads. "Content moderation" is now the critical term of silent editors (some merely algorithms) who monitor what and how we read online. They are supposedly more accurate in identifying and removing problematic content, "policing" texts, and generating satisfying if incomplete answers. But their reach is far with the practice of rewriting classic novels for political correctness a further extension. Agatha Christie, Roald Dahl, and Ian Fleming are already victims.[71] People (editors?) act only as advisors to ensure the proper functioning of the AI-based content moderator system and adjudicate questionable cases. But an AI Bot can do better. If the pixel has replaced words with content moderators acting as editors if not authors, the sentence as an original expression of an individual must struggle for survival. It is no surprise to learn that AI can easily imitate Jane Austen or write a summer romance.[72] Changes, corrections, or manipulations of literary and other texts are now algorithmically generated, mathematical formulas shaping style and remaking sentences. Imitation becomes a new genre, replacing adaptation or parody. The immediacy of web writing has undermined the nature of the "authentic" sentence (written by an individual) which seems, by necessity, to have jettisoned traditional structures.

The perennial question "What is a sentence?" repeated by Jan Mieszkowski at the end of *Crises of the Sentence*, takes on new urgency. With current and future forms of technological expression, the sentence is undergoing an almost endless series of transformations. The challenge becomes "whether anyone has ever truly finished a sentence" or "finished with a sentence"—that is, finished the making of a sentence (Crises 239). Gertrude Stein, in fact, cautioned that there may not be sentences at all. Her epic *The Making of Americans* (1925) may have a modern sequel, "The Making of the American Sentence," to which the current text has gestured. And if "play it safe" was the rubric of earlier writers concerning the form and order of the sentence, the opposite is true today. AI means play it unsafe: experiment, innovate, discover, and uncover the visual and textual potential of the sentence through new means. Machines are already turning the sentence into a performative act but one with a marginalized identity. How American. With the reconstructive ability of the internet, we have fulfilled Gertrude Stein's prophecy: "A sentence has wishes as an event" (H to W 18). It has absolutely become an event, a variable experience in words constantly attuned to the screen.

Notes

1. Pepperell Robert, *The Post-Human Condition* 2nd ed. (Bristol: Intellect Books, 1997) 1; Cary Wolfe, *What Is Posthumanism?* (Minneapolis: University of Minnesota Press, 2010) xii.

2. Alberto Manguel, *A History of Reading* (New York: Knopf, 1996) 43–5. Hereafter Manguel. In his *Confessions*, Augustine said of Ambrose that when he read, "his eyes scanned the page and his heart sought out the meaning, but his voice was silent and his tongue still" (in Manguel 42).

3. The four levels of interpretation according to Ashkenazi Talmudic scholars were the literal, the limited, the rational, and the secret. Reading could, therefore, never be completed (Manguel 90). Asked why the first page of each of section in the Babylonian Talmud was missing, Rabbi Levi Yitzhak explained that the reader was forced to begin on page two because, no matter how many pages the student has read, he must never forget that he has not yet reached the first page (Manguel 90; source: Buber, *Tales of the Hasidim*).

   Anticipating Samuel Morse's transformation of letters into numbers when creating the telegraph was the *gematria*, a Hebrew system of reading the Talmud that transposes letters into numerical equivalents. Rashi, an eleventh-century rabbi, translated Genesis 17 where God tells Abraham his wife Sarah will bear a son, giving each letter a number (Manguel 90). But this was only one manner of reading text. The allegorical, symbolic, and imagistic would follow.

4. Charles Dickens, *Our Mutual Friend* (London: Chapman and Hall, 1865) 162. The description was the original title of T.S. Eliot's long poem retitled *The Waste Land*.

5. For the vocabulary of the screen, see "Screen Language," Simon Fraser University. http://www.sfu.ca/media-lab/426/Screen%20Language.htm. A fuller discussion is *The Syntax of Film, A Glossary*, ed. Mark Bischoff and Ulrike Ordon, 4th ed. (Seesen, GR, 2017). https://www.filmglossar.de/syntax4.pdf. Also see the extensive discussion by James Monaco, "Syntax, The Language of Film: Signs and Syntax," *How to Read a Film*. 4th ed. (New York: Oxford University Press, 2009) 191–249.

6. See Georgia Gowing, "Reading on Screens Instead of Paper Is less Effective Way to Absorb and Retain Information, Suggests Research." *Phys Org*. February 6, 2024 https://phys.org/news/2024-02-screens-paper-effective-absorb-retain.html; Ferris Jabr, "The Reading Brain in the Digital Age: The Science of Paper versus Screens," Scientific American April 11, 2013. https://www.scientificamerican.com/article/reading-paper-screens/; Erik Ofgang, "The Screen Inferiority Effect: How Screens Affect Reading Comprehension," December 4, 2023. Tech & Learning. https://

www.techlearning.com/news/the-screen-inferiority-effect-how-screens-affect-reading-comprehension.

7 Janet Staiger, "The Hollywood Mode of Production to 1930," *The Classical Hollywood Cinema,* ed. D. Bordwell, et al (London: Routledge 1985) 274. Also see her "Blueprints for Feature Films: Hollywood's Continuity Script," *The American Film Industry,* ed. T. Balio (Madison: University of Wisconsin Press, 1976) 173–92.

8 The arrival of sound meant the need for multiple film shots within a scene where dialogue occurs, the camera alternating angles from one speaker to another. Scripts became known as the "master-scene" form.

Useful is "Screenwriting 101: The History of Screenwriting," by Yoran Praet, "Arcadia," 5 February 2023 with valuable details on the evolution of screenwriting and the financing of screenwriters and the studios. See https://www.byarcadia.org/post/screenwriting-101-the-history-of-screenwriting.

Additionally, see S. Field, *Screenplay* (1979), T. Stemple, *Framework: A History of Screenwriting in the American Film* (1998), S. Maras, *Screenwriting: History, Theory and Practice*, and S. Price, *A History of Screenwriting* (2013).

9 Philip Dunne in Pat McGilligan, "Screenwriters of the Golden Age," *Los Angeles Times* December 28, 1986. This is the source for other details in this paragraph. McGillian drew material from her book, *Backstory: Interviews with Screenwriters of Hollywood's Golden Age* (Berkeley: University of California Press, 1986). Robert Altman's satiric film *The Player* (1992) dramatizes the screenwriter/ studio relationship.

10 "The Philadelphia Story Script—Dialogue Transcript," http://www.script-o-rama.com/movie_scripts/p/philadelphia-story-script-transcript-hepburn.html.

11 Robert Towne, *Chinatown,* Screenplay, 3rd Draft, September 1973. https://www.public.asu.edu/~srbeatty/394/Chinatown.pdf. [1–2].

12 For the script, see Quentin Tarantino and Roger Avery, *Pulp Fiction*. Script, 1994 https://script-pdf.s3-us-west-2.amazonaws.com/pulp-fiction-script-pdf.pdf. This is the final draft of May 1993.

13 Following passages are from Virginia Tufte, *Artful Sentences: Syntax as Style* (Cheshire, CT: Graphics Press, 2006): Tennessee Williams 17; Gore Vidal 28.

14 See Jay David Bolter, *Writing Space, the Computer, Hypertext, and the History of Writing* (Mahwah, NJ: Erlbaum Associates, 1991) ix–x. Despite being over thirty years old, the work still offers a set of stimulating ideas. Hereafter Bolter.

15 Anne Carson, *Red Doc>* (New York: Knopf, 2013) 74; Colson Whitehead. *The Underground Railroad* (New York: Doubleday, 2016) 42.

16 Richard A. Lanham, *The Electronic Word, Democracy, Technology, and the Arts* (Chicago: University of Chicago Press, 1993) 34. Hereafter Lanham. Pushing beyond Lanham Is Gregory Ulmer's Earlier *Teletheory: Grammatology in the Age of Video* (New York: Routledge 1989).

17 Craig Baehr, Bob Schaller, *Writing for the Internet, A Guide to Real Communication in Virtual Space* (Westport, CT: Greenwood Press, 2010) 185. Hereafter Wr. Inter.

18 "Structured authoring tools are designed for large teams to produce content by creating workflows, owners, and statuses," writes S. Kingson, author of "Structured Authoring: A Guide for Content Creators," Document 360 February 29, 2024. https://document360.com/blog/structured-authoring/.

Adobe Systems offers a more precise definition:

> Structured authoring is an authoring workflow that lets you define and enforce consistent organization of information in documents. In unstructured publishing, content is written according to rules and approved styles described in style guides and enforced by editors.
>
> In an unstructured authoring workflow, you create relatively free-flow narrative-based documents. For example, you can have headings, followed by paragraphs, or graphics with captions or alternate text. In case of structured authoring, the content rules enforce a consistent structure across similar pieces of information. For example, you can decide to enforce the following content rules:
>
> - A bulleted list must contain at least two items.
> - A heading must be followed by a paragraph.
> - A table must have a heading row.
> - A graphic must have a caption.
>
> These content rules are defined in either a document type definition (DTD) or an XML schema. Conformance to these content rules is automatically checked against the DTD or schema.

See https://help.adobe.com/en_US/framemaker/2017/using/using-framemaker-2017/frm_structauth_sa/Structured_authoring-.htm.

19 The Joyce Project, an interactive hypertext of *Ulysses,* offering textual commentary, visual images and videos, enriches the direct reading of the book (https://www.joyceproject.com/). For Milton, see *Paradise Lost* at the John Milton Reading Room, a similarly interactive text (https://milton.host.dartmouth.edu/reading_room/pl/intro/text.shtml.). The Digital Dante is another powerful reading tool with images, sound, history, and textual details (https://digitaldante.columbia.edu/dante/divine-comedy/). One additional site providing an in-depth study of Pound's monumental poem is "The Cantos Project" at the University of Edinburgh. It provides annotations, resources, publication timeline, and a general bibliography on *The Cantos*. https://ezrapoundcantos.org/about. Annotation and bibliography are its key goals with links to illustrations, textual anomalies, and criticism.

Informative on the practice and use of the hypertext is George P. Landow, *Hypertext 3.0: Critical Theory and New Media in an Era of Globalization* (Baltimore: Johns Hopkins University Press, 2006).

20   St. Teresa, *Complete Works of St. Teresa*, ed. and tr. E. Allison Peers, Vol. 2 (New York: Sheed and Ward, 1972) 88.

21   Bolter 22; also see Dennis Duncan, *Index, A History of the* (New York: Norton, 2023).

22   A predecessor of this form is the poet/critic Kenneth Burke's "Flowerishes" in his *Collected Poems 1915–1967*, precisely anticipating Danielewski's experiment. Text for both authors becomes a writer-controlled entity. For a reproduction of Burke's poem see Lanham 36. Typography becomes quasi-allegorical.

23   Merve Emre, "Introduction to the New Edition," John Guillory, *Cultural Capital* (1993; Chicago: University of Chicago Press, 2023) x, xi. Hereafter, Emre.

Anticipating some of these issues is Johanna Drucker, *The Visible Word, Experimental Typography and Modern Art 1909–1923* (Chicago: University of Chicago Press, 1996). Two further texts that help are *Diagrammatic Writing* (Einhoven, Netherlands: Set Margins, 2013) and *Graphesis: Visual Forms of Knowledge Production* (Cambridge, MA: Harvard University Press, 2014).

24   John Guillory, *Cultural Capital* (1993; Chicago: University of Chicago Press, 2023) 258–9. Hereafter CCapital.

25   John Guillory, *Professing Criticism, Essays on the Organization of Literary Study* (Chicago: University of Chicago Press, 2022) 127. Hereafter G.

26   "The end of rhetoric is concurrent with the *extension* of literacy to the populace as a whole," Guillory claims (G 129). Rhetoric would die when the classical languages no longer dominated the educational system, although demands for vernacular writing were growing.

On Barthes and the demise of rhetoric see Guillory 125–6. Also useful is Guillory, "Mercury's Words: The End of Rhetoric and the Beginning of Prose," *Representations* 138 (2017) 59–86. Guillory argues for the emergence of the plain style as a result of recognizing prose itself as a medium of composition. This liberated prose from its subordination to the system of rhetoric and its link to oratory which had triumphed over narrative. He offers special credit to Richard Foster Jones writing in the late seventeenth century on the Royal Society and its program of language reform in support of "the plain style" whose most important sites were preaching and philosophy (Guillory 67, 69). *"Elocutio"* or ornament, long a feature of rhetoric, lost favor.

27 For an important bibliographical summary of the decline of rhetoric, see G 130 ftnt. 10. For Guillory's complaint on the failure of memory training and its impact on the decline of rhetoric and pedagogy with consequences for cognitive development, see 145. Memory was no longer an art and rhetoric lost its prominence as a system for training cognition. The reduction of rhetoric to a form of elocution marked its demise (G 148). It was no longer an art, a *techné* (craft) distinguished from *epistemé* or scientific knowledge and, on the other hand, *praxis* or pure action (G 127–8 nt.5). Information in the modern age depends on the idea of information "as disembodied knowledge" (G 160). Method becomes the new means of transmitting knowledge through practice.

28 Joseph Glanville, *An Essay Concerning Preaching* (London, 1678) 25.

29 James Gleick, *The Information, A History, A Theory, A Flood* (New York: Pantheon, 2011) 3–9.

30 Hilary Mantel, *Wolf Hall* (New York: Henry Holt, 2009) 394.

31 See Michael E. Hobart and Zachary S. Schiffman, *Information Ages: Literacy, Numeracy and the Computer Revolution* (Baltimore: Johns Hopkins University Press, 1998) 5. Also helpful is Alan Liu's website "Palinurus," focusing on teaching the humanities in a restructured world. http://palinurus.english.ucsb.edu/index2.html and his "Voice of the Shuttle," focusing on history and humanities research: https://teachinghistory.org/history-content/website-reviews/22869. On the insufficiencies of writing as taught today, Guillory argues that the reading of the population today is "quantitatively less and qualitatively simpler" than necessary for producing writing competency (G 308).

32 See Merve Emre, *Paraliterary: The Making of Bad Readers in Postwar America* (Chicago: University of Chicago Press, 2017) passim.

33 His essay "The Memo and Modernity," *Critical Inquiry* Vol.31 (2004): 108–32 is useful on this point.

34 Dai Yong Jin, Artificial Intelligence in Cultural Production, Critical Perspectives on Digital Platforms (London: Routledge, 2021) 2.

35 See Michel Foucault, "Appendix, the Discourse on Language," *The Archeology of Knowledge and the Discourse on Language* (New York: Pantheon, 1972) 216. William Bullokar's *Pamphlet for Grammar*, first, published in 1586, was modeled on William Lily's Latin grammar, *Rudimenta Grammatices* (1534) which was being studied in schools in the mid-sixteenth century.

36 The short grammar appears in volume seven of *The Works of Ben Jonson* (1756) [1640]. In addition to the grammar, the volume includes "Timber; or, Discoveries made upon men and matter. Horace, or the art of poetry.

The English grammar. Leges convivales, Rules for the Tavern Academy, and The Case is Altered."

37 See Beth Barton Schweiger, "A Social History of English Grammar in the Early United States," *Journal of the Early Republic* Vol.30 No.4 (2010): 533–55.

38 Gertrude Stein, "A Grammarian," *How to Write* (1931; West Glover, VT.: Something Else Press, 1973) 107, 109. Hereafter H to W.

39 Natalie Simpson, *What Is a Sentence: Gertrude Stein and Sentence Theory*, MA thesis University of Calgary (May 2001) 9. https://prism.ucalgary.ca/server/api/core/bitstreams/c4baef91-1ec3-4ec7-bfc1-74783440fe3b/content.

Gertrude Stein, "How Writing is Written," (1935), *How Writing Is Written*, ed. Robert Bartlett Haas (Boston: Black Sparrow Press, 1974) 153. In the same essay she explains that "I was trying to get this present immediacy without trying to drag in anything else. I had to use present participles, new constructions of grammar. The grammar-constructions are correct, but they are changed, in order to get this immediacy" ("How Writing" 155). Also instructive is her essay "More Grammar for a Sentence" (1930) in *As fine as Melanctha*, Vol. 4 *Unpub. Writings* (Freeport, NY: Books for Libraries Press, 1969) 361–78. "What is a sentence and why cannot it be natural. Because it is a sentence," she writes in contradictory fashion ("More Grammar for a Sentence" 375). Two pages later she notes that "a sentence it is so easy to lose what a sentence is" (377).

40 Stein, "Lecture 2," *Narration* (Westport, CT: Greenwood, 1969) 142, 18. It has been suggested that "Gertrude Stein's resistance to conventional grammar is also a resistance to the patriarchy of language" (Simpson 105). Her writing generates, rather than represents, meaning (Simpson 106). Grammar is in some sense the enemy: "Grammar is a system that subordinates elements of language to other elements in a drive towards meaningful referentiality—grammar organizes sentences to have use values and exchange values" (Simpson 107). But for Stein, her words possess an equivalency of stress; replacing the linearity of syntax is a sentence whose construction is spatial and all parts of speech are equal units. Democratic syntax is the result.

"Sentences and Paragraphs" is another useful essay. And for more detail on sentences, see Ulla E. Dydo with William Rice, "1928–30: Grammar," *Gertrude Stein: The Language that Rises 1923–1934* (Evanston, IL: Northwestern University Press, 2003) 339–409.

41 Mark Danielewski, *House of Leaves* (New York: Pantheon, 2000) 217–31. Hereafter H of L.

42 John Dos Passos, "The Camera Eye (28)," "1919," *U.S.A* (New York: Library of America, 1996) 368. On the subject of blanks, see Jonathan

Sawday, *Blanks, Print, Space and Void in English Renaissance Literature* (Oxford: Oxford University Press, 2024).

43 Danielewski's *Only Revolutions* (New York: Pantheon, 2006) is even more radical. On a single page the top half of the text reads left to right but you must turn the book around to read the bottom text which becomes the new top text but is also in a different type. Columns also appear near the gutter to further embroil the reader. This upside-down book challenges the concentration of readers as it tells the story from two different directions by two different narrators: Sam in one direction, Hailey in another. In this work, the reader loses control of the sentences which are defined by their performativity.

For an earlier example of a challenging typographic novel reconstituting what is a text, and by extension what is a sentence, see *Limbo* (1952) by Bernard Wolfe. Essentially a sci-fi novel told through the notebooks of a Dr. Martine who left a medical post in the Third World War and escaped to a Pacific Island., it destabilizes the idea of a text as contained and embodied only within its typographic markers.

44 Helen DeWitt, *The Last Samurai* (London: Chatto and Windus, 2000) 33, 40. Hereafter LSam.

45 Helen DeWitt, "Entourage," *Some Trick* (New York: New Directions, 2018) 183–93.

46 For these and parallel ideas see the MIT Media Lab website, https://www.media.mit.edu/.

Among texts that address these issues, see Jay David Bolter's early *Writing Space, The Computer, Hypertext, and the History of writing* (1991) to Craig Baehr and Bob Schaller's *Writing for the Internet* (2010), and Ethan Zuckerman's *Rewire, Digital Cosmopolitans in the Age of Connection* (2013). More recent are the works by Ray Kurzwil, *The Singularity Is Nearer* (2024) and his earlier *The Singularity Is Near* (2005). Every twenty minutes, it seems, another work on the life of writing and the internet appears. It is no surprise that the Modern Language Association has published a second edition Ellen C. Carillo's *MLA Guide to Digital Literacy* (2nd ed., 2022), described as providing students with "strategies for reading and analysing data visualizations" (Advt. MLA). New to the second ed. is the ethical dimension of digital technology and "Composing in Digital Spaces," instruction in multimodal composition with writing at the center, although framed by new methods including speech to text software (and the reverse). Lateral and vertical readings are also discussed plus the conversational model of the World Wide Web which continues to influence written style.

The MLA has also published N. Katherine Hayles's "How We Read: Close, Hyper, Machine," in the *ADE Bulletin* (ADE Bulletin 150 [2010] 62–79) and, most recently, Hui Wu and Matthew Kelly, "Professionalizing the English

Major in the Information Age: A Case Study in Designing a Digital Minor," *ADE Bulletin* Vol.160 (2023): 99–108. As early as 1994 the MLA published *Literacy and Computers,* ed. Cynthia L. Selfe and Susan Hilligoss.

Hayles, in 1999, published *How We Became Posthuman, Virtual Bodes in Cybernetics, Literature and Informatics* (Chicago: University of Chicago Press, 1999).

47 Cited in Joi Ito and Jeff Howe, *Whiplash, How to Survive Our Faster Future* (New York: Grand Central Publishing, 2016) 21.

48 McLuhan, "Effect of the Printed Book on Language in the 16th Century," *Explorations* 7 (1957) rpt. in *Marshall McLuhan Unbound*, ed. Eric McLuhan Terrence Gordon (Richmond: CA: Gingko Press, 2005) 11.

49 This is from Stony Brook University's course "Digital Composition, Storytelling & Multimodal literacy." Also see "Digital Storytelling" at Ohio State University and the excellent "Creating Multimodal texts" from the University of Melbourne.

In the simplest of terms, applying unsupervised or self-supervised machine learning to a data set creates a generative AI system.

50 See https://louis.pressbooks.pub/englishcomp2/.

51 Also see Vernor Vinge, "The Coming Technological Singularity: How to Survive in the Post-Human Era," *Vision 21: Interdisciplinary Science and Engineering in the era of Cyberspace*, ed. G.A. Landis (NASA, 1993): 11–22 and Ray Kurzweil's, *The Singularity Is Near* (New York: Viking, 2005) and *The Singularity Is Nearer: When We Merge with AI* (New York: Viking, 2024).

52 Anne Carson, "Seated Figure with Red Angle (1988) by Betty Goodwin," *Decreation* (New York: Knopf, 2005) 95–101. For a discussion, see chapter 3. Susann Howe's *That This* (2010) and *Debths* (2017), especially the "Tom Tit Tot" section with its overlapping, incomplete, and almost unreadable poems are further examples of what one might label corrugated texts.

53 Anne Carson, "Love's Long Lost," *Red Doc>* (New York: Knopf, 2013) 14.

54 On further acronyms, see Kevan lee, "The Definitive List of Social Media Acronyms and Abbreviations, Defined," March 27, 2023. https://buffer.com/library/social-media-acronyms-abbreviations/. On the new language of teenagers, see Stephen Marche, "Today's Teenagers Have Invented a Language That Captures the World Perfectly," *The New York Times*, June 25, 2024. https://www.nytimes.com/2024/06/25/opinion/gen-z-slang-language.html.

55 On deceased celebrities making audio books, see Samantha Murphy Kelly, "Hollywood Stars' Estates Agree to the Use of Their Voices with AI," CNN Business July 3, 2024. https://www.cnn.com/2024/07/03/tech/elevenlabs-ai-celebrity-voices/index.html.

For the virtual boyfriend, see Clare Duffy, "Woman Codes ChatGPT to Be Her Boyfriend," CNN Business. July 8, 2024; https://www.cnn.com/2024/07/08/business/video/ai-boyfriend-chatgpt-digvid.

56   Lucy Knight, "From Books to Bot, Bookmarks," *The Guardian* July 14, 2021. The Guardian info@editorial.theguardian.com.

57   Rachel Metz, "OpenAI Scale Ranks Progress toward 'Human-level' Problem Solving," *Bloomberg News* July 11, 2024. https://www.bloomberg.com/news/articles/2024-07-11/openai-sets-levels-to-track-progress-toward-superintelligent-ai. There are five levels to track the progress of AI capable of outperforming humans: Chatbots (AI with conversational language); Reasoners (human-level problem-solving); Agents (systems that can take actions); Innovators (AI that can aid in invention); Organizations (AI that can do the work of an organization). One worry, however, is that AI systems might become autonomous, able to act on their own initiative without human direction. We literally enter the realm of the posthuman.

58   Jana Schaich Borg, Vincent Conitzer and Walter Sinnott-Armstrong, *Moral AI and How We Get There* (London: Penguin 2024), Shannon Vallor, *The AI Mirror, How to Reclaim Our Humanity in an Age of Machine Thinking* (Oxford: Oxford University Press, 2024), and Neil D. Lawrence, *The Atomic Human, Understanding Ourselves in the Age of AI* (London: Penguin, 2024) are the authors and full titles.

59   A mid-August 2024 British Library newsletter explains that the recovery of all BL systems is not yet complete because of the need to comply to new security standards requiring a newly built computer infrastructure for the entire Library including all servers, networks, and data. For updates on worldwide cyberattacks see the Washington, DC\-based Center for Strategic & International Studies cyber incident page. The future of national security is the mandate of the Center. See https://www.csis.org/programs/strategic-technologies-program/significant-cyber-incidents.

60   On the book wheel, see John Guillory, "How Scholars Read," *ADE Bulletin* Vol.146 (Fall 2008) 11. His source is G. Cavallo and R. Chartier, *A History of Reading in the West* (1999): 25. For images of the book wheel, see "16th Century Bookwheels," Open Culture July 3, 2020. https://www.openculture.com/2020/07/16th-century-bookwheels-the-e-readers-of-the-renaissance-get-brought-to-life-by-21st-century-designers.html. Also, "Behold the 'BookWheel:' The Renaissance Invention Created to Make Books Portable," Open Culture September 25, 2017. https://www.openculture.com/2017/09/behold-the-book-wheel-the-renaissance-invention-created-to-make-books-portable-help-scholars-study-1588.html.

61   Leopold Aschenbrenner, "Situational Awareness, the Decade Ahead," 47. https://situational-awareness.ai/parting-thoughts/. Hereafter Asch.

62 See "Tapping into the Power of Metaphors." FrameWorks Institute, 2020. https://www.frameworksinstitute.org/article/tapping-into-the-power-of-metaphors/ and the FrameWorks Institute. "Homepage," 2020. https://www.frameworksinstitute.org/. Framing theory encourages the reforming of the sentence.

What is framing theory? Essentially, the knowledge that media focuses attention on certain events and then places them with a field of meaning. It is a theory of mass communication and how the media packages and presents information. It focuses on the issues at hand, not just on a particular topic. Gregory Bateson first proposed the theory in 1972 followed by Irving Goffman, under the title of *Frame Analysis* (1974). A frame is a system of preconceived ideas used to interpret and organize new information. Writing becomes a communications strategy, writing, sentences solutions to problems expressing ideas. See "Framing Theory,' Communication Studies https://www.communicationstudies.com/communication-theories/framing-theory.

Also, Dietram A. Scheufele, "Framing as a Theory of Media Effects," *Journal of Communication* Vol.49 No.4 (1999): 103–22.

63 Among many recent studies, see Jefferson Bailey, "Disrespect Des Fonds: Rethinking Arrangement and Description in Born-Digital Archives," *Archive Journal*, 2013. https://web.archive.org/web/20170919162159/http://www.archivejournal.net/essays/disrespect-des-fonds-rethinking-arrangement-and-description-in-born-digital-archives/ and Benjamin H. Bratton, *The Stack: On Software and Sovereignty* (Cambridge, MA: MIT Press, 2016). https://doi.org/10.7551/mitpress. Bratton explains how the stack can function, partly through cloud platforms creating new forms of expressing knowledge. The Stack quickly becomes a computational apparatus and a new governing architecture.

64 Donald Justice, "For the Suicides of 1962," *Poetry* Vol.105 No.6 (1965): 350.

65 See Bruno Latour, "On Technical Mediation: Philosophy, Sociology, Geneaology," *Common Knowledge* Vol.3 No.2 (1994): 29–64.

66 For Frost, see Ellen Bryant Voigt, *The Art of Syntax* (St. Paul, MN: Graywolf Press, 2009) 123. Also see Alan Liu, "N + 1: A Plea for Cross-Domain Data in the Digital Humanities," *Debates in the Digital Humanities* (Minneapolis: University of Minnesota Press, 2016): 559–68.

67 Roland Allen, *The Notebook, A History of Thinking on Paper* (London: Profile Books, 2024).

68 Lydia Davis, *Essays One* (New York: Farrar, Straus, Giroux, 2019) 170–1.

69 Joan Didion, "On Keeping a Notebook," *Slouching Toward Bethlehem*, Intro. Elizabeth Hardwick (New York: Modern Library, 2000) 120, 122.

70 Henry Miller, *Henry Miller on Writing*, sel. Thomas H. Moore (New York: New Directions, 1964) 86, 74.

71 Alexandra Alter and Elizabeth A. Harris, "As Classic Novels Get Revised for Today's Readers, a Debate about Where to Draw the Line," *The New York Times* April 5, 2023. https://www.nytimes.com/2023/04/03/books/classic-novels-revisions-agatha-christie-roald-dahl.html.

72 See Aatish Bhatia, "Watch an AI Learn to Write by Reading Nothing but Jane Austen," *The New York Times* April 27, 2023. https://www.nytimes.com/interactive/2023/04/26/upshot/gpt-from-scratch.html?pgtype=Article&action=click&module=RelatedLinks/ and

Curtis Sittenfeld "ChatGPT vs. Me: Who Will Write a Better Beach Read?" *The New York Times* July 9, 2024. https://www.nytimes.com/2024/07/09/opinion/chatgpt-beach-read.html.

Conclusion: Dancing Periods

It is my ambition to say in ten sentences what others say in a whole book.

FRIEDRICH NIETZSCHE, *TWILIGHT OF THE IDOLS* (1888)

Are good sentences why we read? Is that what draws us into a story or a novel? Is it what draws in the writer, as well? Lydia Davis has remarked that often "a line or sentence occurs to me, or even just a sentence containing an idea for a story" and she begins.[1] The exchange between the sentence and the imagination is reciprocal. In her collection *Essays One*, Davis discusses how a sentence discovered out of context can light an entire narrative. The author Grant Faulkner considers sound an essential ingredient: a successful writer, he explains, listens "for the peal of vowels and sibilance of constants, identifying the acoustical zones of a sentence" (Brevity 129). Sound is sometimes the forgotten feature of a sentence. Gary Lutz in "The Sentence Is a Lonely Place," agrees, adding that "the words in the sentence must bear some physical and sonic resemblance to each other" (Brevity 130). Cadence can carry a sentence, while "[s]entences are like people" short or tall, thin or rotund (Brevity 131). Some even expand: "Space, Whether and Why," a short story by Ted McLoof, is told in a single sentence of 1,394 words, contradicting William Strunk's principle that "when a sentence is made stronger, it usually becomes shorter." Brevity may be the product of vigor but it's not always possible. As Pascal explained, "[I]f I had more time, I would have written a shorter letter."[2]

But in the world of shorter writing, generated by screens and encouraged by Instagram, Facebook, memes, X, ChatGPT, and other platforms, what is the future of the American Sentence? Will it continue to vacillate between the oracular and the minimal, or will it become increasingly deconstructed into a series of fragments or algorithmic compositions? Will AI take full control or will authors still have a creative role in expressing thought through their own words, ideas, arguments, facts, and voices? Will the manufactured sentence replace the creative? Will reading itself become competitive as certain apps are now promoting?[3] Or will we race to decipher the conscious scrambling of sentences expressed through a language virus descending upon us as Samuel R. Delaney depicts in *Babel 17* (1966)? "Sentence Babel" may actually be the fate of the American (and other) Sentences and weaken the view that a sentence "is a small, sealed vessel for holding meaning." Periods may, indeed, go dancing.[4]

Nevertheless, the American Sentence presents a history of American writing that alternates between high rhetoric and direct expression. To create the perfect sentence became an obsession as seen in the hero of William H. Gass's 2013 novel, *Middle C*. A supposed specialist in Arnold Schoenberg and atonal music, throughout the work Joseph Skizzen fixates on revising a single sentence: "The fear that the human race might not survive has been replaced by the fear that it will endure."[5] Variations of the sentence appear throughout the book in a quest for syntactic perfection but it is unobtainable: "[T]he sentence had simply passed through his ears and lodged in his head like a random bullet from a drive-by gang" (Gass 27). His alterations, however, are a metaphor of the writer's perpetual search for the exact expression of an idea, event or feeling. Skizzen, never satisfied, embodies the well-known anecdote of Oscar Wilde: at a country house, Wilde once told his hostess that he was working all morning on the proof of one of his poems and took out a comma. "And in the afternoon?" she asked. "In the afternoon, I put it back in."[6]

The narrative of the American Sentence has been the shift away from biblical oratory, scriptural typology, and cultural hegemony to the plain style, writing as a soloist, not a member of the chorus. Of course, there were exceptions—James, DeLillo, Pynchon, David Foster Wallace—but the preference was for syntactic independence, the current American Sentence emerging as a reaction against the enclosing, erudite, convoluted language of early American rhetoric. But such weighty syntax, clauses, and phrases clashed with modern American sensibilities and culture, although a hidden energy and tension of styles remained described by Joan Acocella. In her essay "Finding Augie March/ Saul Bellow," after quoting a lengthy sentence from *Augie March* on how Augie and a friend rode the elevator at City Hall for amusement "rubbing elbows with bigshots and operators, commissioners, grabbers, heelers, tipsters, hoodlums, wolves, [and] fixers," she writes that such sentences "occur on almost every page. They are like hall closets; you open them and everything falls out."[7] In this period of the 1950s, there was a need to reclaim the prewar experience of material excess expressed through abundant verbalization—in contrast to the later, spare, post-atomic style of a Raymond Carver, Cormac McCarthy, or Anne Tyler. Styles altered with the times; the times altered with style.[8]

But to replace creative sentences with OpenAI is a risky business as seen in the answer ChatGPT 4.0 offered to the following question asked in the summer of 2024: "What is the style of the modern American Sentence?" The answer appeared in approximately 5–7 seconds. The characteristics of the following additional four answers offer seemingly substantial, if abbreviated, declarative replies, although the answers to my fourth and fifth questions list books that have never been written (with one exception). The questions and answers:

1. "What is the style of the modern American Sentence?"

The style of the modern American sentence, as influenced by various literary and linguistic trends, can be characterized by several key features:

    1   **Clarity and Precision**: Modern American sentences often aim for clarity and directness. There is an emphasis on being

straightforward and avoiding unnecessary complexity. This style values sentences that convey meaning efficiently and clearly.

2. **Conciseness**: There is a tendency toward brevity. Unnecessary words are often omitted, and sentences are typically shorter. The goal is to be as succinct as possible while still conveying the intended message.

3. **Active Voice**: The use of active voice is preferred over passive voice. Active voice tends to be more direct and dynamic, making sentences more engaging and easier to understand.

4. **Informality**: Modern American writing can be informal, reflecting the conversational tone of spoken English. Contractions, colloquialisms, and a relaxed tone are common, especially in personal or less formal contexts.

5. **Variation in Sentence Structure**: While clarity and conciseness are valued, there is also an appreciation for variety in sentence structure. Mixing short, punchy sentences with longer, more complex ones can create a more engaging and dynamic text.

6. **Personal Voice**: There is a strong emphasis on individuality and personal voice. Writers often strive to make their unique style and perspective come through, even in more formal writing.

7. **Imagery and Sensory Details**: In narrative and descriptive writing, there is often a rich use of imagery and sensory details to create a vivid picture in the reader's mind.

8. **Adaptability**: The style can vary greatly depending on the context and audience. For example, technical writing will differ significantly from creative writing, but both will still reflect the overall trends toward clarity, conciseness, and engagement.

These elements together form the backbone of the modern American sentence, making it a flexible and effective tool for communication in a wide range of contexts.

2. "What is the style of the nineteenth-century American Sentence?" This answer is more informed

The style of the nineteenth-century American sentence is distinct from modern styles and can be characterized by several key features:

1. **Length and Complexity**: Sentences were often longer and more complex. Writers frequently used multiple clauses, creating elaborate and detailed structures that conveyed nuanced ideas and descriptions.
2. **Formal Tone**: The tone was generally more formal compared to modern writing. This formality reflected the conventions of the time and the influence of classical education on writing styles.
3. **Elaborate Descriptions**: There was a strong emphasis on descriptive language. Writers often used detailed and vivid descriptions to paint pictures with words, focusing on the sensory and the specific to evoke a clear image or mood.
4. **Ornate and Rhetorical Flourishes**: The use of rhetorical devices such as parallelism, anaphora, and antithesis was common. These flourishes added a sense of grandeur and artistry to the prose.
5. **Moral and Philosophical Reflection**: Sentences often contained moral, philosophical, or didactic reflections. Writers used their prose to explore deep and complex themes, reflecting the intellectual currents of the time.
6. **Subordination**: There was a frequent use of subordinate clauses, which added depth and complexity to sentences. This structure allowed for the exploration of multiple ideas and details within a single sentence.
7. **Period Style**: The period style often featured balanced sentences with a clear, rhythmic quality. This balance added a musicality to the prose, making it more engaging and memorable.

8. **Influence of Classical Literature**: Many writers were influenced by classical literature, which was reflected in their sentence construction. They often emulated the styles of ancient Greek and Roman authors, incorporating their techniques and rhetorical devices.

9. **Use of Passive Voice**: While the active voice was certainly present, the passive voice was also commonly used. This added to the formality and sometimes created a sense of objectivity or detachment.

10. **Introspection and Narration**: First-person introspection and detailed third-person narration were prevalent, allowing for deep character exploration and rich narrative development.

Authors like Nathaniel Hawthorne, Herman Melville, and Henry James exemplified these characteristics in their writing, creating works that were dense, richly textured, and intellectually engaging.

3. "What is the style of the eighteenth-century American Sentence?"

The style of the eighteenth-century American sentence reflects the literary and rhetorical conventions of the Enlightenment period, characterized by several distinct features:

1. **Formality and Eloquence**: The tone was highly formal and eloquent. Sentences often aimed to reflect the writer's education and intellectual sophistication, using elevated diction and complex syntax.

2. **Balanced and Periodic Structure**: Sentences frequently employed balanced and periodic structures, where the main clause or predicate is placed at the end of the sentence. This created a sense of anticipation and emphasis, often making the sentence more impactful.

3. **Complex Syntax**: Similar to the nineteenth century, sentences were often complex, with multiple subordinate clauses. This complexity allowed for detailed and nuanced expression of ideas.

4. **Rhetorical Devices**: The use of rhetorical devices such as parallelism, antithesis, and anaphora was common. These devices added a persuasive and ornate quality to the writing, reflecting the influence of classical rhetoric.

5. **Philosophical and Moral Reflections**: Sentences often contained philosophical and moral reflections, echoing the Enlightenment's emphasis on reason, ethics, and human nature. Writers used their prose to explore and convey complex ideas and principles.

6. **Expository and Argumentative Style**: Much of the writing was expository and argumentative, especially in political and philosophical texts. Sentences were crafted to persuade and inform, often presenting logical arguments and evidence in a structured manner.

7. **Politeness and Deference**: The style often included expressions of politeness and deference, reflecting the social norms and hierarchies of the time. This could involve elaborate courtesy phrases and respectful language.

8. **Use of Latin and Classical References**: Writers frequently incorporated Latin phrases and references to classical literature and history. This demonstrated their education and connected their ideas to a broader intellectual tradition.

9. **Ornate and Decorative Language**: The language was often ornate and decorative, with a preference for elaborate descriptions and flowery expressions. This added a sense of grandeur and beauty to the prose.

10. **Clarity and Precision**: Despite the complexity and formality, there was an emphasis on clarity and precision. Enlightenment writers aimed to communicate their ideas as clearly and logically as possible.

Authors like Benjamin Franklin, Thomas Jefferson, and Thomas Paine exemplified these characteristics in their writing, creating works that were intellectually rigorous, persuasive, and reflective of the cultural and intellectual milieu of the eighteenth century.

4. But then, this curious reply to "who has written the best history of the sentence?" curious because two of the four suggested titles do not exist

One of the most highly regarded books on the history of the sentence is "*The Art of Syntax: Rhythm of Thought, Rhythm of Song*" by Ellen Bryant Voigt. (**Valid**). In this book, Voigt, a poet and essayist, explores the structure and function of sentences in literature, combining analysis with examples from a wide range of literary texts. She delves into the rhythmic and musical qualities of sentences, offering insights into how syntax shapes meaning and emotional impact.

Another notable work is "*Verbal Style and the Genesis of Modernist Narrative*" by James Phelan, (**Invalid**). No title under this name) which examines the evolution of sentence style and narrative techniques in literature, particularly focusing on the transition to modernist writing. Phelan's analysis of sentence construction in different historical contexts provides a comprehensive overview of the changes in prose style over time.

For a broader historical and theoretical perspective, Stanley Fish's "*How to Write a Sentence: And How to Read One*" (**Valid**) is also influential. Fish, a literary theorist, not only provides a history of sentence styles but also offers practical advice on writing and appreciating well-crafted sentences.

While these works may not be a single comprehensive history of the sentence, they collectively provide a deep understanding of how sentence styles have evolved and how they function in various literary traditions.

5. And then, the answer to "Who has written the best history of the American Sentence?"

One of the most comprehensive and insightful books on the history of the American sentence is "*The American Sentence: Modernity and Style in the Age of New Deal Liberalism*" by Douglas Mao (**Invalid**). Mao, a prominent literary scholar, examines how American sentences have evolved, particularly in the context of twentieth-century modernist literature. He explores the impact of social, political, and cultural changes on sentence structure and style, offering a detailed analysis of how American writers have adapted and transformed their prose to reflect contemporary realities.

For a broader historical perspective that includes the evolution of the American sentence, you might consider *"A New History of the Sentence: The American Prose Tradition"* by Jeffrey F. Lavoie (**Invalid**). This book traces the development of the American sentence from the colonial period to the present, analyzing key texts and authors who have shaped the American prose style. Lavoie provides a thorough examination of the changes in syntax, diction, and rhetorical strategies across different literary periods.

While there may not be a single definitive "best" history of the American sentence, these works are highly regarded for their thorough research and insightful analysis, making significant contributions to our understanding of American prose style and its development.

All of these replies attempt breadth and comprehensiveness, although some of the titles are fabrications. The historical summaries select and evaluate useful characteristics, but when dealing with specifics, ChatGPT 4.0 is still shaky.

****

Is there a "Crises of the Sentence" as Jan Mieszkowski titles his 2019 study? The answer depends on what is meant by crisis. With the impact of AI and computer-generated sentences, the balance, creativity, and individuality of sentence writing are clearly in jeopardy. "Collaborative discourse" has become the new guide. Literary networks, redefinitions of canons, and the interactivity of electronic literature threaten the uniqueness of the writer. Social media facilitate the appearance of new kinds of writing and authors, creating questionable affordances, the qualities of an object that defines its possible uses.[9] The de-materializing of reading, turning it into a screen-oriented, electronic experience, has made literary curation on social media a medley of commentary and reference while creating entirely new communities of readers.

But even with the growth of AI-generated fiction and writing, there are still elements of writing sentences that remain, notably narrative energy, forms of expression that generate value. Emily Dickinson realized this when, in a letter of 1872 to her first cousin, Louisa Norcross, she wrote:

> Do you remember what you said the night you came to me? I secure that sentence. If I should see your face no more it will be your portrait, and if I should, more vivid than your mortal face .... A word left careless on a page May Consecrate an eye When folded in perpetual seam.[10]

A sentence read and kept resonates and gains emotional value. It resonates with its drama and meaning, substituting for one's presence. It supersedes the physical, generating a condition beyond even the written. The responsibility of every sentence is to state, to question and, for the reader, to remember.

The ambiguity often produced by grammar insures that the sentence continues off the page and beyond. In multiple ways. The sentence survives and so does language under scrutiny becoming in Dickinson's words, a "portrait."

And this is exactly what a sentence should do according to Gertrude Stein: "[A] sentence should force itself upon you, make you know yourself knowing it." With Steinian comedy, she adds that "I return to sentences as a refreshment."[11] Accompanying this position is a line from Joseph Joubert, quoted by Lydia Davis: "Everything that is exact is short ... because what is isolated can be seen better."[12] Exactness and precision are the goals. This extends to Davis's belief that there are two types of reading: immersive where the reader forgets herself and the self-conscious where the reader becomes self-consciously aware of the text, itself a visible object of interest by its language and form (Essays One 222–4). Such circumscribed writing may be a response to the "philosophical problem of seeing the written thing replace the subject of the writing" (Essays One 225). But it is attention to detail that matters, as Ezra Pound suggested: the "fundamental accuracy of statement is the ONE sole morality of writing," an aphorism Raymond Carver supposedly had pinned above his desk.[13]

But has the Americanness of the American Sentence endured? The answer in part is "yes" in its applicability to the American narrative, often incorporating dialect and regional features. The power of setting remains, whether Bellow's Chicago in *The Adventures of Augie March* (1953) or Hernan Diaz's New York in *Trust* (2022). The responsibilities of the American Sentence, recognized by American authors, continue as seen in Edward P. Jones's *The Known World* (2003), recently ranked #4 in *The New York Times* poll of the top works of literature of the twenty-first century and the highest ranking work of fiction by an American author on the list. It's nineteenth-century rural Virginia setting appropriates the American Sentence to a specific time and place, a dark and troubling period in American history just ahead of the Civil War.[14] And language itself becomes its subject.

Early in the novel, the ill and bedridden Black slave owner Henry Townsend is asked if he'd like to hear some Milton or the Bible? He tells his wife Caldonia that "'I been so weary of Milton,' adding that 'the Bible suits me better in the day, when there's sun and I can see what all God gave me'"[15] But at that moment, neither voice seems right. He prefers his own or that of his slaves, simple, direct, and plain. This is a novel about freedom bought and earned for the sentence as much as for the slaves, the sentence freed from the elaborate rhetoric of the Bible or the epic style of Milton. There is no hiding, rhetorically or otherwise, in the language of the South or plantation culture. Later, when Loretta, Henry's maid, tells Elias, another slave, that Henry has just died, he's skeptical. She replies with "He dead, thas all … I know dead when I see it, Elias. It don't put on a face to make look like nothin else but dead. Master dead" (KWorld 59). The impact of her two words and forceful delivery eliminate any doubt, underscored by repetition. But Elias does not understand, noting that he never heard Loretta use "Master" before. It "compelled [him] to repeat her words, as if to make it so once and for all. 'Master dead'" (KWorld 59). Language confirms reality.

The novel takes its title from a 300-year-old map hanging in the jail of a Virginia sheriff and reflects the backwardness of such a document. But metaphorically, it shows how sentences do double duty: they offer an archaeology of the past and a glimpse of the future, while incorporating the present, what the author writes and what the reader, reading, understands. At one point, even the slave Moses experiences this double-time: "[H]e was standing less than 10 feet from the spot where he would die one morning" (KWorld 125).

The structure of the novel parallels that of the American Sentence itself: the first half is about accumulation: of clauses, images, and elaborate syntax parallel with status, money, security through the lives of Henry Townsend, his wife, his parents, his slaves; the second half is of their decline and emergence of simplified, concise vocabulary marked by the unraveling of Townsend's legacy and the lives of the surviving characters. Sentences themselves have come undone as the novel struggles over the question of freedom, words syntactically escaping to freedom, much the way a woman, after diving into a well, was able to swim to freedom. Afterward, the owners would not permit access to the slaves, although "every slave on the place wanted to taste the water that gave a woman the power of a fish." The white people bricked it over after likely poisoning the water (KWorld 296).

Late in the novel, Sheriff Skiffington remarks that "he was beginning to feel that matters were getting beyond his control" (KWorld 322). Slaves disappear, violence flares, others die. The world had changed, and speech goes through another transformation testing the limits of formality and slang (see 330–1; 362). In the final pages, Mildred, protecting the slave Moses from Sheriff Skiffington, refuses to "surrender the property": "No more. No more men from here. No more men from anywhere. Not one more," she exclaims (KWorld 364). But her resilience meets death, accidentally (it seems) shot with a rifle. After a search in her house for the missing Moses, Counsel, Skiffington's cousin from North Carolina and his aide, announces in a biblical tone, "I found him not" (KWorld 369). In the moments that follow, he kills the sheriff with a single shot. The traditional rhetoric of the American Sentence, with its biblical overtones, has also been killed, leaving confusion, illustrated by the reaction of the sheriff's horse now "caught between wanting to be away from a dead man and wanting to be near its master" (KWorld 370).[16] Sentences are themselves in limbo, prompting one character to ask, "What are you meaning" (KWorld 372)? There is no simple answer.

At the center of this paradox between a conflicted narrative form and constantly changing sentence structures is prose which itself can be frustrating as Flaubert experienced:

> What a bitch of a thing prose is! It's never finished; there's always something to redo. Yet I think one can give it the consistency of verse. A good sentence in prose should be like a good line in poetry, *unchangeable*, as rhythmic, as sonorous.

Yet, he added, "[T]o be simple is no small matter."[17]

A sentence is always contingent, questioning and destabilizing fixed units, whether a clause, paragraph, chapter, or book of their structure and meaning. But while offering American prose new energy, even its impact can be chancy as a teacher explains to a student after a fistfight in *The Known World*: "[T]he hitter can never be the judge. Only the receiver of the blow can tell you how hard it was, whether it would kill a man or make a baby just yawn" (KWorld 181). Lethem's "The King of Sentences" may have been dethroned but not the impact of what he attempted.

****

The argument here has been that the elusive American Sentence, from its beginnings in the American Sermon to its treatment on both the large and small screen, has been shaped by four distinct forms of communication. Beginning with the sermon, one witnesses the shift from formal, Latinate, impressive structures spoken above the heads of the audience, to something approaching a direct "arrow to the heart" in an effort to speak *to* the assembled. Audience, rather than rhetoric, took control. One had to be understood before one could process the religious references, allusions, and meanings.

Extending the need to comprehend through clear expression, now reinforced by economics, was the telegraph where one paid by the word and sometimes the letter. Its importance was lasting becoming both the vehicle of new expressions, often abbreviated and in code, and a new style. It also became the subject of stories, poems, and even romance. An entire telegraph literature emerged which, in terms of style, crossed over to the newspaper and its emphasis on succinct expression. Again, no room to expand or to be prolix. Space was at a premium, mostly set aside for advertising revenue. News, especially crime news, had to be sharp, limited but exact, if not always accurate.

From newsprint to the screen was a natural progression as communication became quick and electric. The emergence of the screen, first in films, then the computer and most recently the smartphone meant adjustments to the American Sentence. Codes, a carry-over from the telegraph days, took the form of abbreviations that had odd and often indecipherable meanings.

The filmscript was an important influence where action needed to be conveyed through words as well as movement. This meant a curt, often incomplete style which the computer also promoted. Electronic transmission was fast and statements had to be quick, which the smartphone only intensified. In short, the sentence became unstable, impacted most recently by the effort of Generative AI where answers to complex questions appear in seconds, sometimes useful and sometimes not.

The drive for speed throughout all of these communication forms ties both the historical periods and methods of sharing together. News, gossip, information, bulletins, and alerts became normal while generating new forms of expression.

No paradigm for the American Sentence exists, simply a set of inputs that shape and pull at its form which constantly renews itself and offers new discoveries, much of them unknown. In many ways, it is a "time of suspense" as James writes in *The Golden Bowl* (1904) optimistically adding, however, that "the equilibrium, the precious condition, lasted in spite of rearrangement; there had been a fresh distribution of the different weights, but the balance persisted and triumphed."[18] The challenge of communication and style continues.

Notes

1   Lydia Davis in Grant Faulkner, *The Art of Brevity, Crafting the Very Short Story* (Albuquerque: University of New Mexico Press, 2023) 128, 129. Hereafter Brevity.

   Davis's work as a translator may have contributed to her awareness of individual sentences. Her translation of Proust's *Swann's Way* appeared in 2003, attempting to retain the original rhythms of the French syntax, trying to translate "comma for comma." She also has a passion for grammar and collects foreign grammars, often the subject of her short short stories. "Honoring the Subjunctive" and "Examples of a Continuing Past Tense in a Hotel Room," and "Grammar Question" are three. And in a 2018 interview, she explains that very few of her short stories are spontaneous. They benefit from revision, "a lot of revision! Changing one word and changing it back." See Davis in Lola Boorman, "'Honor the Syntax': An Interview with Lydia Davis," *Post45* October 22, 2018. https://post45.org/2018/10/honor-the-syntax-an-interview-with-lydia-davis/.

2   William Strunk and E.B. White, "Rule 14," *The Elements of Style*, 1918; 4th ed. (Boston: Allyn & Bacon, 2000) [19].

The original French, from Pascal's letter of 1657, reads "*Je n'ai fait celle-ci plus longue que parce que je n'ai pas eu le loisir de la faire plus courte.*" Translated, it reads "I have made this longer than usual because I have not had time to make it shorter." "If I had more time, I would have written a shorter letter" is the contemporary translation. QuoteInvestigaror, April 28, 2012. https://quoteinvestigator.com/2012/04/28/shorter-letter/. The website offers a list of other authors from Benjamin Franklin to John Locke and Mark Twain who provide variations of the statement.

3   Reading goals have become a new "sport." Nearly 8 million joined the Goodreads Reading Challenge (Goodreads is an Amazon subsidiary) in 2024, while StoryGraph, which sets out charts on data about top genres, and while the goal of ReadOn, launched by the London Libraries, is to make reading a habit. The key feature of ReadOn is that it allows you track your time spent reading not the number of books read. Ella Creamer, "Competitive Reading," *The Guardian* July 21, 2024. https://deal.town/the-guardian/should-you-set-reading-goals-bookmarks-FKCTD5YET2M.

4   Joe Moran, "Good Sentences Are Why We Read," *Literary Hub* August 30, 2019. https://lithub.com/good-sentences-are-why-we-read/?fbclid=IwAR0jdX649ml_K24Q3L8Dh0nYxbthOg-d2cBREkJzZiBZjZEYBMv64bCrCyc. This is an excerpt from *First You Write a Sentence, The Elements of Reading, Writing … and Life* (London: Penguin 2019). Also helpful is "Sentences" on the Language Hat blog: https://languagehat.com/?s=sentences and "Sentences" from the Language Log plus posts on Lingua Franca.

For a piece on the long sentence, see Gerald Murnane, "In Praise of the Long Sentence," *Meanjin*, Autumn 2016. https://meanjin.com.au/essays/in-praise-of-the-long-sentence/. The essay is partly a challenge to Frank Kermode and his review of Thomas Pynchon's *Vineland* and the long sentence.

The phrase "dancing periods" comes from Jackson Cope's discussion of Joseph Glanvill (1636–80) in Robert Adolph, *The Rise of Modern Prose Style* (Cambridge, MA: MIT Press, 1968) 81.

5   William H. Gass, *Middle C* (New York: Knopf, 2013) 22. Hereafter Gass.

6   Sources for the anecdote are varied; see John Cooper, "Oscar Wilde in America," https://www.oscarwildeinamerica.org/quotations/took-out-a-comma.html. Another variation: "in the morning I took out a comma, but on mature reflection, I put it back again." Ibid.

7   Joan Acocella, "Finding Augie March/ Saul Bellow," *Twenty-eight Artists and Two Saints: Essays* (New York: Pantheon, 2007) 388. *Augie*

appeared in 1953; Ellison's *The Invisible Man*, a novel of equal rhetorical power, the preceding year.

8   Today, there is a spare writing website (http://www.hiwrite.com/spare.html) and a One Sentence website, highlighting single sentences of literary merit (bendolnick@substack.com.). It also features titles of a minimalist nature such as Raymond Carver's "Bicycles, Muscles, Cigarettes," a short story.

9   On these developments, see Bronwen Thomas, *Literature and Social Media* (London: Routledge, 2020). Chapters 3 and 4 are especially useful.

10 Emily Dickinson to Louisa Norcross in Fiona Green "Scattered Effects," *TLS* August 16, 2024: 19. This is a review of the *Letters of Emily Dickinson* ed. Cristanne Miller and Domhnall Mitchell (Cambridge, MA: Harvard University Press, 2024).

11 Stein, "Poetry and Grammar," *Lectures in America* (1935; London: Virago, 1988) 221; "Sentences and Paragraphs," *How to Write* (West Glover, VT: Something Else Press, 1973) 26.

12 Joseph Joubert in Lydia Davis, "Fragmentary or Unfinished," *Essays One* ([1942]; Garden City, New York: Doubleday, 1956), ix.

13 Shaun Belcher, "Pound V Frost: Left V Right?" Dark Weather, November 18, 2014. https://shaunbelcher.com/writing/?p=978. Also see James Ley, "The Writers' Writer's Writing," *Sydney Review of Books* May 22, 2020. https://sydneyreviewofbooks.com/review/lydia-davis-essays/. Also Raymond Carver, "On Writing," *Fires: Essays, Poems, Stories* (Vintage Books, 1984) 23.

14 Formally titled "The 100 Best Books of the 21st Century," *The New York Times* July 14, 2024. Shaping the list were 503 writers and critics each asked to name the ten best books published since January 1, 2000. https://www.nytimes.com/interactive/2024/books/best-books-21st-century.html.

15 Edward P. Jones, *The Known World* (New York: Harper Collins, 2003) 6. Hereafter KWorld.

16 Alfred Kazin alluded to this paradox when he wrote in *On Native Grounds* that the most absorbing fact about "modern American writing" is "our writers' absorption in every last detail of their American world together with their deep and subtle alienation from it" (Kazin, *On Native Grounds, An Interpretation of Modern American Prose Literature* [1942; Garden City, NY: Doubleday,1956] ix).

17 Gustave Flaubert in Lydia Davis, "Flaubert's *Madame Bovary*," *Essays One* 335, 321.

18 Henry James, "The Golden Bowl," *Novels 1903–1911* (New York: Library of America, 2010) 477, 781.

Bibliography

Acocella, Joan. "Finding Augie March/ Saul Bellow," *Twenty-Eight Artists and Two Saints: Essays*. New York: Pantheon, 2007.
Adams Cable Codex. 7th ed. Boston, MA: E.A. Adams, 1894.
Adams, Henry. "The Education of Henry Adams," *Novels, Mont Saint Michel, The Education*, ed. Jane Samuels and Ernest Samuels. New York: Library of America, 1983. 715–1192.
Adorno, Theodore. "Punctuation Marks," tr. Shierry Weber Nicholsen, *Antioch Review* Vol.48 No.3 (1990): 300–5.
Agee, James. *A Death in the Family*. New York: Avon, 1966.
Allen, Roland. *The Notebook, a History of Thinking on Paper*. London: Profile Books, 2024.
Alter, Alexandra and Elizabeth A. Harris. "As Classic Novels Get Revised for Today's Readers, a Debate about Where to Draw the Line," *The New York Times*, April 5, 2023. https://www.nytimes.com/2023/04/03/books/classic-novels-revisions-agatha-christie-roald-dahl.html.
Alter, Robert. *Pen of Iron, American Prose and the King James Bible*. Princeton: Princeton University Press, 2010.
American Heritage Dictionary of the English Language. 5th ed. New York: Harper Collins, 2018. https://www.ahdictionary.com/word/search.html?q=sentence.
Anderson, Sam. "Stalking the Gramno," *New York Magazine*, February 27, 2008. https://nymag.com/arts/books/reviews/44616/.
Anon. "Theatres," *The Satirist or the Censor of the Times*, September 13, 1846: 294.
Armitage, Kay. "Gertrude Stein's Radical Grammar," *The Walrus*, February 12, 2007. https://thewalrus.ca/2007-02-language/.
Aschenbrenner, Leopold. "Situational Awareness, The Decade Ahead," 47. https://situational-awareness.ai/parting-thoughts/.
Baehr, Craig and Bob Schaller. *Writing for the Internet: A Guide to Real Communication in Virtua Space*. Westport, CT: Greenwood Press, 2010.
Bailey, Jefferson. "Disrespect Des Fonds: Rethinking Arrangement and Description in Born-Digital Archives," *Archive Journal*, 2013. https://web.archive.org/web/20170919162159/http://www.archivejournal.net/essays/

disrespect-des-fonds-rethinking-arrangement-and-description-in-born-digital-archives/.
Banville, John. *The Infinities*. London: Picador, 2009.
Barthelme, Donald. "Sentence," *New Yorker*, March 7, 1970. https://www.newyorker.com/magazine/1970/03/07sentences.
Barthes, Roland. "Flaubert and the Sentence," *New Critical Essays*, tr. Richard Howard. New York: Hill and Wang, 1980. 69–78.
Barthes, Roland. "Writing Degree Zero," *Writing Degree Zero and Elements of Semiology*, Preface by Susan Sontag. Boston, MA: Beacon Press, 1970. 1–88.
Beckett, Samuel. "Dante ... Bruno. Vico... Joyce," *Our Exagmination Round His Factification for Incamination of Work in Progress*. 1929; New York: New Directions, 1972.
Beckett, Samuel. *Waiting for Godot*. New York: Grove Press, 1982.
Belcher, Shaun. "Pound V Frost: Left V Right?" *Dark Weather*, November 18, 2014. https://shaunbelcher.com/writing/?p=978.
Bercovitch, Sacvan. *Puritan Origins of the American Self*. New Haven, CT: Yale University Press, 1975.
Bercovitch, Sacvan. *The American Jeremiad*. Madison: University of Wisconsin Press, 1978.
Bergengruen, Vera. "How Telegram Became the Digital Battlefield in the Russia-Ukraine War," *Time*, March 21, 2022. https://time.com/6158437/telegram-russia-ukraine-information-war/.
Bezanson, Walter. "Moby Dick: Work of Art," *Moby Dick*, Norton Critical Edition, 2nd ed., ed. Hershel Parker and Harrison Hayford. New York: Norton, 2001.
Bhatia, Aatish. "Watch an AI Learn to Write by Reading Nothing but Jane Austen," *The New York Times*, April 27, 2023. https://www.nytimes.com/interactive/2023/04/26/upshot/gpt-from-scratch.html?pgtype=Article&action=click&module=RelatedLinks/.
Bolter, Jay David. *Writing Space, the Computer, Hypertext, and the History of Writing*. Mahwah, NJ: Erlbaum Associates, 1991.
Borg, Jana Schaich, Vincent Conitzer and Walter Sinnott-Armstrong. *Moral AI and How We Get There*. London: Penguin, 2024.
Bovsun, Mara. "NYC Photographer Fatally Shoots Wife," *New York Daily News*, July 28, 2024.
Brand, Max (aka Frederick Faust). *The Notebooks and Poems of Max Brand*, ed. John Schoolcraft. New York: Dodd, Mead, 1957.
Bratton, Benjamin H. *The Stack: On Software and Sovereignty*. Cambridge, MA: MIT Press, 2016. https://doi.org/10.7551/mitpress.
Bridgman, Richard. *The Colloquial Style in America*. New York: Oxford University Press, 1966.
Brown, Keith and Jim Miller. *Syntax: A Linguistic Introduction to Sentence Structure*. 2nd ed. London: Routledge, 1994.
Burgess, Anthony. *Earthly Powers*. London: Hutchinson, 1980.
Burroughs, William S. *Rub Out the Words: The Letters of William S. Burroughs 1959–1974*, ed. Bill Morgan. New York: Ecco, 2012.

Burroughs, William S. *The Ticket That Exploded*. New York: Grove Press, 1967.
Burroughs, William S. and Brion Gysin. *Third Mind*. New York: Viking, 1978.
Bushman, Richard. *From Puritan to Yankee: Character and the Social Order in Connecticut 1690–1765*. Cambridge, MA: Harvard University Press, 1967.
Cain, Paul. *Fast One*. London: No Exit Press, 1989.
Cambridge Dictionary. https://dictionary.cambridge.org/dictionary/english/sentence.
Careau, Rachel in Joseph Schreiber. "You Who Have Loved Me: *Chéeri* and *The End of Chéri*," *Rough Ghosts*, June 9, 2022. https://roughghosts.com/2022/06/09/you-who-have-loved-me-cheri-and-the-end-of-cheri-by-colette-a-new-translation-by-rachel-careau/.
Carroll, R. S. *Studies in the Background and Practice of Prose Style in New England 1640–1750*. Cambridge, MA: Unpub. Harvard thesis, 1951.
Carson, Anne. *Decreation*. New York: Knopf, 2005.
Carson, Anne. "Love's Long Lost," *Red Doc>*. New York: Knopf, 2013. 14.
Carson, Anne. *Red Doc>*. New York: Knopf, 2013.
Carson, Anne. "Seated Figure with Red Angle (1988) by Betty Goodwin," *Decreation, Poetry Essays, Opera*. New York: Knopf, 2005. 95–101.
Carson, Anne. *Short Talks*. Kingston, ON: Brick Books, 1992.
Carson, Anne. "The Glass Essay," The Poetry Foundation. https://www.poetryfoundation.org/poems/48636/the-glass-essay.
Cather, Willa. "The Professor's House," *Later Novels*, ed. Sharon O'Brien. New York: Library of America, 1990. 99–271.
Chandler, Raymond. "Farewell, My Lovely," *Stories and Early Novels*, ed. Frank MacShane. New York: Library of America, 1995. 765–984.
Chandler, Raymond. "On English and American Style," *Later Novels and Other Writings*, ed. Frank MacShane. New York: Library of America, 1995. 1012–16.
Chandler, Raymond. "Red Wind," *Pulp Fiction: The Crimefighters*, ed. Otto Penzler, Intr. Harlan Coben. New York: Quercus, 2006. 189–229.
Chandler, Raymond. *Selected Letters of Raymond Chandler*, ed. Frank Macshane. New York: Columbia University Press, 1981. 159–60.
Chandler, Raymond. *The Glass Key*. London: Orion Books, 2002.
Chandler, Raymond. *The High Window*. New York: Vintage Books, 1976.
Chandler, Raymond. "The Simple Art of Murder," *Later Novels and Other Writings*, ed. Frank MacShane. New York: Library of America, 1995. 977–92.
Chandler, Raymond. "Trouble Is My Business," *Stories and Early Novels*, ed. Frank MacShane. 1934; New York: Library of America, 1995. 514–68.
"Character of Puritan Preaching, Part 4," Place for Truth, biblical doctrine from the Alliance of Confessing Evangelicals. https://www.placefortruth.org/blog/the-character-of-puritan-preaching-part-4.
Chase, Mary Ellen. *The Bible and the Common Reader*. London: Palgrave Macmillan, 1948.
Cmiel, Kenneth. "Broad Fluid Language of Democracy: Discovering the American Idiom," *Journal of American History* Vol.79 (1992): 913–36.
Cmiel, Kenneth. *Democratic Eloquence: The Fight over Popular Speech in Nineteenth-Century America*. New York: William Morrow, 1990.

Coe, Lewis. *The Telegraph*. Jefferson, NC: McFarland, 1993.
Cohen, Daniel A. *Pillars of Salt, Monuments of Grace, New England Crime Literature and the Origins of American Popular Culture, 1674–1860*. New York: Oxford University Press, 1993.
Cooper, John. "Oscar Wilde in America," https://www.oscarwildeinamerica.org/quotations/took-out-a-comma.html.
Danielewski, Mark Z. *House of Leaves*. 2nd ed. New York: Pantheon Books, 2000.
Danielewski, Mark. *Only Revolutions*. New York: Pantheon Books, 2006.
Davis, Frederick C. and Robert Sidney Bowen. "Memoirs," *Cheap Thrills: An Informal History of the Pulp Magazines,* ed. Ron Goulart. New Rochelle, NY: Arlington House, 1972. 190.
Davis, Lydia. "A Double Negative," *Samuel Johnson Is Indignant*. Brooklyn, NY: McSweeney's Books, 2001. 66.
Davis, Lydia. *Can't and Won't*. New York: Farrar, Straus and Giroux, 2014.
Davis, Lydia. "Index Entry," *Varieties of Disturbance*. New York: Farrar, Straus and Giroux, 2007. 199.
Davis, Lydia. "Suddenly Afraid," *Varieties of Disturbance*. New York: Farrar Straus Giroux, 2007. 189.
Davis, Lydia in Grant Faulkner. *The Art of Brevity: Crafting the Very Short Story*. Albuquerque: University of New Mexico Press, 2023.
De Barros, Deborah Paes. "Driving That Highway to Consciousness: Late Twentieth-Century American Travel Literature," *The Cambridge Companion to American Travel Writing*, ed. Alfred Bendixen and Judith Hamera. Cambridge: Cambridge University Press, 2009. 228–43.
DeLillo, Don. *Mao II*. New York: Viking, 1991.
DeLillo, Don. *Underworld*. New York: Scribner, 1997.
DeLillo, Don. *White Noise*. New York: Penguin, 1986.
DeWitt, Helen. "Entourage," *Some Trick*. New York: New Directions, 2018. 183–93.
DeWitt, Helen. *The Last Samurai*. London: Chatto and Windus, 2000.
Dickens, Charles. *Charles Dickens's Book of Memoranda.* Transcribed and annotated by Fred Kaplan. New York: New York Public Library, 1981.
Dickens, Charles. *Our Mutual Friend*. London: Chapman and Hall, 1865.
Dickens, Charles. *Pickwick Papers*, ed. Robert L. Patten. London: Penguin 1972.
Dickinson, Emily. "Tell All the Truth," Poetry Foundation. https://www.poetryfoundation.org/poems/56824/tell-all-the-truth-but-tell-it-slant-1263.
Didion, Joan. "On Keeping a Notebook," *Slouching Toward Bethlehem*, Intro. by Elizabeth Hardwick. New York: Modern Library, 2000. 117–26.
"Digital Composition, Storytelling & Multimodal Literacy," Stony Brook University.
Digital Dante. https://digitaldante.columbia.edu/dante/divine-comedy/.
Dillard, Annie. *The Abundance, Narrative Essays Old and New*. Forward Geoff Dyer. New York: Ecco/Harper Collins, 2016.

Dillard, Annie. "The Writing Life," *The Abundance*. New York: Ecco/ Harper Collins, 2016. 110.

Dos Passos, John. "The Camera Eye (28)," "1919," *U.S.A.* New York: Library of America, 1996. 368–70.

Duffy, Clare. "Woman Codes ChatGPT to Be Her Boyfriend," *CNN Business*, July 8, 2024. https://www.cnn.com/2024/07/08/business/video/ai-boyfriend-chatgpt-digvid.

Duffy, Enda. *The Speed Handbook: Velocity, Pleasure, Modernism*. Durham, NC: Duke University Press 2009.

Duncan, Dennis. *Index, A History of the*. New York: Norton, 2023.

Dunne, Philip in Pat McGilligan. "Screenwriters of the Golden Age," *Los Angeles Times*, December 28, 1986.

Dydo, Ulla E. with William Rice. "1928–30: Grammar," *Gertrude Stein: The Language That Rises 1923–1934*. Evanston, IL: Northwestern University Press, 2003.

Electric Telegraph, an Historical Anthology, ed. George Shiers. New York: Arro Press, 1977.

Elliott, Emory. *Power and the Pulpit in Puritan New England*. Princeton: Princeton University Press, 1975.

Ellison, Ralph. *Going to the Territory.* New York: Vintage Books, 1987.

Ellison, Ralph. *Invisible Man*. 1952; New York: Modern Library, 1994.

Ellison, Ralph. *Selected Letters*, ed. John Callahan and Marc C. Conner. New York: Random House, 2019.

Emerson, Ralph Waldo. *Journal*, June 1840 in Gay Wilson Allen, "Plain Talk from Ralph Waldo Emerson," *American Heritage* Vol. 37 No.4 (June/July 1986). https://www.americanheritage.com/plain-talk-ralph-waldo-emerson.

Emerson, Ralph Waldo. "The Poet," *Essays Second Series* (1844) 21. Emerson Central. https://emersoncentral.com/ebook/The%20Poet.pdf.

Emre, Merve. "Introduction to the New Edition," John Guillory, *Cultural Capital*. Chicago, IL: University of Chicago Press, 1993. vii–xxxi.

Emre, Merve. *Paraliterary: The Making of Bad Readers in Postwar America*. Chicago, IL: University of Chicago Press, 2017.

Fante, John. *Ask the Dust*. 1939; New York: Harper Perennial, 2006.

Feidelson, Charles Jr. *Symbolism and American Literature*. Chicago, IL: University of Chicago Press, 1953.

Fenelon, Felix. *Novels in Three Lines*, tr. Luc Sante. New York: New York Review Books, 2007.

Fisher, Anne and Anne Fisher. *A Practical New Grammar*. London, 1759 in Cynthia Wall, *Grammars of Approach, Landscape, Narrative, and the Linguistic Picturesque*. Chicago, IL: University of Chicago Press, 2019.

Fishkin, Shelley Fisher. *From Fact to Fiction: Journalism & Imaginative Writing in America.* Baltimore, MD: Johns Hopkins University Press, 1985.

Fitzgerald, F. Scott. *The Great Gatsby*. New York: Scribner's, 1925.

Flaubert, Gustave in Lydia Davis. "Flaubert's *Madame Bovary*," *Essays One*. New York: Farrar, Straus and Giroux, 2019. 321–41.

Fleming, John Ambrose. *Wireless Telegraphist's Pocket Book of Notes, Formulae and Calculations*. Glasgow: Wireless Press, 1915.

Foucault, Michel. "Appendix, the Discourse on Language," *The Archeology of Knowledge and the Discourse on Language*, tr. A. M. Sheridan Smith. New York: Pantheon, 1972. 214–16.

"Framing Theory," Communication Studies. https://www.communicationstudies.com/communication-theories/framing-theory.

Francescani, Chris. "'Killer' Librarian Retiring after 34 Years," *Suffolk Times*, August 8, 2024: 1.

Franklin, Benjamin. "Autobiography," *Autobiography, Poor Richard, and Later Writings*, ed. J. A. Leo Lemay. New York: Library of America, 1997. 525–729.

"From Australia to Zimmermann: A Brief History of Cable Telegraphy during WWI," Part of Innovating in Combat: Telecommunications and Intellectual Property in the First World War. https://blogs.mhs.ox.ac.uk/innovatingincombat/files/2013/03/Innovating-in-Combat-educational-resources-telegraph-cable-draft_FIN.pdf.

Frost, Robert. "Interview," with William Stanley Braithwaite. *Boston Evening Transcript*, May 8, 1915. https://udallasclassics.org/wp-content/uploads/maurer_files/Frost.pdf.

Gass, William H. *Middle C*. New York: Knopf, 2013.

Gibson, Walker. *Tough, Sweet & Stuffy, an Essay on Modern American Prose Styles*. Bloomington: Indiana University Press, 1966.

Glanville, Joseph. *An Essay Concerning Preaching*. London, 1678.

Gleick, James. *The Information: A History, a Theory, a Flood*. New York: Pantheon, 2011.

Glück, Louise. "Ersatz Thought," *American Originality: Essays on Poetry*. New York: Farrar, Strauss and Giroux, 2017.

Gorbach, Julian. *Notorious Ben Hecht*. West Lafayette, IN: Purdue University Press, 2019.

Gowing, Georgia. "Reading on Screens Instead of Paper Is Less Effective Way to Absorb and Retain Information, Suggests Research." *Phys Org*, February 6, 2024. https://phys.org/news/2024-02-screens-paper-effective-absorb-retain.html.

"Grammar and Syntax," *Telegraph Style Guide*, January 23, 2018. https://www.telegraph.co.uk/style-book/grammar-and-syntax/.

Griffin, Peter. *Along with Youth: Hemingway, the Early Years*. New York: Oxford University Press, 1985.

Guillemin, Amédée. "Telegraphic Apparatus for Rapid Transmission," rev. and ed. Silvanus P. Thompson, *Electric Telegraph, an Historical Anthology*. New York: Arno Press, 1977. 625–56.

Guillory, John. *Cultural Capital*. 1993; Chicago, IL: University of Chicago Press, 2023.

Guillory, John. "How Scholars Read," *ADE Bulletin* Vol.146 (Fall 2008): 11.

Guillory, John. "Mercury's Words: The End of Rhetoric and the Beginning of Prose," *Representations* Vol.138 (2017): 59–86.

Guillory, John. *Professing Criticism: Essays on the Organization of Literary Study*. Chicago, IL: University Chicago Press, 2022.

Guillory, John. "The Memo and Modernity," *Critical Inquiry* Vol.31 (2004): 108–32.

Hammett, Dashiell in Anne Diebel. "Dashiell Hammett's Strange Career," *Paris Review*, September 14, 2018. https://www.theparisreview.org/blog/2018/09/14/dashiell-hammetts-strange-career/.

Hammett, Dashiell. *Red Harvest*. New York: Vintage Books, 1972.

Hammett, Dashiell. *The Glass Key*. London: Orion Books, 2002.

Hammett, Dashiell. *The Maltese Falcon*. New York: Vintage Books, 1992.

Hardwick, Elizabeth. "Billie Holiday," *New York Review of Books*, March 4, 1976. https://www-nybooks-com.eu1.proxy.openathens.net/articles/1976/03/04/billie-holiday/.

Hardwick, Elizabeth. "Grub Street, New York," *The Collected Essays of Elizabeth Hardwick*, sel. Darryl Pinckney. New York: New York Review of Books, 2017. 125–9.

Hardwick, Elizabeth. *Sleepless Nights*. 1979; New York: Vintage Books, 1980

Hardwick, Elizabeth. "Wives and Mistresses," *Collected Essays of Elizabeth Hardwick*, sel. Darryl Pinckney. New York: New York Review of Books, 2017. 174–93.

Hardwick, Elizabeth in Brian Dillon. *Suppose a Sentence*. New York: New York Review of Books, 2020.

Hayles, N. Katherine. *How We Became Posthuman: Virtual Bodes in Cybernetics, Literature and Informatics.* Chicago, IL: University of Chicago Press, 1999.

Hayles, N. Katherine. "How We Read: Close, Hyper, Machine," *ADE Bulletin*, New York: ADE Bulletin, 2010. 150.

Hecht, Ben. "Man Hunt," *A Thousand and One Afternoons in Chicago*. Chicago, IL: Covici Friede, 1927. 35–8.

Hecht, Ben and Charles McArthur. *The Front Page*. Chicago, IL: Covici Friede, 1928.

Hemingway, Ernest. *A Farewell to Arms*. 1929; London: Jonathan Cape, 1933.

Hemingway, Ernest. *Death in the Afternoon.* New York: Scribner's, 1932.

Hendrickson, Paul. *Hemingway at Eighteen*. Chicago, IL: Chicago Review Press, 2018.

Heschel, Abraham Joshua. "What We Might Do Together," *American Sermons: The Pilgrims to Martin Luther King, Jr*. New York: Library of America, 1999. 865–7.

Hobart, Michael E. and Zachary S. Schiffman. *Information Ages: Literacy, Numeracy and the Computer Revolution.* Baltimore, MD: Johns Hopkins University Press, 1998.

Hochfelder, David. *The Telegraph in America 1832–1920.* Baltimore, MD: Johns Hopkins University Press, 2012.

Hoffman, Adina. *Ben Hecht, Fighting Words, Moving Pictures*. New Haven, CT: Yale University Press, 2019.

"Hold Divorcee as Slayer of Auto Salesman," *Chicago Tribune*, June 6, 1924.
Howe, Susan. *My Emily Dickinson*. Berkeley, CA: North Atlantic Books, 1985.
Howe, Susan. "Secret History of the Dividing Line," *Frame Structures: Early Poems 1974-1979*. New York: New Directions, 1996.
Howe, Susan. "Where Should the Commander Be?" *Writing* Vol.19 (Vancouver) November 1987: 3–20; rpt. *The Quarry: Essays. New York*: New Directions, 2015.
Hughes, Langston. "Poor Little Black Fellow," *The Ways of White Folks*. 1934; New York: Knopf, 1969. 155.
Huxley, Aldous. "Wanted, a New Pleasure," *Aldous Huxley: Complete Essays* Vol. 3, ed. Robert S. Baker and James Sexton. Chicago, IL: Ivan R. Dee, 2001. 260–3.
"Influence of the Telegraph upon Literature," *Democratic Review* Vol.22 (May 1848): 409–13.
Ito, Joi and Jeff Howe. *Whiplash: How to Survive Our Faster Future*. New York: Grand Central Publishing, 2016.
Jabr, Ferris. "The Reading Brain in the Digital Age: The Science of Paper versus Screens," *Scientific American*, April 11, 2013. https://www.scientificamerican.com/article/reading-paper-screens/.
James, Henry. "Daniel Deronda," *The Nation*, February 24, 1876: 131. Unsigned review.
James, Henry. "The Portrait of a Lady," *Novels 1881–1886*, ed. William T. Stafford. New York: Library of America, 1985. 191–800.
Jin, Dai Yong. *Artificial Intelligence in Cultural Production: Critical Perspectives on Digital Platforms*. London: Routledge, 2021.
John Milton Reading Room. https://milton.host.dartmouth.edu/reading_room/pl/intro/text.shtml.
Jones, Edward P. *The Known World*. New York: Amistad, 2003.
Jones, Howard Mumford. "American Prose Style 1700–1770," *Huntington Library Bulletin* No. 6 (November 1934): 115–51.
Jonson, Ben. "The English Grammar," *The Works of Ben Jonson* Vol.7 (1756).
Joubert, Joseph in Lydia Davis. "Fragmentary or Unfinished," *Essays One*. New York: Farrar, Straus, Giroux, 2019. 204–25.
Joyce, James to Harriet Shaw Weaver, November 24, 1926. *Selected Letters of James Joyce*, ed. Richard Ellmann. New York: Viking Press, 1975.
Joyce Project. https://www.joyceproject.com/.
Justice, Donald. "For the Suicides of 1962," *Poetry* Vol.105 No.6 (1965): 350.
Kanderovskis, Karlis. "Telegraph," University of Chicago Theories of Media, Keywords Glossary, 2007. https://csmt.uchicago.edu/glossary2004/telegraph.htm.
Kazin, Alfred. *On Native Grounds*. 1942; Garden City, NY: Doubleday, 1956.
Kelly, Samantha Murphy. "Hollywood Stars' Estates Agree to the Use of Their Voices with AI," *CNN Business*, July 3, 2024. https://www.cnn.com/2024/07/03/tech/elevenlabs-ai-celebrity-voices/index.html.

Kerouac, Jack. "On the Road," *Road Novels 1957–1960*, ed. Douglas Brinkley. New York: Library of America, 2007. 3–278.

Kingson, S. "Structured Authoring: A Guide for Content Creators," *Document 360*, February 29, 2024. https://document360.com/blog/structured-authoring/.

Kipling, Rudyard. *Letters of Rudyard Kipling, Volume 3: 1900–1910*, ed. Thomas Pinney. London: Palgrave Macmillan, 1995.

Knight, Lucy. "From Books to Bot, Bookmarks," *The Guardian*, July 14, 2021. info@editorial.theguardian.com.

Koestenbaum, Wayne. "'Every Gesture Is Gloved:' Wayne Koestenbaum on Elizabeth Hardwick," Pen America, Blog PEN America, Blog, November 17, 2007. http://penamerica.blogspot.com/2007/12/every-gesture-is-gloved-wayne.html.

Kretzoi, Charlotte. "Attitude and Form: Puritan Style in 17th Century American Prose," *Hungarian Studies in English* Vol.14 (1981): 57–68.

Kurzweil, Ray. *The Singularity Is Near*. New York: Viking, 2005.

Kurzweil, Ray. *The Singularity Is Nearer: When We Merge with AI*. New York: Viking, 2024.

Landow, George P. *Hypertext 3.0: Critical Theory and New Media in an Era of Globalization*. Baltimore, MD: Johns Hopkins University Press, 2006.

Lanham, Richard A. *The Electronic Word, Democracy, Technology, and the Arts*. Chicago, IL: University of Chicago Press, 1993.

Lapore, Jill. *A Is for American: Letters and Other Characters in the Newly United States*. New York: Knopf, 2002.

Latour, Bruno. "On Technical Mediation: Philosophy, Sociology, Geneaology," *Common Knowledge* Vol.3 No.2 (1994): 29–64.

Lawrence, David Herbert *Studies in Classic American Literature*. 1923; New York: Viking, 1964.

Lawrence, Neil D. *The Atomic Human: Understanding Ourselves in the Age of AI*. London: Penguin, 2024.

Lee, Kevan. "The Definitive List of Social Media Acronyms and Abbreviations, Defined," March 27, 2023. https://buffer.com/library/social-media-acronyms-abbreviations/.

Leech, Geoffrey and Mick Short. *Style in Fiction: A Linguistic Introduction to English Fictional Prose*. 2nd ed. London: Routledge, 2007.

Lemke, Sieglinde. *The Vernacular Matters of American Literature.* New York: Palgrave Macmillan, 2009.

Lethem, Jonathan. *Motherless Brooklyn*. 1999; New York: Vintage Books, 2000.

Liu, Alan. "N + 1: A Plea for Cross-Domain Data in the Digital Humanities," *Debates in the Digital Humanities.* Minneapolis: University of Minnesota Press, 2016. 559–68.

Liu, Alan. "Palinurus." http://palinurus.english.ucsb.edu/index2.html.

Liu, Alan. "Voice of the Shuttle." https://teachinghistory.org/history-content/website-reviews/22869.

Lorentzen, Christian. "Lewis Lapham Knew That a Great Editor Was an Artful Thief," *The Washington Post*, July 26, 2024. https://www.washingtonpost.com/books/2024/07/26/lewis-lapham-appraisal/.

Love, Glenn A. "*The Professor's House*: Cather, Hemingway and the Chastening of American Prose Style," *Western American Literature* Vol.24 No.4 (1990): 295–311.

Lutz, Garielle. "The Sentence Is a Lonely Place," *The Believer* Vol.59 (January 2009). www.thebeliever.net/the-sentence-is-a-lonely-place.

Macdonald, Ross. *Self-Portrait*. Santa Barbara, CA: Capra Press, 1981.

Maclean, Norman. *A River Runs through It and Other Stories*. Chicago, IL: University of Chicago Press, 1976.

Mailer, Norman. *An American Dream*. London: Andre Deutsch, 1965.

Mailer, Norman. "Introduction to the 50th Anniversary Edition [of *The Naked and the Dead*]," *The Naked and the Dead & Selected Letters 1945–1946*, ed. J. Michael Lennon. New York: Library of America, 2023. 796–7.

Mailer, Norman. *Miami and the Siege of Chicago*. 1968; New York: New York Review Books, 2008.

Mailer, Norman. "On Lies, Power, and Obscenity," *Mind of an Outlaw: Selected Essays*, ed. Phillip Sipiora. Intr. Jonathan Lethem. New York: Random House, 2013. 28–32.

Manguel, Alberto. *A History of Reading*. New York: Knopf, 1996.

Manning, Molly Guptill. *The War of Words: How America's GI Journalists Battled Censorship and Propaganda to Help Win World War II*. Ashland, OR: Blackstone, 2023.

Mantel, Hilary. *Wolf Hall*. New York: Henry Holt, 2009.

Marx, Leo. *The Machine in the Garden*. New York: Oxford University Press, 1964.

Mather, Increase. *The Puritans*, ed. Perry Miller and Thomas H. Johnson. Rev. ed. New York: Harper and Row, 1963. II.

McCarthy, Cormac. *The Orchard Keeper*. London: Andre Deutsch, 1966.

McCarthy, Cormac. *The Road*. New York: Vintage Books, 2006.

McGurl, Mark. *The Program Era: Postwar Fiction and the Rise of Creative Writing*. Cambridge, MA: Harvard University Press, 2011.

McLuhan, Marshall. "Effect of the Printed Book on Language in the 16th Century," *Explorations* 7 (1957) rpt. in *Marshall McLuhan Unbound*, ed. Eric Mcluhan and W. Terrence Gordon. Richmond, CA: Gingko Press, 2005. 99–108.

McWhorter, John. "The Softening of American Conversation," *The New York Times*. August 27, 2021. https://www.nytimes.com/2021/08/27/opinion/uptalk-English-language-coarsening.html.

Melville, Herman. "Moby Dick," *Redburn, White-Jacket, Moby Dick*, ed. G. Thomas Tanselle. New York: Library of America, 1983. 771–1408.

Melville, Herman. "White-Jacket," *Herman Melville, Redburn, White-Jacket, Moby-Dick*, ed. G. Thomas Tanselle. New York: Library of America, 1983. 341–770.

Menke, Richard. *Telegraphic Realism*. Stanford, CA: Stanford University Press, 2008.

Messent, Peter and Louis J. Buddy, eds. *A Companion to Mark Twain*. Malden, MA: Blackwell, 2005.

Metz, Rachel. "OpenAI Scale Ranks Progress toward 'Human-Level' Problem Solving," *Bloomberg News*, July 11, 2024. https://www.bloomberg.com/news/articles/2024-07-11/openai-sets-levels-to-track-progress-toward-superintelligent-ai.

Meyer, Nicholas. *Sherlock Holmes and the Telegram from Hell*. New York: Penzler Publishers, 2024.

Meyers, B. R. "A Reader's Manifesto," *Atlantic*, July/August 2001. https://www.theatlantic.com/magazine/archive/2001/07/a-readers-manifesto/302270/.

Mieszkowski, Jan. *Crises of the Sentence*. Chicago, IL: University of Chicago Press, 2019.

Miller, Henry. *Henry Miller on Writing*, sel. Thomas H. Moore. New York: New Directions, 1964.

Miller, Henry. *The Air-Conditioned Nightmare* in Norman Mailer, *Genius and Lust: A Journey through the Major Writings of Henry Miller*. New York: Grove Press, 1976.

Miller, Perry. "An American Language," *Nature's Nation*. Cambridge, MA: Belknap, 1967. 208–40.

Miller, Perry. "Declension in a Bible Commonwealth," *Nature's Nation*. Cambridge, MA: Belknap Press, 1967. 14–49.

Millie. "Black Mask Magazine," *Dark and Stormy Night Mysteries*, May 14, 2014. https://darkandstormynightmysteries.com/wordpress/?p=838.

Moran, Joe. *First You Write a Sentence: The Elements of Reading, Writing ... and Life*. London: Penguin, 2019.

Moran, Joe. "Good Sentences Are Why We Read," *Literary Hub*, August 30, 2019. https://lithub.com/good-sentences-are-why-we-read/?fbclid=IwAR0jdX649ml_K24Q3L8Dh0nYxbthOg-d2cBREkJzZiBZjZEYBMv64bCrCyc.

Murnane, Gerald. "In Praise of the Long Sentence," *Meanjin*, Autumn 2016. https://meanjin.com.au/essays/in-praise-of-the-long-sentence/.

Museum of Global Communications, Porthcurno, Cornwall, UK. https://pkporthcurno.com/.

Muzny, Grace, Mark Algree-Hewitt, Dan Jurafsky. "Dialogism in the Novel: A Computational Model of the Dialogic Nature of Narration and Quotations," *Digital Scholarship in the Humanities* Vol.32 No.2 (December 2017): ii31–ii52. https://doi.org/10.1093/llc/fqx031. Detailed, algorithmic analysis of dialogue https://academic.oup.com/dsh/article/32/suppl_2/ii31/3978683.

Nashe, Thomas. *The Unfortunate Traveller*. Intro. by Edmund Gosse. London: Chiswick Press, 1892. Project Gutenberg. https://www.gutenberg.org/files/21338/21338-h/21338-h.htm.

Nelson, Paul E. *American Sentences: One Sentence, Every Day, Fourteen Years* (2015). https://www.paulenelson.com/wp-content/uploads/2014/12/1.-American-Sentences-MS-10.27.14.pdf.

New York Herald Tribune Books, August 23, 1942: 17 in a review of Chandler's *The High Window*.

Nickles, David Paul. *Under the Wire: How the Telegraph Changed Diplomacy*. Cambridge, MA: Harvard University Press, 2003.

Norris, Frank. *The Octopus: A Story of California*. Garden City, NY: Doubleday, Page, 1903.

O'Grady, William. *Syntactic Carpentry*. Mahwah, NJ: Erlbaum Associates, 2005.

O'Toole, Garson. "Briefest Correspondence," *Quote Investigator*, June 14, 2014. https://quoteinvestigator.com/?s=Brief+correspondence.

Ofgang, Erik. "The Screen Inferiority Effect: How Screens Affect Reading Comprehension," December 4, 2023. Tech & Learning. https://www.techlearning.com/news/the-screen-inferiority-effect-how-screens-affect-reading-comprehension.

Ong, Walter J. *Orality and Literacy: The Technologizing of the Word*. London: Methuen, 1982.

Pascal, Blaise. Lettres Provinciales (1657) in Quote Investigator. https://quoteinvestigator.com/2012/04/28/shorter-letter/#google_vignette.

Pepperell, Robert. *The Post-Human Condition*. 2nd ed. Bristol: Intellect Books, 1997.

Perelman, Bob. "Parataxis and Narration: The New Sentence in Theory and Practice," *American Literature* Vol.65 No.2 (1993): 313–24.

Peterson, Britt. "The Golden Age of Telegraph Literature," *Slate*, November 11, 2014. https://slate.com/technology/2014/11/telegraph-literature-from-19th-century-was-surprisingly-modern.html.

Phelps, Robert. *Belles Saisons: A Colette Scrapbook*. New York: Farrar, Straus and Giroux, 1978.

"*Philadelphia Story Script*—Dialogue transcript," http://www.script-o-rama.com/movie_scripts/p/philadelphia-story-script-transcript-hepburn.html.

Phillips, Ronnie. "Digital Technology and Institutional Change … The Impact of the Telegraph and the Internet," *Journal of Economic Issues* Vol.34 No.2 (2000): 267–89.

Picasso, Pablo in Grant Faulkner. *The Art of Brevity*. Albuquerque: University of New Mexico Press, 2023.

Poirier, Richard. *A World Elsewhere: The Place of Style in American Literature*. New York: Oxford University Press, 1966.

Praet, Yoran. "Screenwriting 101: The History of Screenwriting," *Arcadia* February 5, 2023. https://www.byarcadia.org/post/screenwriting-101-the-history-of-screenwriting.

"Preface," *The Adams Cable Codex*, 7th ed. Boston, MA: E.A. Adams, 1894.

Price, Richard. *Lush Life*. New York: Farrar, Straus and Giroux, 2008.

Pulp Magazine Project. https://www.pulpmags.org/index.htm.

Pynchon, Thomas. *Gravity's Rainbow*. 1973; New York: Bantam, 1974.
Review, "Paul Cain, *Fast One*," *The New York Times*, October 19, 1933.
Roberson, Susan. *Emerson in His Sermons: A Man-Made Self*. Columbia: University of Missouri Press, 1995.
Robinson, Ian. *The Establishment of Modern English Prose in the Reformation and the Enlightenment*. Cambridge: Cambridge University Press, 1998.
Rosenkrantz, Linda. *Telegram! Modern History as Told through More than 400 … Telegrams*. New York: Henry Holt, 2003.
Ross, Nelson E. "How to Write Telegrams Properly," (1928) at "The Telegraph Office." https://web.archive.org/web/20170315175434fw_/http://www.telegraph-office.com/pages/telegram.html.
Roth, Philip. *Deception*. New York: Vintage Books, 1990.
Roth, Philip. *Nemesis*. Boston, MA: Houghton Mifflin, 2010.
Roth, Philip. *Philip Roth at 80.*. New York: Library of America, 2014.
Roth, Philip. *The Counterlife*. New York: Farrar, Straus and Giroux, 1986.
Rougeux, Nicholas. *Between the Words: Exploring the Punctuation in Literary Classics*. Poster, 2016. https://www.c82.net/work/?id=347.
Ruttenburg, Nancy. *Democratic Personality: Popular Voice and the Trial of American Authorship*. Stanford, CA: Stanford University Press, 1998.
Ryken, Leland. *Worldly Saints: The Puritans as They Really Were*. Grand Rapids, MI: Zondervan, 1986.
Said, Edward in Frank Lentricchia. *After the New Criticism*. Chicago, IL: Chicago: University of Chicago Press, 1980.
Salinger, Jerome David. "A Girl I Knew," *Good Housekeeping* Vol.126 No.37 (February 1, 1948): 186–96.
Salle, David in Janet Malcolm. "Forty-One False Starts," *Forty-One False Starts: Essays on Artists and Writers*. New York: Farrar, Straus and Giroux, 2013. 37–8.
Salter, James. *Light Years*. New York: Random House, 1975.
Saul Bellow. *Adventures of Augie March*. New York: Viking, 1953.
Sawday, Jonathan. *Blanks, Print, Space and Void in English Renaissance Literature: An Archaeology of Absence*. Oxford: Oxford University Press, 2024.
Schiferli, Victor. "Marga Minco … Dies at 103," *The New York Times*, July 15, 2023. https://www.nytimes.com/2023/07/15/books/marga-minco-dead.html?action=click&module=Well&pgtype=Homepage§ion=Obituaries.
Schweiger, Beth Barton Schweiger. "A Social History of English Grammar in the Early United States," *Journal of the Early Republic* Vol.30 No.4 (2010): 533–55.
Scott, Donald M. "Print and the Public Lecture System, 1840–60," *Printing and Society in Early America*, ed. William L. Joyce, *et al*. Worcester, MA: American Antiquarian Society, 1983. 278–99.
Silliman, Ron. *The New Sentence*. New York: Roof Books, 1987.
Simpson, Hannah. "Samuel Beckett and the Nobel *Catastrophe*," *Samuel Beckett Today* Vol.30 No.2 (2018): 337–52.
Simpson, Natalie. *What Is a Sentence: Gertrude Stein and Sentence Theory*, MA thesis University of Calgary (May 2001): 9. https://prism.ucalgary.ca/server/api/core/bitstreams/c4baef91-1ec3-4ec7-bfc1-74783440fe3b/content.

Sittenfeld, Curtis. "ChatGPT vs. Me: Who Will Write a Better Beach Read?" *The New York Times*, July 9, 2024. https://www.nytimes.com/2024/07/09/opinion/chatgpt-beach-read.html.
Smith, Ali. "Being Quick," *The Whole Story and Other Stories*. London: Hamish Hamilton, 2003. 23–43.
Smith, Erin A. *Hard Boiled: Working Class Readers and Pulp Magazines*. Philadelphia, PA: Temple University Press, 2000.
Smith, Henry. "A Glass for Drunkards," *The Works of Henry Smith, Including Sermons, Treatises, Prayers, and Poems*, Vol.I. Edinburgh: James Nichol, 1866. 304–5. https://dn790008.ca.archive.org/0/items/worksofhenrysmit01smit/worksofhenrysmit01smit.pdf.
Smith, Henry Justin. "Preface," Hecht, *A Thousand and One Afternoons in Chicago*. Chicago, IL: Covici Friede, 1927. i–v.
Smith, Zadie. *Swing Time*. London: Hamish Hamilton, 2016.
Sontag, Susan. "The Aesthetics of Silence," *Styles of Radical Will*, ed. Sontag. New York: Farrar, Strauss and Giroux, 1969. 3–33.
Sontag, Susan. "The Conscience of Words," *At the Same Time: Essays and Speeches*, ed. Paolo Dilonardo and Anne Jump, Foreword by David Rieff. New York: Farrar, Straus and Giroux, 2007. 145–55.
Sorrentino, Gilbert. *Mulligan's Stew*. New York: Grove Press, 1979.
Spahr, Juliana. *Du Bois's Telegram*. Cambridge, MA: Harvard University Press, 2018.
Spillane, Mickey. "One Lonely Night," *The Hammer Strikes Again*, ed. Mickey Spillane. New York: Avenel Books, 1989. 1–172.
Staiger, Janet. "Blueprints for Feature Films: Hollywood's Continuity Script," *The American Film Industry*, ed. Tino Balio. Madison: University of Wisconsin Press, 1976. 173–92.
Staiger, Janet. "The Hollywood Mode of Production to 1930," *The Classical Hollywood Cinema*, ed. David Bordwell, *et al.* London: Routledge, 1985. 271–8.
Standage, Tom. *The Victorian Internet*. New York: Walker, 1998.
Steele, Joseph. "A Classical Analysis of Puritan Preaching," *Reformation 21*, August 23, 2010. https://www.reformation21.org/articles/a-classical-analysis-of-puritan-preaching.php.
Stein, Gertrude. "A Grammarian," *How to Write*. 1931; West Glover, VT, and New York: Something Else Press, 1973. 109–18.
Stein, Gertrude in Donald Sutherland. "An Interview with Gertrude Stein," *Gertrude Stein: A Biography of Her Work*. New Haven, CT: Yale University Press, 1951. 180–203.
Stein, Gertrude. *How to Write*. West Glover, VT: Something Else Press, 1973.
Stein, Gertrude. "How Writing Is Written," (1935), *How Writing Is Written*, ed. Robert Bartlett Haas. Boston, MA: Black Sparrow Press, 1974. 151–60.
Stein, Gertrude. "Lecture 2," *Narration: Four Lectures*. Westport, CT: Greenwood Press, 1969. 16–29.

Stein, Gertrude. "Poetry and Grammar," *Lectures in America*. 1935; London: Virago, 1988. 209–46.
Stein, Gertrude. "Sentences and Paragraphs," *How to Write*. West Glover, VT: Something Else Press, 1973. 19–32.
Stein, Gertrude. *Tender Buttons*. New York: Claire Marie, 1914.
Stein, Gertrude. *Useful Knowledge*. New York: Payson & Clarke, 1928.
Stein, Gertrude. *Wars I Have Seen*. New York: Random House, 1945.
Steinbeck, John. *The Winter of Our Discontent*. New York: Viking, 1960.
Stout, Harry S. *The New England Soul: Preaching and Religious Culture in Colonial New England*. New York: Oxford University Press, 1986.
"Structured Authoring," Adobe Systems. https://help.adobe.com/en_US/framemaker/2017/using/using-framemaker-2017/frm_structauth_sa/Structured_authoring-.htm.
Strunk, William and Elwyn Brooks White. "Rule 14," *The Elements of Style*, 1918, 4th ed. Boston, MA: Allyn & Bacon, 2000.
"Tapping into the Power of Metaphors," FrameWorks Institute, 2020. https://www.frameworksinstitute.org/article/tapping-into-the-power-of-metaphors/.
Tarantino, Quentin and Roger Avery. *Pulp Fiction*. Script, 1994. https://script-pdf.s3-us-west-2.amazonaws.com/pulp-fiction-script-pdf.pdf.
Tawil, Ezra. *Literature, American Style: The Originality of Imitation in the Early Republic*. Philadelphia: University of Pennsylvania Press, 2018.
"Telegram Writing," Pearson Longman textbook for India and South Africa. See "Telegram Writing," https://www.scribd.com/document/191373376/Telegram-writing-1-pdf plus https://za.pearson.com/content/dam/region-growth/south-africa/pearson-south-africa/TeacherResourceMaterial/pea_9781447978671_m09_pep_lag_pr6_tg_eng_ng.pdf.
Teresa, St. *Complete Works of St. Teresa*, ed. and tr E. Allison Peers, Vol. 2. New York: Sheed and Ward, 1972.
"The 100 Best Books of the 21st Century," *The New York Times*. July 14, 2024. https://www.nytimes.com/interactive/2024/books/best-books-21st-century.html.
The Electric Telegraph, an Historical Anthology, ed. George Shiers. New York: Arno Press, 1977.
Thomas, Bronwen. *Literature and Social Media*. London: Routledge, 2020.
Thoreau, Henry David. "Journal Passages," January 1842. American Transcendentalism Web. https://archive.vcu.edu/english/engweb/transcendentalism/authors/thoreau/index.html.
Tichi, Cecelia. "Twentieth Century Limited: William Carlos Williams' Poetics of High-Speed America," *William Carlos Williams Review* Vol.9 No.1, 2 (Fall 1983): 49–73.
Towne, Robert. *Chinatown*, Screenplay, 3rd Draft, September 10, 1973. https://www.public.asu.edu/~srbeatty/394/Chinatown.pdf.
Traugott, Elizabeth Closs. *A History of English Syntax*. New York: Holt, Rinehart and Winston, 1972.

Trotter, David. "Telegraphy," *On Style in Victorian Fiction*, ed. Daniel Tyler. Cambridge: Cambridge University Press, 2021. 93–108.
Trotter, David. *The Literature of Connection*. Oxford: Oxford University Press, 2020.
Tufte, Virginia. *Artful Sentences, Syntax as Style*. Cheshire, CT: Graphics Press, 2006.
Twain, Mark. "'Autobiography' in Thomas D. Zlatic, 'I Don't Know A from B:': Mark Twain and Orality," *A Companion to Mark Twain*, ed. Peter Messent and Louis J. Buddy. Malden, MA: Blackwell, 2005. 211–27.
Twain, Mark. (Samuel L. Clemens), *Adventures of Huckleberry Finn*. 2nd ed., ed. Sculley Bradley, *et al.* New York: Norton, 1977.
Updike, John. "Hub Fans Bid Kid Adieu," *New Yorker*, October 22, 1960. https://www.newyorker.com/magazine/1960/10/22/hub-fans-bid-kid-adieu.
Vallor, Shannon. *The AI Mirror: How to Reclaim Our Humanity in an Age of Machine Thinking*. Oxford: Oxford University Press, 2024.
Vinge, Vernor. "The Coming Technological Singularity: How to Survive in the Post-Human Era," *Vision 21: Interdisciplinary Science and Engineering in the Era of Cyberspace*, ed. Geoffrey A. Landis. NASA, 1993. 11–22.
Voigt, Ellen Bryant. *The Art of Syntax*. Saint Paul, MN: Graywolf Press, 2009.
Walker, Sue. "The American Sentence," Blog, Negative Capability Press, April 5, 2015. http://www.negativecapabilitypress.org/blog/theamericansentence.
Walsh, Thomas. "Double Check," *Pulp Fiction: The Crimefighters*, ed. Otto Penzler. Intro. by Harlan Coben. London: Quercus Books, 2006. 137–56.
War Communication during WWI. " National Museum of the Marine Corps," https://www.usmcmuseum.com/uploads/6/0/3/6/60364049/nmmc_wwi_military_communication_resource_packet.pdf.
Warner, Michael. "Note on the Sermon Form," *American Sermons: The Pilgrims to Martin Luther King, Jr*. New York: Library of America, 1999. 889–90.
Watkins, Maurine. "Demand Noose for 'Prettiest' Woman Slayer," *Chicago Tribune*, April 4, 1924. https://chicagology.com/notorious-chicago/beaulahandbelva/.
Webster, Noah. *An American Dictionary of the English Language* (1828) Vol. 2 (539). https://webstersdictionary1828.com/Dictionary/sentence.
Webster, Noah in Gunnel Tottie. *An Introduction to American English*. Malden, MA: Blackwell, 2002.
Weijie Liu. "Linguist Features of British and American Literary Works from a Cross-Cultural Perspective," *International Journal of Art Innovation and Development* Vol.1 No.3 (2020): 45–56.
Welch, Kathleen Welch. *Electric Rhetoric: Classical Rhetoric, Oralism and a New Literacy*. Cambridge, MA: MIT Press, 1999.
Wharton, Edith. "The Custom of the Country," *Novels*, ed. R. W. B. Lewis. New York: Library of America, 1985. 621–1014.
"When William Faulkner Set the World Record for Writing the Longest Sentence in Literature," *Open Culture*, March 14, 2019. https://www.

openculture.com/2019/03/when-william-faulkner-set-the-world-record-for-writing-the-longest-sentence-in-literature.html.

Whitehead, Colin. *The Underground Railroad*. New York: Doubleday, 2016.

Whitehead, Colson. *Harlem Shuffle*. New York: Bond Street Books, 2021.

Whitman, Walt. "Democratic Vistas," *The Portable Walt Whitman*, ed. Mark Van Doren. New York: Viking, 1945. 395–462.

Whitman, Walt. "Preface," 1855 Edition, *Leaves of Grass*, Whitman Archive, ed. Ed Folsom and Kenneth M. Price. http://whitmanarchive.org/published/LG/1855/whole.html.

Wilde, Oscar. *Oscar Wilde*, Oxford Authors Series. Oxford: Oxford University Press, 1989. 571–2.

Williams, William Carlos. *Autobiography*. New York: New Directions, 1967.

Williams, William Carlos. *Imaginations*. New York: New Directions, 1971.

Williams, William Carlos. *In the American Grain*. 1925; New York: New Directions, 1956.

Williams, William Carlos. *Selected Essays*. 1954; New York: New Directions, 1969.

Williams, William Carlos. *The Embodiment of Knowledge*, ed. Ron Loewinsohn. New York: New Directions, 1974.

Wilson, Christopher P. *The Labor of Words Literary Professionalism in the Progressive Era*. Athens: University of Georgia Press, 1985.

Wilson, Edmund. *Patriotic Gore: Studies in the Literature of the American Civil War*. 1962; New York: Norton, 1994.

Wolfe, Cary. *What Is Posthumanism?* Minneapolis: University of Minnesota Press, 2010.

Wood, James. "Say What?" *New Yorker*, March 31, 2008. https://www.newyorker.com/magazine/2008/04/07/say-what.

Woodruff, Douglas. *Plato's American Republic*. New York: Dutton, 1926.

Woolf, Virginia. *A Room of One's Own*. London: Hogarth Press, 1929.

Woolf, Virginia. *Letters*, Vol. III 1923–1928, ed. Nigel Nicolson and Joanne Trautmann. New York: Harcourt Brace, 1978.

Woolf, Virginia. *The Years*, ed. Hermione Lee. Oxford: Oxford University Press, 2009.

Woolf, Virginia. *To the Lighthouse*, ed. David Bradshaw. Oxford: Oxford University Press, 2006.

Wortman, Zack. "Ernest Hemingway's Six-Word Sequels," *New Yorker*, September 11, 2016. https://www.newyorker.com/humor/daily-shouts/ernest-hemingways-six-word-sequels.

Yang, Andrew. "Words on the Wire," UX Collective, April 1, 2020. https://uxdesign.cc/words-on-the-wire-8ee91b75e894.

"Zimmermann Telegram," National WWI Museum and Memorial, Kansas City, MO. https://www.theworldwar.org/learn/about-wwi/zimmermann-telegram.

Index

abbreviations 168
Acocella, Joan 189
   "Finding Augie March" 189
Adams, Henry 30, 58, 90
   Education of Henry Adams 58, 90
   Mont Saint Michel and Chartres 58
Adams Cable Codex 70–1
AI 141, 155–6, 159–60, 168–71, 173–5, 188, 195–6, 200
Allen, Roland 172
Alter, Robert 41, 45
American Heritage Dictionary 18, 148
Anderson, Sam 127
   Winesburg, Ohio 22
Angelou, Maya 83
Aquinas 142
Aristotle 86
Aschenbrenner, Leopold 167, 170
   "Situational Awareness" 167, 170
Associated Press 72
audience 42–3, 45, 47, 49–51, 54–5, 100, 116, 118, 120, 128, 146, 153, 190, 199
Augustine 142
Austen, Jane 12, 143, 175

Ballantyne, R.M. 79
   The Battery and the Boiler 79
   Post Haste: A Tale of Her Majesty's Mails 79

Banville, John 12
   The Infinites 12
Barthelme, Donald 1, 25
   "Sentence" 1
Barthes, Roland 4–6, 120, 158
   "Flaubert and the Sentence" 4
Baxter, Richard 46
Bay Psalm Book 50
Beach, Sylvia 69
Beckett, Samuel 4, 68, 82
   Waiting for Godot 4
Bellow, Saul 13, 20, 29, 52, 189, 197
   The Adventures of Augie March 13, 189, 197
Bercovitch, Sacvan 41, 43–4, 52
   The American Jeremiad 43
Berendt, John 103
   Midnight in the Garden of Good and Evil 103
Berkeley, Bishop George 8, 55
Bible 44–5, 52–3, 143, 197
Black Mask 101, 106, 120
Bolter, Jay David 154
   Writing Space 177 n14
Borges, Jorge Luis 5, 158
   "Library of Babel" 158
Boston News-Letter 50
Bowen, Robert Sidney 119
Bradford, William 50
Brand, Max 123
Bridgman, Richard 30, 54
   The Colloquial Style in America 30

Index

British Library 169
Bronte, Charlotte 79
   Jane Eyre 79
   Wuthering Heights 12
Bulgakov, Mikhail 68
   Master and Margarita 68
Burgess, Anthony 13
   Earthly Powers 13
Burroughs, William 22, 24, 30–1, 79, 91
   The Third Mind 24
   The Ticket That Exploded 24, 31–2

Cain, James M. 31, 107
   The Postman Always Rings Twice 31
Cain, Paul 117
   Fast One 117–18
Cambridge Dictionary 18
Canaanites 6
Carnegie, Andrew 76
Carson, Anne 126, 130–1, 152, 167
   "The Anthropology of Water" 130
   Autobiography of Red 167
   "The Glass Essay" 131
   "Love's Long Lost" 167–8
   Red Doc> 152, 167
   "Seated Figure with Red Angle" 130, 167
   Short Talks 130
   Wrong Norma 131
Carver, Raymond 20, 25, 30
Cather, Willa 29–30
   "On the Art of Fiction" 29
   The Professor's House 29–30
Céline, Louis-Ferdinand 31
Chandler, Raymond 23, 29, 106–8, 120–1, 132, 189, 197
   The High Window 121
   "Red Wind" 107
   "Trouble is my Business" 23, 37 n29
Chicago Daily News 111–12
Chicago Times 99–100

Chicago Tribune 99–100, 110
Christie, Agatha 119, 121, 175
   The Mysterious Affair at Styles 119
Cicero 7, 55–6, 85, 100
Civil War 58, 66, 72, 83, 87–8, 197
Clarendon, Earl of 87
Clark, S.W. 87
Cmiel, Kenneth 85
code/s 4, 68, 70–1, 74–6, 81, 88, 92 n2, n3, 94 n32, 141, 156, 165, 168, 171, 174, 199–200
codices distincti 7
Cohen, Leonard 4, 173
   The Favorite Game 4
Collette 112, 131, 139 n69
colloquial 18, 22, 30–1, 54, 116, 124
Commercial Advertiser 99
"Content moderation" 174–5
Cooper, James Fenimore 10, 52
Corinthians 7
Covici, Pascal 112
Crèvecoeur, J. Hector St. John 9, 20–1
   Letters from an American Farmer 9–10, 21
Cuba 143
Cukor, George 145
   The Philadelphia Story 145–7

Dadaists 155
Dahl, Roald 175
Daily Telegraph Style Book 77
Danforth, Samuel 43
Danielewski, Mark 23, 28, 30, 32, 79, 155, 161, 163, 182 n43
   House of Leaves 23, 28, 155, 161, 163
Darrow, Clarence 110
Davis, Frederick C. 119
Davis, Lydia 2, 4, 20, 86, 126–7, 155, 173, 187, 196, 200 n1
   Break It Down 127
   "Can't and Won't" 127
   "A DOUBLE NEGATIVE" 126

Essays One 187
"Local Obits" 127
"Revising One Sentence" 173
"Suddenly Afraid" 127
"THEY TAKE TURNS" 127
"We Miss You" 127
Delaney, Samuel R. 188
　Babel 17 188
Delbanco, Andrew 41
DeLillo, Don 2, 6, 13, 25, 27, 86, 109, 123, 189
　Mao II 6, 13, 25
　Underworld 13
　White Noise 86
Deming, Richard 119
DeWitt, Helen 163
　"Entourage" 164–5
　The Last Samurai 163–5
Dialog 32, 89, 113, 116–18, 120, 122, 141–5, 148, 150
Diaz, Hernan 197
　Trust 197
Dickens, Charles 79, 81, 143
　Our Mutual Friend 143
　The Pickwick Papers 81
　"The Signal Man" 79
Dickinson, Emily 7, 89, 105, 129, 196
Didion, Joan 83, 126, 173
　"On Keeping a Notebook" 173
Dillard, Annie 126–8, 130
Dillon, Brian 1
　Suppose a Sentence 1
"dime novels" 101
diplomacy 87–8
Dos Passos 18, 21, 29, 79, 86, 162
　1919 163
Doyle, Conan 121
Dreiser, Theodore 18, 21
Dreyfus Affair 66
Du Bois, W.E.B. 68
Duchamp, Marcel 89

Ede, Lisa and Andrea Lunsford 159
　Singular Texts/ Plural Authors 159
Edison, Thomas 76

Edwards, Johnathan 8–9, 20
　Daniel Deronda 80–1
Elliott, Emory 56
　Power and the Pulpit 56
Ellison, Ralph 21–3, 26, 32, 36–7 n27
　Going to the Territory 23
　Invisible Man 26–7, 32
Ellmann, Lucy 19
　Ducks, Newburyport 19
Emerson, Ralph Waldo 22, 33, 57, 83–4, 104
　"Divinity School Address" 57
Emre, Merve 157
English Standard Version of the Bible 47–8
Epstein, Julius 145
Esquire 25
Ezekiel 151

Fante, John 3
　Ask the Dust 3
Faraday, Michael 69
Faulkner, Grant 187
Faulkner, William 19, 26, 45, 52, 109, 123–4
　Absalom, Absalom! 19, 22
Fish, Stanley 1, 194
　How to Write a Sentence 1, 194
Fitzgerald, F. Scott 5
　The Great Gatsby 5
Flaubert, Gustave 4–5, 199
Fleming, Ian 175
Fleming, John Ambrose 72
　Wireless Telegraphist's Pocket Book of Notes 72
Forster, E.M. 169
　"The Machine Stops" 169–70
Foucault, Michel 160
Franklin, Benjamin 2, 9, 20, 51, 83, 194
　Autobiography 9
　Poor Richard's Almanac 9
Frost, Robert 2, 21–2, 172
Futurists 155

Gaelic 7
Gardner, Earl Stanley 119, 132
Gass, William H. 188
  Middle C 188
Ginsberg, Allen 18–19, 24
  Cosmopolitan Greetings 19
Glanville, Joseph 158
Gleick, James 158
  The Information 158
Glück, Louise 19
  American Originality 19
  "Ersatz Thought" 19
Gould, Glenn 164
Gould, Jay 78
grammar 6–7, 23–5, 29, 47, 52, 77, 87, 91, 141, 143, 160–1, 163, 172, 181 n39, n40, 196, 201 n1
Grant, Cary 145
Grant, Ulysses S. 30
Greek 7, 51, 158, 163–5, 172
Guillory, John 156–7, 159, 165–6, 172
  Cultural Capital 156
  Professing Criticism 165–6

Hammett, Dashiell 23, 107, 119–21
  The Big Knockover 120
  The Dain Curse 120
  The Glass Key 108, 120
  The Maltese Falcon 120–1
  Red Harvest 119–20
  "The Road Home" 120
Hardwick, Elizabeth 6, 15 n14, 126
  Sleepless Nights 6
Hardy, Thomas 12, 27
  Jude the Obscure 12
Hawthorne, Nathaniel 21, 45, 53, 192
Hayles, N. Katherine 172
  How We Became Posthuman 172
Headlines 102–3
Hearst William Randolph 102
Hecht, Ben 111–17, 144–5
  The Front Page 113–17
  "The Man Hunt" 111–12

Heller, Joseph 88
Hemingway, Ernest 17, 19, 23, 29–30, 53, 67, 82–3, 85, 89, 124
  Death in the Afternoon 29
  A Farewell to Arms 18
Hempel, Amy 25, 32
  "Beg, Sl Tog, Inc, Cont, Rep." 32
  Reasons to Live 25
Hemyng, Bracebridge 79
  Telegraphic Secrets 79
Hepburn, Katherine 145
Heschel, Abraham Joshua 51
Hochfelder, David 72–4, 83
Holmes, Sherlock 79
  "The Adventure of the Copper Beeches" 79
  "The Adventure of the Naval Treaty" 79
  "The Adventures of the Blue Carbuncle" 79
  "The Adventures of the Creeping Man" 79
  "The Adventures of the Second Stain" 79
  "The Sign of Three" 79
  A Study in Scarlet 79
Homiletics 54
Hooker, Thomas 55–6
  A Survey of the Summe of Church-Discipline 55–6
Hopper, Kenneth and William 41
"How to Save Words" 71
Howe, Susan 7, 128–30
  My Emily Dickinson 129
Hubbard, William 57
  Huckleberry Finn 53–4
Huebsch, Ben 68
Hughes, Langston 89
  "Poor Little Black Fellow" 89
Hugo, Victor 80
Hull, Cordell 87
Huxley, Aldous 79
hypertext 152, 154

International Telegraph Union 75–6
Irving, Washington 21
    Sketch Book 21
Isaiah 46
Italy 7

James, Henry 2, 4, 20, 31, 59, 68, 80, 86, 123, 173, 189, 192, 200
    The Ambassadors 4–5
    The Golden Bowl 4, 200
    "In the Cage" 60, 68, 70, 80
    The Portrait of a Lady 59, 70
Jamestown 8
Jefferson, Thomas 194
Jeremiad 41–4
Jin, Dal Yong 159
    Artificial Intelligence in Cultural Production 159
Johnson, Dr. Samuel 8, 155
    An English grammar 160
Johnson, Rev. Dr. Samuel Johnson 160
Jones, Edward P. 197
    The Known World 197–9
Jones, James 88
Jonson, Ben 7, 160
    "The English Grammar" 160
    Poetaster 7
Joubert, Joseph 196
Joyce, James 68–9, 91, 128, 154, 178 n19
    Finnegans Wake 82
    Ulysses 68–9
Justice, Donald 172

Kafka, Franz 131, 173
Kazin, Alfred 20
Kerouac, Jack 13, 21
    On the Road 13, 16 n31, 21
Kipling, Rudyard 80
Koestenbaum, Wayne 6
Krasna, Norman 145

Lanham, Richard A. 155
Lardner, Dionysius 81
    The Electric Telegraph Popularised 81
Latin 6–7, 51, 141, 158, 160, 163, 167, 193
Lawrence, D.H. 25
    Studies in Classic American Literature 25
Leopold and Loeb 110
Lethem, Jonathan 1, 24, 28, 33, 199
    "The King of Sentences" 1, 199
    Motherless Brooklyn 24, 28, 33
Lewis, Sinclair 21
Lightning Flashes and Electric Dashes 80
Lincoln, Abraham 30, 65
Lish, Gordon 25
    English Grammar 25
Liu, Alan 170–1
Lloyd-Jones, Martyn 47
Locke, John 8
    An Essay on Human Understanding 8
Longfellow, Henry Wadsworth 53
Love's Telegraph 81
Luke 57
Lutz, Gary 187
    "The Sentence is a Lonely Place" 187

MacArthur, Charles 113
Macdonald, Ross 121
Maclean, Norman 2–3, 17, 21
    "A River Runs through It" 2
Magnalia Christi Americana 51
Magnet Telegraph Company 74
Mailer, Norman 3, 17, 21, 83, 88, 91, 109, 118, 123, 126, 155
    An American Dream 17
    The Executioner's Song 123
    The Naked and the Dead 3

Index

"On Lies, Power and Obscenity" 118
"Quickly: A Column for Slow Readers" 118
Malcolm, Janet 126
Manguel, Alberto 142
   History of Reading 142
Mankiewicz, Herman J. 144
Manovich, Lev 172
   The Language of New Media 172
Mantel, Hilary 158–9
Marinetti, Filippo Tommaso 155
Marx, Leo 58
Massachusetts Bay Colony 8
Mather, Cotton 51–2, 57
Mather, Increase 41, 43, 50, 57
   An Arrow Against Profane and Promiscuous Dancing 50–1
   A Wicked Man's Portion 50
Mather, Richard 41, 150
McBain, Ed 119
McCarthy, Cormac 2, 4, 18–20, 23, 25, 27, 86, 126, 189
   The Orchard Keeper 86
   The Road 23, 27
McCullers, Carson 27
   The Heart is a Lonely Hunter 27
McLoof, Ted 187
   "Space, Whether and Why" 187
McLuhan, Marshall 165
McWhorter, John 32
Melville, Herman 20–1, 45, 52–3, 123–5, 192
   Moby Dick 124–5, 130
   White-Jacket 21, 35 n14
Menke, Richard 81
Merkoski, Jason 144
   Burning the Page 144
Middle English 6
Midrash 143
Mieszkowski, Jan 1, 15 n19, 32, 166, 174–5, 195
   Crises of the Sentence 1, 175, 195

Miller, Henry 72, 82–3, 174
Miller, Perry 8–9, 42, 52–3
   "An American Language" 52
   Errand into the Wilderness 52
Milton, John 30, 154, 197
Mitchell, Jonathan 43, 56
Mitchell, Margaret 83
Moore, Laurie 126
Moore, Marianne 89
Moore's law 165
Moran, Joe 1
   First you Write a Sentence 1
Morrison, Toni 28, 52, 109, 123, 173
   Beloved 28
Morse, Samuel 65–6, 69, 72, 74, 167, 176 n3
Morse code 66–7, 72, 75–6, 80, 141–2

Nashe, Thomas 24
   The Unfortunate Traveller 24
Nebel, Frederick 117
   Sleepers East 117
Nehemiah on the Wall 56
New York Daily News 105, 111
The New York Gazette 50
New York Herald 99
New York Times 117, 197
New York World 102
Nietzsche, Friedrich 187
Nobel Prize 67–8
Nollet, Jean-Antoine 69
Norris, Frank 58
   The Octopus 58
notebooks 172–3

O'Hara, John 68
Oates, Joyce Carol 18, 25
Odyssey 165
Operator, The 78
Oxenbridge, John 57

Paine, Thomas 100, 194
Pascal, Blaise 187, 201 n2

Pearl Harbor 87
Perkins, William 46
   Art of Prophecying 47
Petrarch 142
Picasso, Pablo 127
plain style 19–20, 44, 46–8, 53, 55, 100, 158, 179 n26, 188
Poe, Edgar Allen 53, 121
Poirier, Richard 26, 28
   A World Elsewhere 26
posthuman 141–2, 167
Pound, Ezra 89, 197
   Cantos 89
preaching 45–7
Price, Richard 99, 122–3
   Lush Life 99, 122–3
print 50–1, 80, 141, 152–3, 165
Proust, Marcel 4, 127, 173
   Sodom and Gomorrah 4
   Swann's Way 127
Puchner, Martin 169
Pulitzer, Joseph 102
pulpit 29, 48–9, 125
pulpit style 20, 41, 44
punctuation 7, 24, 28, 32, 75, 77, 79, 96 n52, 142, 161
Puritans 8, 20–1, 41–2, 44, 46–7, 52–5, 65, 107
Pynchon 5, 109, 123, 189
   Gravity's Rainbow 5

Quinby, Ione 112

reading 29, 31, 48, 70, 76, 80, 112, 118–19, 128–9, 142–3, 152–8, 162–3, 165–6, 170, 173, 176 n6, 180 n31, 188, 196, 198, 201 n3
Renaissance Book Wheel 170
Roberts-Miller, Patricia 41
Robinson, Ian 7
Roth, Philip 11, 22, 24, 124, 134 n19
   The Anatomy Lesson 11
   The Counterlife 22
   Deception 22
Ryken, Leland 47

Salinger, J.D. 10, 20, 88–9
   "For Esme—with Love and Squalor" 89
   "A Girl I Knew" 10
Salle, David 126
Salter, James 3
   Light Years 3
Saunders, George 18
Schoenberg, Arnold 164, 188
screen 141–2, 144, 152, 154–6, 165–8, 171, 174–5, 188, 196, 200
screenwriting 144–5
Seneca 55–6, 86
sermon 41–2, 44, 46–51, 53–4, 56, 124, 171, 199
Shakespeare 30, 89, 169
   Hamlet 173
Shannon, Claude 158
Shaw, Irwin 88
Shockproof 168
Silliman, Ron 25, 174
   The New Sentence 174
Simenon, Georges 119
Smith, Ali 90
   "Being Quick" 90
Smith, Francis O.J. 75
   Secret Corresponding Vocabulary 75
Smith, Henry 55
Smith, Zadie 12, 155
   Swing Time 12
Sontag, Susan 27–8, 83, 131
   "The Aesthetics of Silence" 27–8
Sorrentino, Gilbert 79
Speed 60, 72–4, 76–9, 89–90, 97 n56, 110, 117, 119, 143, 165, 200
Spillane, Mickey 107–8, 132
   One Lonely Night 108
Sprat, Bishop Thomas 55
St. Teresa 154
St. Valentine's Day Massacre 110
Steffens, Lincoln 82

Stein, Gertrude 2, 7, 11, 18, 33, 75,
    86–7, 91, 130, 141, 160–1,
    175, 196
  "A Grammarian" 160
  How to Write 87
  Lectures in America 87
  The Making of Americans 175
  "More Grammar for a Sentence"
    141, 160–1
  Narration 161
  "Poetry and Grammar" 160–1
  Tender Buttons 2
  Useful Knowledge 21
Steinbeck, John 68, 91
Stewart, Donald Ogden 145
Stewart, James 145
stile coupe 85
Stoughton, William 43
Stout, Harry 42, 49
  New England Soul 42
structured authoring 153–5, 160,
    165, 178 n18
Strunk, William and E.B. White 71,
    125, 187
  The Elements of Style 71, 125
Swift, Jonathan 100
syntax 4, 6, 8–9, 18, 20–1, 23, 25,
    28–9, 31, 33, 38 n49, 44, 48,
    51–2, 56, 59, 70, 89–90, 100,
    108–9, 112, 124, 144, 152,
    160, 172, 189, 192–5, 198,
    201 n1

Tarantino, Quentin 148
  Pulp Fiction 148–51
Tawil, Ezra 8, 10
  Literature, American Style 8
telegraph 31, 60, 65–6, 84, 171, 199
Thackeray, William Makepeace 13
  Vanity Fair 13
Thatcher, Thomas 57
Thayer, Ella Cheever 78
  Wired Love 78
Thompson, Jim 104, 119, 133
  After Dark, My Sweet 133
  The Killer Inside Me 104, 119

Thoreau, Henry David 18, 21, 58, 83
  Walden Pond 58
  *Week on the Concord and
    Merrimack Rivers* 21
Thornton, John Wingate 49
  "Pulpit of the American
    Revolution" 49
Todd, Obbie Tylor 47
  "Preach like a Puritan" 47
Tolstoy, Sofia 126
  War and Peace 126
Torah 143
Towne, Robert 147
  Chinatown 147–8
Transcendentalists 65
travel narrative 21–3
Trilling, Lionel 58
  "Reality in America" 58
Trollope, Anthony 68, 79
  "Telegraph Girl" 79
Trollope, Frances 84
Tufte, Virginia 109
  Artful Sentences 109, 134 n17
Twain, Mark 10, 18, 21, 51, 53, 83
  Autobiography 51
  Huckleberry Finn 54
  Innocents Abroad 21
Tyler, Anne 189

Updike, John 25, 109
Uris, Leon 88–9

Vidal, Gore 109, 151
  Washington, D.C. 151–2
Village Voice 118
Voigt, Ellen Bryant 194
  The Art of Syntax 194

Walden Font Co. 62 n15
Wallace, David Foster 2, 19, 189
  Infinite Jest 19
Walsh, Thomas 99, 105
  "Diamonds Mean Death" 99
  "Double Check" 105
Watt, Ian 4–5
Waugh, Evelyn 68

Weaver, Harriet Shaw 68
Webster, Noah 8, 52, 83, 85, 160
   An American Dictionary of the English Language 52
   Dissertation on the English Language 52
   A grammatical institute of the English language 160
   A Philosophical and Practical Grammar of the English Language 160
Western Union 67, 72, 75–6, 78
Wharton, Edith 81, 86
   The Custom of the Country 81
Whitehead, Colson 2, 29, 108–9, 152
   Harlem Shuffle 108–9
   The Underground Railroad 152–3
Whitman, Walt 22, 31, 84, 102
   Democratic Vistas 31
   Leaves of Grass 102
Whittier, John Greenleaf 53
Wilde, Oscar 80, 188
Willard, Samuel 57
Williams, William Carlos 89–90, 97 n56
   Autobiography 89
   In the American Grain 90
Wilson, Edmund 30
   "The Chastening of the American Prose Style" 30
   Patriotic Gore 30
Wolfe, Bernard 172
Wolfe, Thomas 20, 83
Wood, James 123
Woodhouse, P.G. 68
Woolf, Virginia 11
   To the Lighthouse 11–12
   The Years 12, 14
World War I 66–7, 74, 87, 173
World War II 87
Wouk, Herman 88
Wright, Richard 52, 132
   Native Son 132

Yates, Frances A. 142
   The Art of Memory 142
Yellow Journalism 102, 111

Ziff, Larzar 41
Zimmerman, Arthur 66
Zimmerman telegram 66